WIDESPREAD PRAISE
FOR GRANDMASTER Y. K. KIM

"Y. K. Kim has shown that the American dream is still a reality. He is a pioneer in the truest sense. What he has accomplished I would call a miracle if I had not seen him do it with sweat, spirit, and a keen intelligence.

He has lived by the principles about which he writes. His action philosophy is the product of an alert, intelligent mind learning from the most demanding school of all, 'life.' That he has lived and learned in two worlds, East and West, makes his observations all the richer."

—**CHARLEY REESE**, *The Orlando Sentinel*

"I found my new life. My father abandoned me as a child, resulting in my being placed in foster homes. I grew up angry and my heart was full of poison and hate for what my father did to me.

One day while listening to a motivational speech about Master Kim's modern philosophy I became paralyzed by the power of forgiveness. It changed my way of thinking.

Since then I searched and found my father, forgave him for abandoning me and built a strong relationship with him.

Now I am anger-free and have peace in my heart, which strengthens my mind, body and life. I love my life. I feel I can do anything. Now I can focus on higher goals.

I am very lucky to have Y. K. Kim as my personal coach and best friend."

—**KEITH WINKLE**

"As a young man I worked as a daily laborer. I was unable to advance into a better career because I lacked the proper skills. I felt hopeless and unwanted.

During that time I met Master Kim. He taught me about his modern philosophy. I was amazed.

I had a strong body but my mind was undernourished.

He opened my mind and changed my way of thinking, making me more optimistic and taught me to set higher goals for myself.

He helped me change my life dramatically. I became more confident and gained personal respect. Now I am the director of a YMCA that is responsible for 90 employees and 6,000 members. I met a very lovely lady whom I married. I now have real passion in my life.

I would like to give many thanks to my close friend and mentor Y. K. Kim for helping me develop my personal growth."

—VINCENT HIRSCH

WINNING
is a CHOICE

Maximize Your Life
with the Seven Steps
to Build Physical, Mental,
and Moral Fitness

Y. K. KIM

healthyliving**books**

NEW YORK · LONDON

A Healthy Living Book
Published by Hatherleigh Press
5-22 46th Avenue, Suite 200
Long Island City, NY 11101
www.hatherleighpress.com

Kim, Y. K.
   Winning is a Choice! : maximize your life with the seven steps to build phys-
ical, mental, and moral fitness / Y.K. Kim.
      p. cm.
   Includes index.
   ISBN 1-57826-211-9
1. Success 2. Kim, Y. K.   I. Title.
BJ1611.2.K56   2005
158--dc22

                              2005021997

Winning Is a Choice is available for bulk purchase, special promotions, and
premiums. For information on reselling and special purchase opportunities, call
1-800-528-2550 and ask for the Special Sales Manager.

Interior design by Eugenie S. Delaney, Jacinta M. Monniere, and Deborah Miller
Cover design by Y.K. Kim Productions and Deborah Miller
Author photographs by Y.K. Kim Productions

10 9 8 7 6 5 4 3 2 1
Printed in the United States

DEDICATION

*To my family
and my Martial Arts World family.*

Special Thanks

MY PARENTS AND LIFETIME ADVISORS:

I have to give my first, my last, and my deepest gratitude to my parents. Without my mother, Hyung Sook Kang, there would never have been *Winning Is a Choice*. She showed me the meaning of love, dedication, and indomitable spirit. Every word I have written, every good thing I have ever done, is because of her teaching. My late father Wan Soo Kim's spirit of loyalty and self-sacrifice inspired me always to strive to become more than I was.

MY MASTER AND SPIRITUAL ADVISOR:

My Martial arts father, the late Master Choong Hyup Lee, who taught me the philosophy of winning that changed my life and became the basis for this book.

MY FAMILY AND DAILY ADVISORS:

My strongest supporter, my beloved wife Sonja Kim, has brought meaning to my life beyond my work. Her unwavering support, along with sacrifices of my daughter Hyungjung Jackie Kim and my son Min Chul (Tae Min) Kim, have allowed me to write this book. I owe them everything.

PROFESSIONAL ADVISORS:

I am so also fortunate to have the special advice of two media personalities: Mr. Charley Reese, my adopted brother, who is a nationally syndicated columnist (former *Orlando Sentinel* columnist) who taught me fairness, balance, and justice, which became a way of life that energized me and encouraged me to finished this book.

Ms. Nickie Sarner, my adopted sister, who was the Public Relations Director and on-air personality at WKMG TV, who taught me the meaning of generosity; and her journalistic guidance changed this book 180 degrees and inspired me to become a better writer.

EXECUTIVE ADVISORS:

Master Tim McCarthy, my business partner, personal advisor and my best friend, whose intelligent and philosophical advice and accurate help during the final editing made this book move up to next level.

Master Kirk Pelt, my business partner and professional advisor; my daily discussions of every aspect of this book with him helped me maximize my potential to finish this book. Without his undying daily support, this book would still be on the shelf.

EDITORS:

Master Joseph Diamand, whose keen personal advice and editing helped improve the quality of this book.

Mr. Jeff Gardenour, a former reporter for *USA Today*, whose special editing talent and journalistic advice helped define the form of this book.

Mr. Jesse Bradley, my adopted nephew and editor, whose honesty, support, research, and knowledge of grammar helped continue my education on a daily basis, and develop this book into its final form.

SCIENTIFIC ADVISORS:

Dr. Gideon G. Lewis, M.D., P.A., whose special contributions on physiology helped make the advice in the book more scientifically sound.

Dr. Thomas Fisher, Jr., professor of psychology at the University of Central Florida, whose professional advice helped clarify key personal concepts.

Dr. Roland Thompkins, Florida Department of Corrections Senior Psychologist and professor at Valancia Community College, whose professional advice helped define human relationships.

CONTENT ADVISORS:

Ms. Crissy Vega, practicing psychologist; Dr Pearl K. Burns, D.D.S.; Reverend J. Dunn, clinical director; Master Keith Winkle; Mr. R. Allan Lougheed, President of Lougheed Resource Group, Inc.; Instructor Rodney Robertson; Mr. Drew Washburn, engineer; Instructor Nick Zambri, former high school principal,

All of these professional people gave their personal, honest opinions and practical suggestions, which changed the content of this book dramatically.

I truly appreciate all of you from the bottom of my heart for your guidance, support, editing, and personal and professional advice. I respect and love each one of you.

WINNING
is a CHOICE

Contents

DEAR LEADER,

Welcome and thank you for choosing *Winning is a Choice*. I have been passionately researching, writing, editing and rewriting this book since 1978. I have learned remarkable lessons about personal and professional improvement, which has changed my life dramatically. I realized I have only one life; I will have no second chance…the same as you. We are all special and unique; within each of us there is a tremendous potential power: the power to succeed. We have no reason to minimize our lives, to be weak, poor, or to have an unhappy life. We have every reason to maximize our lives, to be strong, rich, and to have a successful life. You and I have the choice to maximize our lives.

How? The answers are right here in this book.

Winning Is a Choice is an uncommon blend of the best of Eastern and Western culture, creating a new way of thinking. I was fortunate enough to live half of my life in the East and the other half in the West. This unique perspective has helped me create a simple, practical step-by-step process of self-improvement.

No matter who you are, *Winning Is a Choice* will help you become healthier, stronger, wiser, happier, wealthier, and more successful through these 7 Steps to Maximize Your Life:

WINNING IS A CHOICE. How to develop a new way of thinking to win in your life.

BE A LEADER, NOT A FOLLOWER. How to develop the leader within.

DEVELOP PERSONAL POWER. How to unleash the real power inside of you.

BUILD WIN-WIN RELATIONSHIPS. How to inspire others for success.

CREATE DYNAMIC ORGANIZATIONS. How to develop a winning team that will triumph.

LEAD THE REAL WORLD. How to make your dream come true no matter what roadblock is in your way.

SUCCESS IS YOUR CHOICE. How to maximize your potential and become successful. Push the limit, success is easy.

The most powerful leaders in the world have advisors that they turn to for guidance. The greatest athletes in the world have coaches to direct them in becoming great players. Everyone, no matter how successful, needs advisors or coaches in order to improve.

This book contains the principles of success that I have taught to thousands of people over time and all over the world. I hope that, in some small way, I can become your advisor or coach.

In addition, we all need good friends to make our lives more enjoyable. Perhaps eventually, I can be your friend…even your best friend. As friends we can help each other by sharing our experiences, thoughts, ideas, and feelings in our never-ending quest to be winners.

Please, after you've finished this book, share your thoughts and comments with me at YKKim@YKKimProductions.com. If you see me at a seminar, meeting, party, or even in an airport, please say hello and share your success story.

I hope you enjoy listening to this book as much as I enjoyed researching and writing it. And my friend: Maximize your life.

Winning Is a Choice

Be a victor, not a victim

WINNING IS A CHOICE, NOT A RESULT. YOU are the one who decides whether you win or lose. No matter what the odds, no matter how tough the competition, you can win every time, every place, if you know how. Be a victor, not a victim, by winning.

Deep within us, we all have a strong burning desire to win in everything that we do: games, races, fights, and all of life's battles.

The undeniable desire to win and hatred of losing is human nature, driven by the one law that all life on Earth obeys: the survival of the fittest. This inherited instinct explains why everyone likes to win and no one likes to lose.

Our winning instinct manifests in us at a very young age. In class, we competed for the teacher's attention when we had a right answer. When it was time to get into a car or on a school bus, we competed for the best seat.

This winning instinct carries over into adulthood. Think of the winners and losers on Election Day or in the Super Bowl. Notice how the winners scream, dance, and wildly celebrate while the losers grieve and

mourn with long faces. Now think about how you feel when your candidate or team wins. You feel like a victor, don't you? However, when they lose, you feel disappointed, don't you? These aren't learned responses; they are your winning instinct, which is human nature.

> **Winning is a choice, not a result.**

So if it's human nature that everyone wants to win and no one wants to lose, then why are only 5% of people in our society winners while 95% are just potential winners? Before I answer this monumental question, let me illustrate how I arrived at these figures.

Every year on January 1st, most of us enthusiastically make New Year's resolutions—to exercise more, to lose weight, or to quit smoking. When the end of the year comes, only a few have stuck to them. Surveys show that less than 3% of people who made these New Year's resolutions followed through with them, so my estimate of 95% of the population being potential winners might be generous.

Ask yourself: are you a winner, or just a potential winner?

To better understand the concept of winners versus potential winners, we must start from the beginning: the survival of the fittest fuels the desire to win.

Let's examine the roots of this idea in the animal world: every animal wants to win because winning means survival. If they don't have a strong enough desire to survive, they die. Watch a nature documentary and see what happens when lions chase zebras. The lions are focused and in control during the hunt, singling out a weak or slow zebra for the kill. The zebras are frightened and confused. The lions revel at their opportunities and enjoy their lives. Their hunt demonstrates the natural order of victors and victims in the food chain. Our human society is no different.

In the jungle of life, there are some real-world consequences of winning and losing. When we win, we become a victor and get pleasure, joy, and happiness. When we lose, we become a victim and get pain and suffering. Beyond the natural desire to win are the natural consequences of winning and losing, which reinforce our desire to win. In modern terms, when we win, we get the cash; when we lose, we get the trash. Winning means success.

UNLIKE ANIMALS, who can't change their place in the food chain, humans can break their limitations to become winners because there is no absolute rule that determines who is a winner or just a potential winner in life. A rabbit can intensively train to be stronger and faster, but that rabbit will never be a tiger. Nature may give us the desire to win, but the choice of what we become is up to us. We must make that choice to win: winning is a choice.

> Only you can break the chains of your limitations to become a victor.

Throughout my life, I have watched so many people suffer, from students, to housewives, to celebrities. They didn't realize they were limiting themselves because they simply didn't know what it takes to win in life. I, too, had a great deal of suffering—more than some, not as much as others—then, one fateful day in the middle of my life-long battle to win, I had an epiphany that made everything clear. It changed my life. I'd like to share with you how I discovered how to win every competition, every place, every time.

FROM THE EAST...

When I was a kid, I thought that life's winners were those who were rich or from a powerful family. I believed that people who were born taller, bigger, faster, smarter, or more handsome than me were also life's winners. I was a short and frail child and my family was poor and powerless. These thoughts bled over into my daily life; comparing myself to others like this shattered my self-confidence and made me constantly doubt myself.

Anyone who was stronger, faster, taller, or better-looking easily intimidated me. My insecurities made me so depressed, so angry, even incredibly afraid of meeting new people; it felt almost impossible to make new friends. I lived in a waking nightmare. So I wished as hard as I could every day and every night to be bigger, stronger, taller, faster, smarter, richer, to be better than anyone else.

My desire to win only got stronger, consuming me to the point that it would make me sick to my stomach. I desperately needed to discover the secret weapon that would make me a winner in life. All I thought was "win, Win, WIN!"

As I walked around my neighborhood one day, I was thinking of ways I could defend myself against bullies because I was constantly being picked on for being small and weak. Then I heard a lot of people yelling all at once. I ran towards the sound and saw what was going on: people wearing white uniforms simultaneously throwing kicks and punches. It seemed that they all had so much power, yet they didn't look big or tough. I asked someone what those people were doing; it was the martial arts. "I could do this. I could learn how to defend myself like this," I thought. I ran home and begged my mother to let me take lessons. Once she said, "Yes," I knew that my life would start to change, but I didn't quite realize how.

Eventually, I got my first look at the school's master, and my first impression was, "How is this guy a martial arts master? He's not big, strong, or tough looking. How is this possible?" Once the master showed he could easily defeat bigger and stronger opponents, my doubts were put to rest. From that day on, I dedicated myself to the martial arts, believing that they would lead to the secrets of winning.

My desire and drive to win fueled my intense training regimen, making me physically and mentally stronger. After years of training and hard work, I became an instructor. No longer was I intimidated by anyone.

However, even with this newly found strength and ability, my pockets were still empty. My insecurities, depression, anger, and fear kept

growing. On top of that, I began doubting my master. Even though he could defeat opponents of superior size and strength with his outstanding fighting techniques, he wasn't wealthy or politically powerful. I began to think that perhaps martial arts weren't the answer to truly winning in life after all.

I still believed in the physical and mental benefits of the martial arts and continued my training, but I had to look elsewhere for the answers I desperately needed.

...TO THE WEST

My search took me around the world, from Korea to South America to the United States. Once I arrived in Chicago, Illinois in 1977, I thought I had finally found what I was looking for.

When I was back home in Korea, I had met Koreans who had emigrated to the United States and told stories of freedom and the countless opportunities of success that America offered. I wanted to be as successful, if not more successful, than they were. I thought that by studying the American formula for success, I could learn how to be a winner.

I always remembered their stories during my travels, using them as a beacon of hope during my struggles to get into America. I thought of them as I taught martial arts in South America because I didn't have the political or financial resources to get a U.S. work visa from Korea. I kept their stories in my brain and in my heart until I finally made it to the U.S. for the World Tae Kwon Do Championships in Chicago, praying that all of my struggles would pay off.

They did. The stories were all true: the freedoms, the countless opportunities, all of it. Just standing outside in the heart of Chicago made me realize that America, this epicenter of world culture, was the place to be. I was used to a culture where travel was restricted by military check-points; where personal freedoms like dress and hairstyle were severely limited, and business opportunities only existed for the chosen few. Finally, I thought, finally I have found what was

needed to be a winner, because I now had the opportunity to become rich and successful.

But the euphoria of my arrival went away quickly as reality set in. After the World Tae Kwon Do Championships in Chicago, I moved to New York City. There, I struggled to make ends meet until I saved barely enough money to move to Orlando, Florida, and opened my own martial arts school in 1978. I worked hard to make the school very successful, believing that my dreams would come true once I attained financial freedom and fame.

Yet, despite all of my hard work, despite my persistence and drive to win in life, still my depression, anger, and fears were with me. I still felt insecure. My frustrations were increasing.

I turned to books because I thought that they had the answers, reading everything I could get my hands on, taking in whatever knowledge I could, but I didn't find what I was looking for.

Then, I attended seminars, believing them to be my last, best hope in figuring out what it took to be a winner. Unfortunately, after listening to the most famous speakers I could find, the answers still eluded me. I didn't know what else to do or where else to turn.

AN EPIPHANY

One morning, I was teaching my students how to defend themselves against multiple opponents. Using ten students as the attackers, I sent them after one of my other students, John. John tried defending himself against them, but they easily overwhelmed him. John looked exhausted and worn-out, so I told the attackers to back off. I explained to the rest of the class that if we tried defending ourselves against all of these opponents simultaneously, we would lose. I then stepped in and demonstrated how to take the attackers one at time without being attacked from behind. As I did this, words that my master once etched in my brain began echoing in my ears:

*"It is much easier to fight only one enemy
than it is to fight many enemies."*

As I continued showing the class how to turn this potentially disastrous situation into a winning one, those same words kept coming back:

*"It is much easier to fight only one enemy
than it is to fight many enemies."*

When I finished, all ten of my opponents were exhausted; they appeared defeated. It was when I looked at each student that another piece of my master's wisdom surged through me:

*"He who competes with others wrongfully, never really wins.
The true winner is he who competes with himself."*

Then it hit me: all my life I had competed with others wrongfully, fighting against multiple opponents in life simultaneously so I could be better than them in every way, much like my student John and his ten attackers. Just when I thought I was richer, stronger, or more successful, someone else with more came along, and I had to defeat him. I had to win, but these opponents seemed endless. I could defeat ten, one hundred, or one thousand people, and still more and more would keep appearing until I collapsed. The entire world was my enemy. Why? By competing with others wrongfully, every man, every woman, every child, everyone is my enemy, and with all of these enemies attacking me at once, I could never win.

It was after that sparring lesson that I realized the enemy I needed to fight the hardest was myself; I was my own worst enemy. Fighting against one enemy was much easier than fighting ten or one hundred or one thousand enemies. In fact, it was my master who always said that my worst enemy was not far away; he was always within me. He also said

that my best friend was also not far away, that he was also always within me. I didn't understand what he meant up until that point in time. I had to team up with my best friend in order to fight and compete within myself, so I could truly win in life.

WOW! After years and years of searching, the answer I needed was within me the entire time! Then, I remembered more of my master's teachings:

"You can lose by winning or losing."
"You can win by losing or winning."

I experienced situations directly related to his words:

"YOU CAN LOSE BY WINNING OR LOSING": I remembered how snobby I was after winning a competition. Victory made me so full of myself that nobody wanted to be around me. When I lost, I got very depressed and dwelled on it for a long time.

"YOU CAN WIN BY LOSING OR WINNING": In defeat, I learned it was better to walk away feeling positive about my efforts than moping over the loss. In winning, I learned to be humble and show respect towards an opponent after a well-fought match.

Finally, I fully understood and appreciated the value of my master's wisdom, realizing that it could be applied to all aspects of life; it was never too late to choose to be a winner at anytime, anywhere. I also understood that no one could make that choice to win for me.

Because I competed with others wrongfully, all I cared about was superficial and material success like being taller, bigger, more handsome, powerful, wealthy, or famous. Thinking that was what it took to be a winner in life, I suffered so much. By learning to compete within myself, I unearthed these winning qualities: a winning spirit, tenacity, an open mind, and a love for learning new ways to improve myself. It was an amazing feeling. In one fell swoop I went from believing that I lacked so many winning qualities to knowing I had tremendous ones. Now, instead of being jealous, doubtful, or hateful towards others because they had what I didn't, I learned to admire, recognize, and respect others for their strong points, positive qualities, and good characteristics, learning from others instead of competing with them wrongfully. The insecurities, the anger, the fear, and the depression that were in me for so long just faded away; finally, I was truly happy with my life and myself, because I finally realized the true concept of winning.

THEN I DISCOVERED that I wasn't the only one who suffered from not knowing what it took to truly win in life. I found that so many people also suffered and limited themselves because they, too, shared the same misconceptions about winning: that the only way to win in life was to be physically stronger, faster, smarter, or

> Winning or Losing in life begins within

richer than everybody else. These misconceptions are actually the wrong way to compete with others. When we compete with others wrongfully, we show how insecure we actually are and how hateful, jealous, and doubtful we are of others. Anyone who wrongfully competes with others loses. The true way to win in life lies in competing within ourselves.

CHANGE THE WORLD: THE EXAMPLES OF MOHANDAS K. GANDHI AND OSAMA BIN LADEN

Now that we know the right concept of winning in life, let's examine two real-life examples to show the personal, professional, and social impact of both the right and wrong concept of winning. Please understand that I am not attacking any religion, race, country, or even the individuals. I am simply examining two well-known people's actions and their

world-changing results, and how they illustrate the right and wrong concepts of winning.

One of the best comparisons of people who embraced the right and wrong concept of winning is that of Mohandas K. Gandhi and Osama Bin Laden. The choices that these men made changed the world in radically different ways.

During Gandhi's time, India was a colony of the British Empire. As a young man, Gandhi resented his country being ruled by another. Many of the young men in India at that time were willing to fight and die to prove their strength and free their country. Gandhi would have the same instincts, but he also strongly believed in nonviolence. This created a fight within him between his positive and negative tendencies.

At the age of 19, Gandhi made a choice. He knew that without knowledge, it is hard to win, especially if the enemy has great power. He chose to go to England to get the best education he could: to study British culture and law. His education, combined with the principle of nonviolence, helped him find another solution. He thought of the consequences of fighting the British with violence, and saw that thousands, maybe millions, would die. Instead, he decided not to fight with the British (competing wrongfully), but to teach his people to fight within themselves, to overcome their instinct to violence, and resist peacefully.

Gandhi led nonviolent marches and went on hunger strikes to influence the people of India. He never gave up as he faced seemingly insurmountable odds. Gandhi showed the people of India, the British Empire, and the world that diplomacy, not violence, was the best solution. His compassion, conviction, and intelligence helped the people of India gain their independence in 1947.

Gandhi's resolve and peaceful resistance enabled great change, helping to free his country from one of the world's greatest colonial powers. His philosophy educated people on the benefits of nonviolence and how they could overcome fear and anger through understanding.

Osama Bin Laden, in contrast, became a player on the world's political and diplomatic scene at the age of 17 by leaping into the battle against Communism and the Soviet Union in Afghanistan. With the aid of the U.S., Afghanistan repelled the Soviet invaders. However, Bin Laden's gratitude for the American aid was short-lived. He became enraged at America during the 1991 Gulf War against Iraq because the U.S. used Saudi Arabian bases as launching points. Like Gandhi, Bin Laden resented the presence of foreigners on his home soil. However, this situation was different in that the foreigners were not there to colonize his country, but to fight a neighboring aggressor who might expand its aggression to his homeland of Saudi Arabia in the near future. Bin Laden apparently felt that the American presence was unacceptable, and allowed his anger to take over. He decided that America must be destroyed in order to protect Saudi Arabia's sovereignty and way of life. Gandhi's example of peaceful resistance was a matter of history and readily available to Bin Laden, but he chose the path of violence over peace. If he thought of the consequences of his actions, he thought only of the destruction of America, and did not take into account the retaliation on his own people and the deaths it might bring. His focus was on competing with others (America) wrongfully rather than on competing with himself by helping his people improve themselves from within.

Bin Laden recruited, indoctrinated, and influenced many Arabic people with money and religious ideology into an organization known as Al-Qaeda. From their ranks, the most devoted to Bin Laden's cause were trained as terrorists for suicidal attacks against Americans. The most devastating of these attacks happened September 11, 2001, which destroyed the World Trade Center towers in New York and killed over 3000 people of different ethnicities and religious backgrounds, including Muslims. In addition, these attacks damaged the Pentagon, killing many civilians and members of the Armed Forces.

Bin Laden's success was only temporary. America quickly retaliated with a military strike on Afghanistan. In striking back at the Al-Qaeda

network and its Taliban hosts in Afghanistan, the U.S. destroyed most of the enemy's terrorist training compounds while capturing or killing many Al-Qaeda and Taliban fighters in the process.

Gandhi realized that what Great Britain was doing to his people was wrong, that they were suffering a great injustice. India's situation upset Gandhi, but he did not allow anger or revenge to influence him in his vision of a free India. He knew that the best way to gain his country's independence was to compete within himself, which would lead him to compete rightfully against Great Britain. Gandhi competed within himself by going to England to study law and their culture, acknowledging their positive qualities, using that knowledge when he returned home to make his vision come true. This course of action makes Gandhi a true winner.

Bin Laden, on the other hand, allowed his emotions to control him. By becoming so enraged at America during the Gulf War, he made the decision to avenge Saudi Arabia by violently striking back at America. When he made the choice to compete with others wrongfully, thousands of lives were lost, the entire Muslim community damaged, and Bin Laden and his followers became hated and hunted criminals Because he did not compete within himself, but repeatedly competed with others wrongfully, Bin Laden is a loser. The results were the death of thousands of innocent people. However, if he were to change and begin to compete with himself by disciplining his anger and choosing his positive side over his negative side, he could become a winner and a powerful force in achieving world peace.

THE DIFFERENCES BETWEEN WINNERS AND LOSERS

Within each of us are two sides: one good and one evil; one positive and one negative; one strong and one weak. The good, positive, and strong side is your best friend. The evil, negative, and weak side is your worst enemy. If you don't fight within yourself, your worst enemy will win naturally, because it takes the path of least resistance. In any hardship, to give up is easy; to continue is difficult. When you fight within yourself, you evaluate the consequences of your actions, and intentionally choose good over evil, positive over negative, strong over weak.

For example, if your friend does well, you have the choice to be jealous or to improve yourself. When you give in to jealousy, you allow the evil, weak, and negative side to win. The consequences are all negative. That is competing with others wrongfully. If you choose to learn from him and improve yourself, you allow the good, positive, and strong side to win. The consequences are all positive. That is competing with others rightfully.

Now let's use this new understanding to examine some of the differences between Gandhi and Bin Laden.

Winners are Respected by Their Enemies, Losers are Hated by Everyone

After the attacks on September 11th, some Muslims said Bin Laden was a hero. However, most Muslims were disgusted by Bin Laden's actions because they conflicted with the teachings of Islam. Some Muslims even gave up practicing their faith because of the attacks. Even the late Palestinian leader Yasser Arafat criticized Bin Laden publicly, warning Osama Bin Laden to stop justifying attacks on Westerners in the name of Palestinian statehood.

"I am telling him directly not to hide behind the Palestinian causes," Arafat was quoted as saying in the Sunday Times of London, "Why is Bin Laden talking about us now? He never helped us. He was working another, completely different area and against our interest."

The Muslim community's shock and disgust of Bin Laden's actions were indicative of the majority opinion: Osama Bin Laden was a terrorist. Mohandis K. Gandhi was viewed internationally as a hero to the nation of India and the rest of the world, even gaining the respect of the British people.

Winners Have Principles, Losers Lack Principles

Competing within creates self-respect and self-confidence. Those who compete with others wrongfully and allow their feelings to control them are not truly self-confident individuals. Gandhi demonstrated that anger wasn't the answer, controlling his emotions even when his situation was at its darkest. Doing so allowed him to maintain his rationality and follow his principles, which dictated he would not act violently even if confronted by violence, continuing to compete within. Bin Laden allowed his emotions and anger to control him, letting his feelings guide him to make rash and dangerous decisions, so that either he did not compete within himself, or if he did compete with himself, he gave up and allowed the negative side to win. Either way, the result was that he competed with others wrongfully.

Winners Have Constructive Vision, Losers are Destructive

What do you think were the differences between Gandhi's fight for his country's independence and Bin Laden's fight for his beliefs? What were their respective outcomes?

Gandhi viewed diplomacy as the only solution in resolving disputes with foreign powers. His vision took root among his people and helped liberate India from Great Britain. Bin Laden's vision of a New World Order for Muslims, free from American influence, backfired with his violent attack against the United States. Al-Qaeda's actions caused the murder of thousands of innocent people, which resulted in America's wrath; Bin Laden's violent methods proved to be destructive to Al-Qaeda. Gandhi walked into the heart of danger when he noticed his people falling into a religious civil war, pitting Hindu against Muslim. He showed no fear as he preached peaceful resistance for the sake of his people, dying with great honor in the process. As Bin Laden's followers were being captured or killed, he was nowhere to be found.

Bin Laden's actions illustrated that he had the wrong concept of

winning. His vision was clouded by anger and hate, culminating in failure for him and his followers. Gandhi had the right concept for winning because he followed a vision based on compassion and diplomacy. By using sound judgment and reason, Gandhi executed his plans with wisdom and intelligence.

It is my opinion that if Bin Laden had possessed the right concept of winning, he could have been a true hero to the people of Islam and others worldwide. Bin Laden could have led and educated his people to a better future. He could have helped in developing a stronger economy and a stronger, socially progressive educational system for his country, which could have led Saudi Arabia to eventually become a world superpower like the U.S. If Bin Laden had chosen education and nonviolence over bloodshed, he could have left a lasting positive impact on not just the Muslim world, but also the entire world.

The Difference Between True Winners and Real Losers

True winners compete within themselves, which leads them to compete with others rightfully. They are very confident, think and act positively, courageously, intelligently, generously, productively, and constantly look for possibilities. They are also honest, responsible, full of integrity and personal leadership ability, which makes them reliable and trustworthy. Winners never quit and always make things happen so they have a successful life.

Real losers don't compete within themselves, which causes them to compete with others wrongfully. They are filled with self-doubt, making them insecure individuals. Losers think and act negatively, cowardly, destructively, unfairly, ignorantly, and selfishly. They are dishonest, irresponsible, and have no personal leadership ability, which makes them unreliable and untrustworthy. When something goes wrong, losers always quit, look for excuses, or blame others. They never make things happen so they live miserable lives.

We have the potential to be true winners or real losers. No one can

decide for us what we will be, but it is our responsibility to choose whether we want to be winners or losers: winning is truly a choice.

So, ARE YOU READY to embrace the right concept of winning? Then please join me so you can discover how to truly win in life through the Three Steps to Win in Your Life.

In order to become a winner, you have to change your mind and change your body, which means your mind and body must work together. Let me give you some examples why the body and mind have to work together to become a winner.

The best golfer in the world is in good physical shape. But if his mind is not focused when he hits the ball, he can end up hitting the ball into the woods.

By the same token, even if the best golfer in the world lets himself get out of shape, it will be difficult for him to remain on top.

Not just in golf, but whatever you do in life, if you want to achieve your goal for success, your mind and body have to work together to maximize your potential.

So, these three steps will take you where you want to be:

1. **CHANGE YOUR MIND:** Changing your mind is the beginning of becoming a winner.
2. **CHANGE YOUR BODY:** Changing your body is the best tool to become a winner.
3. **MAXIMIZE YOUR LIFE:** When you maximize your life, winning is guaranteed.

CHANGE YOUR MIND

People become what they believe about themselves because belief is stronger than fact or truth. If you change what you believe, which is changing your mind, you will change your life.

In the self-improvement series, The Psychology of Achievement, Brian Tracy tells the following story: John was a straight "A" student all through high school. After taking the college entrance exam, John was awarded a scholarship to one of the most prestigious universities in the country. When he entered the university, John met with his counselor to go over his test scores and choose his college classes. At the end of his first semester in college, John's grades were surprisingly low and it looked like he would lose his scholarship.

John's college counselor met with him to figure out what had happened. John explained that he shouldn't be expected to do well because he had a below average IQ of 98. The counselor was puzzled and reviewed his test scores. Realizing what happened, she explained to John that the scores they went over weren't IQ scores but the results of the college entrance exams. John didn't have an IQ of 98; he had scored in the 98th percentile of his class, which meant that he was an excellent student. Finally aware that he wasn't below average, John changed his mind and rededicated himself to his studies, and the next semester earned straight "A's."

John's initial self-evaluation upon entering college is a prime example of why you should never think negatively about yourself. Whenever you label yourself negatively, you limit yourself. However, negative thinkers are NOT what they think they are. Never think of yourself as a failure, unless you want to be one. Never think you can't succeed because of your intellect, your race, your social standing, your body or educational background. Remember, you may not be what you think you are. Change your mind, change what you believe, and you will change your life.

> You become what you think, what you do, and what you feel.

THE MOVIE *Stand and Deliver* gives another example of a positive belief system. *Stand and Deliver* tells the story of Jaime Escalante and his students at Garfield High School in East Los Angeles during the late 1970s and 80s.and how such a positive belief system changed an entire school.

Garfield High had the reputation of being one of the nation's lowest-ranking schools in math. The school's student body was comprised of inner-city kids, many of whom were gang members. The teachers and students both came to believe the students were lazy, uncaring, and incapable of learning. This negative belief system took root in the students and destroyed their desire to learn.

During this time, a new math teacher named Jaime Escalante was hired. He knew the students could do well if he expected them to do well. By believing in his students, he helped them rise to the occasion. Escalante would often push his students by saying, "You have to have *ganas*" (which means "desire" in Spanish). He also encouraged his students, "You guys are great. You're all the best. You can do this. Don't ever forget it." This was the first time these students had anyone push them to learn and do it well.

Escalante's positive belief system soon paid off as some of the students at Garfield actually started to learn and improve their grades in math. The more they believed in themselves, the more they improved. Through Escalante's leadership, students who once believed that they were incapable of learning math were now taking a college-level calculus course while in high school.

When his students were about to take the Advanced Placement Calculus test for college credit, faculty members told Escalante he shouldn't let them take the test because they believed it would destroy his students' self-esteem. Escalante knew his students could do it and told them to take the test anyway. His students didn't just pass the exams; they earned some of the highest scores in the country. But the Educational Testing Service didn't believe the students at Garfield could do that well. They accused Escalante and his students of cheating and invalidated their results. Escalante knew his students were at a breaking point so he encouraged them to retake the test, turning them away from quitting.

They passed the second test; convincing everyone the first success was no fluke. Garfield High School became one of the nation's highest ranked math schools because their students embraced a positive belief system.

These students were a great example of how a change in self-perception can change one's performance and also change how others perceive and feel about them. A positive belief system will make a profound difference in your life. If you want to be brave, change your mind and then think, act, and feel brave. If you want to be intelligent, change your mind then think, act, and feel intelligent by reading, studying, and learning new things. If you tell yourself, "Yes, I can do it!," change your mind, and focus on your goals, you will work confidently and eliminate the limitations you created for yourself. You will be a winner. It doesn't matter who or what you were yesterday. Escalante and his students proved there are no excuses for failing.

ARE YOU A MORNING PERSON or an evening person? If you are a morning person, close your right eye. If you are an evening person, close your left eye. Now open your eyes please.

If you believe you are a morning or evening person, you are not good for anything for half the day, which means you limit yourself. Once you change your mind and you believe you are a 24-hour person, you can maximize your life 24 hours a day. Many people believe that they are a

> You can't change fact or truth, but you can change what you believe.

morning person or an evening person, or that they aren't good at something. Unfortunately, people program themselves to believe such things as fact, thus limiting themselves.

What you think is a fact about yourself isn't fact at all; you are not what you think. At the same time you are what you think you are. You may think that it is a fact that you are just a morning or evening person, or that you are poor or incapable, and because you believe these things as fact, you will continue to be these things since facts cannot be changed. Once you realize that these things are not fact but instead what you think of yourself, you can change the way you think and embrace all the amazing, positive qualities within you.

In order to break your own programming and maximize your potential, always remember that belief is stronger than fact or truth. No one can change fact, which is the past, but everyone can change the present and the future by changing their mind, what they believe about themselves. Once you change your mind, you believe that you are an amazing person with excellent qualities; you will be a winner in life.

> Belief is the wind that keeps winning spirits afloat. Desire is the spark that lights the fire of success.

Compete Within Yourself

No matter who you are, you have two sides within you: One side is your strong points and the other side is your weak points. Your strong points are your positive qualities and your goodness, your weak points are your negative qualities and your evil. The strong, positive, and good side is your best friend. The weak, negative, evil side is your worst enemy.

In order to maximize your life, to win in life, so that you reach your dreams and have peace in your heart, you must compete within yourself and never give up until your best friend wins. If you compete with others, you will compete with others rightfully. You will be a stronger and better person.

If you don't compete within yourself or if you give up, your worst enemy will win, because it is naturally stronger. You will compete with others wrongfully, and you will become weak, negative, and evil. Your worst enemy will have beaten you.

Let me give you a few examples to help you understand this important point. First, let's consider some natural physical reactions. It is natural that when you see delicious food, especially something sweet like a doughnut, that you want to eat it. If you give in to the temptation as most people do, and give in often, you will soon gain weight. This is why 65% of the population is overweight—it is easier to give in to temptation than to fight it. Once you establish a bad habit like smoking, you can become physically addicted to it. That is why people who know that they may die of cancer continue to smoke—the weak side is addicted, and it is easier to give in than to fight it.

Second, look at some mental reactions. If someone humiliates you, the two most common reactions are anger or depression. Aggressive personalities get angry and want to strike back, while passive personalities just get depressed and withdraw. These are both natural mental reactions of the weak side winning. It is much more difficult to discipline yourself to forgive the other person and keep your own positive attitude.

Third, let's look at a common moral reaction. Imagine that someone you know, perhaps a friend or coworker, suddenly gets a big promotion at work. The negative, evil side will be tempted to hurt this person and would enjoy seeing him fail. The positive, good side will congratulate him and truly wish for his continued success, without feeling jealous. In addition, if his success motivates you to learn more, work harder, and improve yourself, then you are competing with others rightfully. You are not trying to beat him, but trying to beat yourself because of his success.

So how do you strengthen your best friend, so that you can always win when you fight within yourself? First, you must love yourself unconditionally. Everyone makes mistakes, so you cannot dislike yourself just because you have made some mistakes. The weak, negative, evil side of you is only part of you. You also have the strong, positive, and good side. Love your whole self, including both sides, so that you will have the self-esteem to win over your worst enemy.

Second, continue to discipline yourself. Discipline is how we develop good habits. Every time you choose positive over negative and

good over evil, you will build your self-confidence. Third, continue to practice fighting within yourself until it becomes a second habit. Never give up and you will become a true winner.

IF YOU DON'T COMPETE within yourself, or if you compete within yourself and give up, the consequences will eventually be disastrous for you, your family, perhaps for your community, your country, and the world. Let me tell you a real life story that illustrates my point.

During the early 1960's, the late Korean President Chung Hee Park was humiliated twice. In the first incident, when President Park was visiting the United States, the U.S. president missed a meeting with him, leaving him to feel personally ignored and politically embarrassed. Then, the Japanese made public some old records showing that President Park had been taught in elementary school by a Japanese teacher, implying that the president of Korea (and therefore all Koreans) were on an elementary level. Park felt that neither of these incidents would have happened if his country had more economic power.

Though these incidents angered him, Park realized that it was important for himself and the good of his nation not to compete with others wrongfully, but to change and compete within. This meant he had to rightfully compete with America and Japan, acknowledging their positive qualities and learning from them instead of humiliating them in return.

Park learned Japanese and American systems of economic development and applied them to his nation's economy. He fired up the Korean people by promoting education and encouraging an uncompromising work ethic, which transformed his nation's economy into a world power; the results were astounding.

Korea became a major player in the world market with the introduction of popular consumer goods such as Hyundai and Kia automobiles and Samsung electronics. The country hosted the most successful summer Olympics in the modern history of the Games in 1988. A little more than a decade later, Korea co-hosted the wildly successful 2002 World Cup, in which the Korean soccer team finished fourth. Korea's economic and social improvement was so impressive that many leaders from undeveloped countries visited Korea to learn its formula for success.

Once Park changed his mind and chose to compete within himself instead of competing with others wrongfully, he himself became rightfully competitive, making him a key factor in Korea's transformation into a world economic power, gaining the respect of not just America and Japan, but the entire world.

If you compete with others wrongfully, it is very difficult to win anything. Even if you are lucky enough to win, you can only win externally. Winning externally can include becoming very wealthy, famous, powerful, or successful. Despite any success you attain, though, when you solely focus on winning externally, your life will be like a beautifully painted house with a completely gutted interior; it may look nice on the outside, but inside it is very ugly and empty.

Take a look at how some of the wealthiest, most famous, most powerful people suffer because they are miserable internally, despite their success. Watch TV or read magazines to see examples of some of the celebrities that constantly abuse drugs and alcohol, trying to numb their internal suffering. Constantly competing with others wrongfully is emotionally and spiritually draining. Those who constantly compete with others wrongfully become uncomfortable with themselves as they allow their insecurities to tear down all that they have achieved. These people get jealous, angry, and lonely when they see others succeed. In order to hide all of these negative emotions, those who compete with others wrongfully create a false self-confidence that easily crumbles under stress. Then, to prevent stress from affecting them, they began escaping life by overeating, fighting with others, joining the wrong crowd, or abusing alcohol and drugs. If you have reached this point, you have begun to lose in life.

Regardless of your wealth, fame, power, or success, when you wrongfully compete with others, you only defeat yourself because the enemies you fight are constant and endless. If you don't know how to compete within to rightfully compete with others, other people easily defeat you because you have already defeated yourself.

But, who does not compete with others?

As much as some of us would like to deny it, we all compete with others because most of us want to be better than other people. In fact, competition is a part of our human nature and very necessary in all aspects of our lives; without it, there would be no progress. As long as we learn from others by competing within to improve ourselves personally and professionally, competing with others rightfully will benefit us because the entire world will no longer be our enemy; the entire world will become our greatest ally. However, the real problem comes from wrongfully competing with others.

Why don't potential winners compete within themselves?

1. They don't know the importance of changing the mind to compete within.
2. Potential winners do not know how to change their minds to compete within; therefore they wrongfully compete with others.
3. Potential winners lack self-esteem and self-confidence, which causes them to be insecure and full of self-doubt, making them unable to compete within themselves.

What drives us to compete within ourselves?

1. Love and belief in ourselves to generate high self-esteem and strong self-confidence.
2. We know the difference between consequences of competing within and others
3. We chose to do the right thing for ourselves and others

How do you find out if you are competing within or wrongfully competing with others?

Ask yourself if you are competing wrongfully or rightfully with others.

If you are hateful, jealous, angry, doubtful, and critical towards others, even going so far as to harm them emotionally and/or physically, you are competing wrongfully. Another sign to look for is what your inner voices say: "You're too short." "You're the wrong color." "You're poor." "You're uneducated." "You're weak." "You're unlucky."

If you've said these things to yourself, you are comparing yourself to others and wrongfully competing with them.

In addition, if you hear, "I am better than others," "I am richer and more famous than others," "I am more educated than others," "I am more powerful than others," and you project these thoughts, then you treat others unfairly and you wrongfully compete with them as well.

If, on the other hand, you try understanding others, recognizing people for their qualities, and appreciating them for the good things they do, you are competing within yourself. You also try to learn from others so you improve yourself.

Why you must compete within yourself?

1. If you don't compete within yourself, your negative qualities and weaknesses will win naturally when you meet an obstacle in achieving your goals because it is easier to walk away than face a struggle.
2. Only when you compete within yourself; can you have true success, internally and externally.
3. If you compete with others, the whole world can be your enemy, but if you compete within yourself, the whole world will be your ally. Remember that it is easier to fight one enemy (yourself) instead of countless enemies at once (others).

How can you compete within yourself to truly win in life?

1. Remember you are your own best friend and your own worst enemy. Your best friend is your positive qualities and strengths. Your worst enemy is your negative qualities and weaknesses. Use your positive qualities to beat your negative qualities to become a positive person.

2. Love and believe in yourself and try to do the right thing for yourself and others.

3. Make fighting within a habit so it never ends. Even after you win, continue this fight within to make it a habit. Once it does, you are successfully competing within.

Winning Is a Personal Choice

Life is about choices. Everyday, we choose what we eat for breakfast, what to wear to work, what kind of effort we give at work, even how we end our day. The choices we make range from small and insignificant to ones that have a lasting impact on our lives. Out of all these choices, the most important is the choice to win. When we choose to win, we choose to live a successful life.

Indeed, winning is a personal choice. Other people can help, coach, or advise you, but no one can change your mind. Only you can change yourself. The decision you make today will change the rest of your life. It doesn't matter what you were like yesterday. Winning is a choice, not a result. If you change your mind and you choose to be a winner, you will become a winner.

CHANGE YOUR BODY

Action makes things happen. Even if you have a great idea or positive goal, you can't actualize your idea or goal without action—and action requires a sound body. Therefore, you must change your body to reach your goals.

People are winners in life because they chose to win, and all of us have the power of choice. So if you choose to win, you can transform from a potential winner to an actual winner, too. One of the best examples of someone who chose to win and became a winner was a frail young American child named Teddy.

Teddy was born to a prominent wealthy family in New York. Unfortunately, as a child, he was sickly and painfully thin and suffered from debilitating asthma and poor eyesight. His parents weren't sure if he would survive.

When Teddy was 12, his father told him, "You have the mind, but you don't have the body, and without changing his body, the mind can only go so far. You must change the body." Teddy took those words to heart and developed his body along with his mind. He worked out with weights, hiked, ice-skated, rowed, hunted, rode horses, boxed, and even practiced Judo. As he grew mentally and physically stronger, he held various positions of leadership, ranging from New York City's Police Commissioner to Vice President of the United States. In 1900, he gave 673 speeches and traveled 20,000 miles while campaigning with President William McKinley. When McKinley was assassinated, this young man stepped up and became President of the United States. His name? Theodore "Teddy" Roosevelt, the man whom British historian Hugh Brogan described as "the ablest man to sit in the White House since Lincoln, the most vigorous since Andrew Jackson, and the most bookish since John Quincy Adams."

In addition to being one of the most scholarly and outspoken Presidents in U.S. history, Roosevelt was the toughest. Even after his Presidency, he constantly drove himself beyond human limits. While preparing to deliver a speech one day, Roosevelt was shot in the chest during an assassination attempt on his life. With a broken rib and a bullet lodged in his chest, the President insisted on delivering his one-hour speech before allowing himself to be taken to the hospital. His actions were indicative of a true winner.

In New York on January 6th, 1919, Roosevelt died in his sleep at his home. Vice-President Thomas Marshall said, "Death had to take him sleeping, for if Roosevelt had been awake, there would have been a fight." When Roosevelt's body was removed from his bed, a book was found under his pillow. Roosevelt strived to learn and improve himself until his final breath.

From a sickly child to President of the United States, Teddy Roosevelt traveled a long road. To rise to the presidency seemed like a miracle for someone who was once puny, nearsighted, and asthmatic. In reality, it was not a miracle; he changed his mind to change his body, it was a choice Roosevelt made—a choice to win. Teddy Roosevelt proved to us, in order to win, we have to make our mind and body work together.

> Your lifestyle and your body run parallel to each other. What you do to your body will affect your lifestyle.

Exercise Daily

Before you try to change your friends, your family, or the world, you have to change yourself first. In order to change yourself, you have to change yourself. How? You must change your body first because of its intimate connection to the mind. Why? When you are stressed out, tired, or ill, it's very easy to lapse into negativity. Being energetic and positive is very difficult because you are fighting against your body. Unlike the philosophy of fighting within to aid self-improvement, fighting the needs of your body and mind isn't wise. Instead, cooperation is more effective.

Through many years of studying the martial arts, I've learned it is better to cooperate with the body and mind than to fight their needs. Use the connection between your body and mind to become more positive. For example, when you move your body, you increase your heart rate, your circulation, and your breathing. In other words, you get excited. When your body gets excited, it's easier to be energetic and positive. The easiest way to change your mind is to change your body.

Whenever I'm tired, I stall in my work. Fatigue blocks my writing, but do I give up? No. I react to the fatigue by taking a break from writing and doing some exercises. Sometimes, I go for a walk, jog, run, or take a bike ride, and the exercise reinvigorates me. When I return to my office, new ideas begin flowing out like spring water from a well.

In fact, exercise has the power to positively change your body. When your body changes, your thinking changes, becoming more positive. When your thinking changes, your actions change into positive ones. When your actions change, you will feel more positive. When you feel more positive, you will keep doing what makes you feel positive, thus changing your habits, which is your attitude. Exercise will change your life, so exercise daily.

Please try the following so you can feel the advantages of cooperating with your body and mind:

1. Sit up straight, with your back away from any backrest. Next, focus on your breathing and tighten your fists and the rest of your body as you inhale deeply through your nose and count to seven. (If you have high blood pressure or a weak heart, tighten your body softly.)

2. As you proceed with the exercise, relax as you exhale through your mouth and count to seven—really relax. Try thinking of your body as a wet rag.

3. Now, close your eyes, and repeat this simple exercise eight more times. Go ahead. The book will be right here when you open your eyes.

4. When you reopen your eyes, stand up, bounce lightly on the balls of your feet and let your arms flap around like wet rags as you turn to the left and then turn back to the right several times, if you have room. (If you're in a place where you can't stand up, twist in your seat to loosen up your back.) Open your mouth and stretch your face a couple of times.

How do you feel? More energetic and positive? Just imagine if you took a walk or a run. If you want to change the way you think and feel, just change your body. Do some exercise to get your blood and energy flowing!

By changing your attitude, you make your fight against mental fat (laziness, negativity, ignorance, and fear) easier. You learn to accept responsibility for the way you feel.

However, habits are habits. You must continue to make the same choices time and time again. If you want to change your body, you need to eat wisely, exercise daily, get proper rest, and think positively. Choose to be a winner like Teddy Roosevelt, compete within yourself to win like Chung Hee Park, choose to believe in yourself like John, the college student, and choose to change your attitude like the students of Garfield High. Make that choice to change your body, so you can change your thinking, and, therefore, change your actions. By repeating these choices, you will have a great attitude that will become a habit—a winning habit.

MAXIMIZE YOUR LIFE

You have no reason to minimize your life, but you have every reason to maximize your mind, body, and life to become successful and win. In order to maximize your life, you must fight for yourself and never give up until you win.

> A winner never quits ... A quitter never wins.

IF THERE IS ONE CONSISTENT QUALITY present in all winners, it's an indomitable spirit; winners fight to win. When I think of who most embodies an indomitable spirit, Abraham Lincoln comes to mind. No matter what hardships he faced, Lincoln refused to give in and maximized his life. His drive to succeed made him one of the greatest Presidents in U.S. history.

On February 12, 1809, Lincoln was born to an extremely poor family in Hodgenville, Kentucky. He grew up to be homely, tall, and gangly. Instead of complaining about his plain looks or poor economic background, Lincoln pushed himself to break his limitations and became remarkably knowledgeable in forensics, philosophy, writing, and law. This extensive self-education turned him into a very capable lawyer, speaker, and politician.

Lincoln's first challenge was starting his own business, but, unfortunately, he lost everything. Instead of giving up, he set a higher goal, running in an Illinois State legislative race at the age of 23. Unfortunately, Lincoln lost. Instead of allowing these devastating setbacks to crush his hopes, Lincoln fought even more. His persistence paid off when he won four consecutive elections to the Illinois House of Representatives, then the U.S. Congress. In 1858, Lincoln challenged Stephen A. Douglas for his seat in the Senate. The election was close, but Douglas managed to hold on to his seat. Yet, Lincoln didn't let it get to him.

His friends saw how determined Lincoln was in achieving his political goals, noting his winning spirit. So in 1860, Lincoln's friends urged him to run for President against his Senate opponent, Douglas. The fact that Douglas beat him two years before didn't intimidate Lincoln. His fighting spirit and tenacity helped him finally defeat Douglas, becoming the 16th President of the United States.

After all of his struggling and fighting, Lincoln was finally beginning to see the fruits of his labors, reaching the highest office in the land. What Lincoln didn't realize was that his greatest test waited for him in the Oval Office: the Civil War.

On the day he was inaugurated, four Southern states seceded from the Union to form the Confederate States of America. At first, Lincoln struggled, lacking the military experience to plan attacks and make decisions that would win or lose battles. In fact, the Union was defeated in battle after battle by the Confederate Army. After the Battle of Gettysburg and the Gettysburg Address, Lincoln's great leadership eventually

came through as he bravely ended slavery and reunited a nation torn apart by war.

Think about the adversity Lincoln faced. When he was young, he was poor and the only way he could be educated was to do it himself. Despite repeated political losses later in his career, he continued overcoming defeat after defeat until he became President. Despite walking into a looming war and lacking military leadership experience, Lincoln used his great leadership skills to help end slavery and the Civil War, which strengthened the spirit of democracy and left a lasting impact on the United States. Lincoln left a defining mark on history because of his indomitable spirit.

IN ORDER TO MAXIMIZE your life, you have to do three things:

1. Set a positive goal.
2. Educate yourself.
3. Never give up.

Setting a positive goal gives you hope, energy, and a deadline. Hope and energy give you strength. A deadline gives you a sense of urgency. When you have hope, strength, and a sense of urgency, you can make things happen and maximize your potential.

Educating yourself helps you know what to do and how to do it. We live in a rapidly changing world. Technology advances by the minute. When you educate yourself you make better plans and better decisions to truly maximize your potential.

Never giving up means you have an indomitable spirit that keeps you from giving up until you reach your goal while having you the flexibility you need to overcome all obstacles. However, you will not develop an indomitable spirit without setting positive goals. Positive goals have the awesome power of keeping hopes and dreams alive, even in our darkest hours.

You must learn to expect challenges. When you expect them, it's easier to get back up after you fall. It may hurt to stumble in life, but the rewards far outweigh the obstacles. Everybody faces challenges. Everybody fails. Winners accept failure as a necessary step on the road to success, so obstacles aren't discouraging. They know the only time they lose is when they quit. That's what separates winners from losers.

Remember that you are your own best friend and your own worst enemy. These two sides of you constantly fight for control of your future. So develop a winning spirit by changing your mind, changing your body and maximizing your Life like Teddy Roosevelt, Chung Hee Park, Abraham Lincoln, and Garfield High math teacher Jaime Escalante and his students. By doing these things, you will become a winner.

THE TOP TEN WINNING HABITS

After you win the battle by mastering the Three Steps to Win in Your Life, you need to maintain your winning drive by following the Top Ten Winning Habits.

ON THE OTHER HAND, life is like art: your mind and body must work together and maximize your life for success, so you can create a life that is as beautiful as a work of art.

Following these habits will transform your life.

> Life is like a war: you have to fight for yourself to win by competing within yourself, so you can create internal strength and inner peace.

1. **SMILE:** Winning begins with a smile.
2. **EAT AND DRINK WISELY:** You are what you eat.
3. **EXERCISE DAILY:** Release stress to shape up.
4. **FOCUS ON THE POSITIVE:** Develop a winning attitude.
5. **MAKE PREPARATION A HABIT:** Preparation is a key to success.

6. **ACT WITH PASSION:** Acting passionately brings you success.

7. **COMMUNICATE CLEARLY:** Winners are good communicators.

8. **SHARE WITH OTHERS:** Generosity creates win-win situations.

9. **LOVE TO LEARN:** Build mental fitness.

10. **FIGHT WITHIN YOURSELF:** Develop personal power.

These winning habits will make your life rich with enjoyment.

HABIT ONE: SMILE

Nobody likes to see an ugly frown or a face that looks angry or depressed because it makes others feel depressed. Everybody likes a smiling face, a face that gives positive energy. If you are smiling, it is impossible to frown. Many times, smiling leads to laughing, and you know what they say about laughing: "Laughter is the best medicine." A smile is the best and most inexpensive exercise for the body, mind, and soul. A smile can:

- ❖ Positively change your lifestyle.
- ❖ Generate great feelings for you and others.
- ❖ Give you the best tool for self-defense.
- ❖ Build golden relationships.
- ❖ Provide you the strongest weapon for emotional control.
- ❖ Release stress to put you in the best mental shape.

How to develop a winning smile habit

- ❖ Initiate a smile campaign. Start smiling now and keep doing so for the rest of your life.
- ❖ Smile a lot. The more smiles you give, the more smiles you will receive.
- ❖ Constantly remind yourself to smile at least 10 times a day until it becomes a habit.
- ❖ Always return a smile with a smile.

If possible, go beyond a smile and laugh. Please try this exercise:

Touch your lower abdomen with your fingertips and push it in a couple of inches. Now, try to laugh and push in your abdomen at the same time. When you are not laughing, your stomach is soft. When you laugh, your stomach gets hard. This tightening and relaxing of your stomach muscles relieves stress and massages your internal organs, dramatically improving your health.

HABIT TWO: EAT AND DRINK WISELY

The saying, "You are what you eat," is absolutely true. If you build your body with junk foods, you will have a junky, out-of-shape body. Much sickness and discomfort come from an improper diet, including obesity. If you build your body with sound nutritional foods, you will be strong and healthy.

Drinking the wrong things can be unhealthy and dangerous. Refrain from drinking alcohol because too much alcohol will leave you inebriated, irreversibly damage your liver, and could get you arrested and thrown in jail. Instead, drink healthy things like water and juices to have control of your senses at all times.

The purer your body, the purer you will be. Never poison your body with harmful drugs. Avoid nicotine in all forms: chewing tobacco, cigarettes, cigars, etc. Nicotine has been proven to cause cancer. Also, avoid illegal drugs. They can cause all sorts of problems, including heart attacks, seizures, and strokes. Don't poison your body. If you poison your body, you will eventually fall ill, even die.

By eating energy-giving and energy-saving foods, you will release stress and gain physical and mental power; this kind of diet is a positive and healthful thing. Eating healthy foods will help you focus better and keep your body looking and feeling younger. Consuming the wrong food and drinks can sabotage your immune system, so don't hurt yourself. In fact you will be surprised how healthy and energetic you feel when you eat and drink healthy things.

- ❖ Drink at least seven cups of water a day. By hydrating yourself, you internally cleanse your body.

- ❖ Avoid drugs, nicotine, junk food, red meat, caffeine, and white-sugar products.

- ❖ Eat healthy foods such as vegetables, fruits, poultry, and fish. If you exercise or work physically a great deal, you'll need to eat good carbohydrates to maintain your energy level. If you want to build muscles, you'll need to eat protein-rich foods. Those who want to learn more about healthy foods can do so through any one of many good nutrition books available at any local library, bookstore, or on the internet.

- ❖ Please don't eat too much at once and thoroughly chew what you eat. Not only is chewing slowly healthy, but it also allows you to savor your food, which can be emotionally pleasing.

HABIT THREE: EXERCISE DAILY

Exercise cleanses your body. When you exercise, you sweat through the pores of your skin, expelling physiological toxins, and you metaphorically sweat through the pores of your brain, expelling psychological toxins. In addition, exercise gives you these benefits:

- ❖ Exercise is the best way to lose fat, gain muscle, and get in shape while releasing stress and tension, and gaining energy.

- ❖ Exercise increases circulation and strengthens your immune system, which helps prevent illness.

- ❖ Exercise will make you healthier, stronger and happier.

- ❖ Exercise will improve your self-confidence.

- ❖ Exercise will turn the idle into the active.

How to exercise daily

- ❖ Smile and laugh (mental and physical exercise).

- ❖ Walk.

- ❖ Lift weights.
- ❖ Do some sort of aerobic activity.
- ❖ Clean the house.
- ❖ Do yard work.
- ❖ Organize your office.
- ❖ Run, bike, or climb.
- ❖ Practice martial arts.

While exercise is very important for good health, it's also prudent that you cooperate and listen to your body, not fight its needs. For example, if you are sleepy, rest then exercise; if you are sick, get better, then exercise.

HABIT FOUR: FOCUS ON THE POSITIVE

When you focus on the negative, you feel discouraged and stressed. When you focus on the positive, you feel encouraged and energized. Positive thoughts bring positive action; continued positive action makes it a winning habit.

Focusing on the positive will help you succeed in life, and it helps you to become an energy magnet, attracting all the positive energy around you.

How to focus on the positive

- ❖ Set positive goals. Hope comes from imagining and believing in a positive future, giving you the energy to overcome any challenge.
- ❖ Focus on your positive goals and see yourself achieving them in order to fuel your passion.
- ❖ Always think, look, listen, talk and act positively.
- ❖ Associate with positive people.

HABIT FIVE: MAKE PREPARATION A HABIT

Preparation allows you to use your time effectively and efficiently. Proper planning enhances performance. Preparation reduces mistakes, stress, and saves time. Proper planning is the foundation of success. A lack of preparation is a plan for failure.

How to make preparation a habit

- ❖ Plan–organize–practice. You must plan because success doesn't happen by accident. Organize for execution if necessary, and then practice, practice, practice when needed so you can successfully execute anything that you do.
- ❖ Write down a daily list of things to do in order to plan and organize your personal or professional schedule and become more effective with time management. Once written down, you can prioritize this list and set about doing it in an organized manner.
- ❖ Get into the habit of preparing for everything.

HABIT SIX: ACT WITH PASSION

Machines can do almost every physical activity that a person can do, and a machine is usually more accurate. However, machines can't create with passion. The difference between the actions of a man and those of a machine is the passion behind the action.

Nothing great has ever been achieved without enthusiasm. You can increase what you get out of any activity by increasing the passion you put into it. Passion will give you double or triple the results in whatever you do, and you are more likable when you show passion.

How to act with passion

- ❖ When you love yourself and love what you do, you will act with passion.
- ❖ Do your best and do so enthusiastically.
- ❖ Have positive goals.

❖ Build self-confidence, and passion will follow.

❖ Always speak and act with conviction.

HABIT SEVEN: COMMUNICATE CLEARLY

One word!
One rude word can leave you feeling miserable.
One warm word can make you feel good.

One careless word can ruin a relationship.
One caring word can build a good relationship.

One critical word can create an enemy.
One motivational word can change someone's life.

One inappropriate word can destroy a person's future.
One appropriate word can save a person's life.

Communication is the tool that builds successful relationships, and it will help you achieve your dreams.

How to communicate clearly

❖ Listen twice as much as you talk.

❖ Try to understand others by verbally relating to them.

❖ What you say is important. How you say it is more important; watch how you communicate with others.

❖ Choose the right word, control your voice, and use your best body language.

❖ If you need to touch someone's ears, then just speak from your mouth. If you need to touch someone's mind, speak from your mind.

❖ If you need to touch someone's heart, speak from your heart.

HABIT EIGHT: SHARE WITH OTHERS

You must share your experiences with others in order to be truly successful. If you don't share them, you have not truly achieved success. Sharing is the foundation of all relationships and the more you share, the more personal power you have. By helping others, you help yourself.

Remember; when you die you cannot take anything with you except your name. Therefore, the more you share, the greater the legacy you will leave behind. Selfishness always creates losing situations.

How to share with others

- ❖ Share more than just your money. Share your knowledge, your heart, and your experiences with love and compassion.
- ❖ Do at least one good thing for yourself and others daily.
- ❖ Be generous to eliminate being selfish.

HABIT NINE: LOVE TO LEARN

Education is mental food and mental exercise, which builds mental muscle. Choose what you study wisely because it can influence your thinking, and you become what you think. If you choose to be uneducated, you limit yourself. You blind yourself to possibilities when you are ignorant. You improve your life by educating yourself.

A winner is a lifelong learner. By enjoying the fruits of knowledge, you maximize your potential in life, build character, and create the opportunity to be successful.

How to love learning

- ❖ Have the desire to constantly improve yourself through education.
- ❖ Life is not merely a course or seminar; it is a lifelong experience. Continue to educate yourself every day and enjoy your life.
- ❖ Be a learner to eliminate being ignorant.
- ❖ Teaching others will also educate you.

- ❖ Remember: learning means you are learning from other people's experience and your own, so read as much as possible and learn from your own experiences.

HABIT TEN: FIGHT WITHIN YOURSELF

True victory is the victory over yourself. By fighting within yourself, you will become a confident individual with balance in your life—a true winner in every situation.

HOW TO FIGHT WITHIN YOURSELF

- ❖ Love yourself unconditionally to eliminate self-doubt, insecurity, and to build self-esteem.
- ❖ Discipline yourself to gain the inner strength needed to compete within.
- ❖ Believe in yourself to lay the foundation of self-confidence.
- ❖ Always be persistent in everything you do.
- ❖ Fight against ignorance by educating yourself.
- ❖ Fight against laziness by leading an active life.
- ❖ Fight against negativity by focusing on the positive.
- ❖ Fight against fear by being courageous.
- ❖ Fight for yourself and never give up until you win!

Winning is Your Choice! Maximize Your Life!

SUMMARY
Be a Victor, Not a Victim

Winning is a choice, not a result. YOU are the one who decides whether you win or lose. No matter what the odds, no matter how tough the competition, you can win every time, every place, if you know how. Be a victor, not a victim by winning.

In life, when you win, you get the cash and become a victor; and when you lose you get the trash and become a victim; the desire to win is human nature. Even if the desire to win is natural, you are just a potential winner until you choose to win; winning is a choice.

From the East to the West

The key to being a winner in life does not lie in other people and other things; the key to winning lies within you.

Change the World

As Gandhi illustrated, competing within yourself won't just make you a winner but will give you the power to change the world. However, as Bin Laden proved, competing wrongfully with others destroys you and poisons the world.

The Three Steps to Win in Your Life

1. Change Your Mind
   - ❖ **CHANGE YOUR WAY OF THINKING:** Belief is stronger than fact or truth. You may NOT be what you think you are. If you think and act like a winner, you will be a winner.
   - ❖ **COMPETE WITHIN YOURSELF:** If you wrongfully compete with others, you only defeat yourself. If you compete within yourself, you will rightfully compete with others and become a true winner.
   - ❖ **CHOOSE TO WIN:** There are millions of different choices you can make in your life. Among all of them is the choice to win,

which is the most important choice you will ever make. Only you can choose to be a winner and change yourself

2. Change Your Body
   - ❖ In order to change your body, get up and move around to get your blood and energy flowing. Exercise time and time again to form winning habits. Changing your body is your choice.
3. Maximize Your Life
   - ❖ **FIGHT TO WIN:** A winner never quits and a quitter never wins. Fight for yourself and never, ever give up. Only then will you be a winner.

The Top Ten Winning Habits
1. Smile.
2. Eat and drink wisely.
3. Exercise daily.
4. Focus on the positive.
5. Make preparation a habit.
6. Act with passion.
7. Communicate clearly.
8. Share with others.
9. Love to learn.
10. Fight within yourself.

REVIEW OF "WINNING IS A CHOICE!"

Are you a winner or a potential winner? Please explain why.

_____

_____

How can you win every game, race, fight, argument, and competition?

_____

_____

Are you a victor or a victim? Please explain why.

_____

_____

Do you think those who are physically strong, smart, rich, or powerful are the only ones who become winners? Please explain your answer.

_____

_____

What is the right and wrong concept of winning?

_____

_____

How can the right concept of winning change your life?

_____

_____

How can the wrong concept of winning endanger society?

_____

_____

What are the differences between true winners and real losers?

_____

_____

What are the three steps to becoming a winner?

_____

_____

How do you change your mind?

_____

_____

Why is believing in yourself so critical for winning in life?

_____

_____

What is the difference between competing with others rightfully and competing with others wrongfully?

_____

_____

How do you know whether you compete within yourself or not?

_____

_____

In life, who is your best friend and your worst enemy? Please explain why.

_____

_____

Why is belief stronger than fact or truth, and how does belief affect your life?

_____

_____

Explain the meaning of the following phrase: "You may not be what you think you are, but you are what you think you are."

_____

_____

Why should you believe you are a 24-hour person instead of just a morning person or an evening person?

_____

_____

How do you compete within yourself to truly win in life?

_____

_____

Why is choosing to win or lose crucial for winning in life?

_____

_____

How do you change your body?

_____

_____

Why is it extremely important for the mind and body to work together in order to become a winner in life?

_____

_____

What is the difference between fighters and quitters?

_____

_____

How do you maximize your life?

_____

_____

How do you become a fighter?

_____

_____

What are the benefits of having the Top Ten Winning Habits?

_____

_____

Be a Leader, Not a Follower

Lead yourself to change the world

IN ORDER TO HAVE PERSONAL FREEDOM we have to be leaders, not followers. I learned this lesson through some very eye-opening experiences of my own.

During my early days in America, I was still learning the quirks of Western culture, one of which I learned the hard way from road rage. I was driving home after teaching a martial arts class when someone drove past and flipped me the bird. At the time, I had no idea what this gesture meant so I just smiled, waved back, and thought, "That was a really nice person."

The next day, I told my students about what happened, and they broke out laughing. "Why are you all laughing at me?" I asked, surprised, and one of them explained that the driver made an obscene gesture, not a friendly one. My face turned red as I bowed my head, and my teeth ground against each other. I was humiliated and angry.

A few days later, another person flipped me off in traffic for no reason, and I snapped. "I'm gonna beat the crap out of this guy," I thought, and the best way I knew how was to follow him until he stopped somewhere. I just happened to follow the driver to his house. When I arrived at his doorstep, the driver was terrified… so terrified that he immediately apologized. I went about my way feeling really good.

Then reality smacked me in the face. "This man could have called the police and got me thrown in jail for trespassing or could've had a gun and killed me," I thought to myself. "What was I thinking?" I realized that by following this man home, I allowed him and my emotions to control me; I was being a follower. I acted in stupidity, not in self-defense. From that point on, I swore that my emotions would never, ever control me again, and that I would always lead myself.

The next time someone gave me the finger in traffic, I gave him back five fingers, waving and smiling. After that, I just smiled at or ignored anyone else who did that to me. I felt powerful and in control; I felt like a leader!

Just this experience with road rage alone helped me to realize how important it is to be a leader, rather than a follower. However, I'm not the only one who needs to be a leader; everyone does. Here's why.

Superstition clips the wings of leadership. What is superstition? Superstitions are beliefs or practices resulting from ignorance, fear of the unknown, trust in magic, or similar influences. We all have been exposed to some sort of superstition at one point or another in our lives. Even though superstitions promote the wrong ideas, they are still widely believed in and practiced.

In Korea, seeing a raven or a crow is considered bad luck; so is the number four. Superstitions are widespread in America too. The number 13, a black cat crossing one's path, breaking a mirror, walking under a ladder, spilling salt on the table, even stepping on a crack in the sidewalk are all considered bad luck. Even athletes have rituals that they believe will bring them luck, like wearing the same pair of socks they had on when hitting a homerun on the day before. Bad weather makes some feel miserable while good weather makes others feel great.

Most of us are exposed to superstition through family, friends, and society because it is a learned behavior that people choose to follow. If you let such superstitions control you, you become a follower, handcuffing yourself in your fight to win in life. How do you prevent superstition from controlling you? Superstition is what you believe, and belief is stronger than fact or truth. You can't change fact or truth, but you certainly can change what you believe. For example, always think that it's a sunny day in your heart so that the weather never controls the way you feel, no matter how nasty it is outside. You can laugh at superstition to take away any power it has. You can defeat superstition by thinking, "Only weak or ignorant people believe in superstition. I am not weak or ignorant. I am strong and intelligent." Or when you see a superstition in action, think, "Oh, bad things happen and good things happen. Something bad has already happened so something good is waiting for me" to control how you react to it. When you do these things, superstition never controls you; you always control yourself, and you will be a leader, not a follower.

How we handle outside influences such as road rage and superstition determines if we are followers or leaders. How we handle compliments and criticism also makes that same determination.

Whether criticism is constructive or destructive, all of us hate it because of criticism's potentially negative impact: it can make us feel angry, humiliated, and even depressed. If you allow any type of criticism to get to you, you will eventually become a follower.

The first thing you should do when listening to criticism is to determine right away if what you are hearing is constructive or destructive criticism. If it is constructive, listen to it and see if you can learn from it. If the criticism is destructive, control your emotions, ignore it, scream or even laugh destructive criticism out. When you control how you respond to any form of criticism, you will become a leader.

The way you respond to compliments can also show if you are a leader or a follower. By believing too much in the compliments or recognition that you receive, you can eventually become so cocky and arrogant that you become a follower. Like criticism, the first thing you should do when you are being complemented is to determine if you are being flattered or sincerely recognized. If it is flattery, say thank you and disregard it. If it's sincere recognition, be humble and show your appreciation: these responses show that you are a leader.

THE DIFFERENCES BETWEEN LEADERS AND FOLLOWERS

During a seminar at a leadership camp deep in the mountains of Virginia, I remember asking my students if they were ready to follow my instructions. All of them said, "Yes!" I asked the same question over and over and over, and they kept replying, "Yes!" louder and with more confidence. Then I asked, "Are you leaders or followers?" Everybody shouted, "Leaders!" After they answered, I waited for a moment until the room was totally silent. "You mean you are not going to follow me?" I asked. Stunned by this question, the students' faces froze in confusion. I waited a moment, grinned at them and said; "I got you." After we laughed, I reassured them they weren't the only ones who got confused about understanding the differences between leaders and followers.

Leaders follow values (principles) and learn from them because leaders believe in values. Followers follow their feelings (emotions) and allow their feelings to guide them because followers are weak and easily led into temptation.

All great leaders have studied and learned through the example of other great leaders directly and indirectly at some point. If Plato had not met Socrates and studied under him, the world wouldn't probably/ know Plato's brilliant philosophical teachings. Thomas Jefferson may not have become America's third President had he not worked under George Washington as his Secretary of State.

Leaders Are Intelligent and Confident, Followers Are Ignorant and Cowardly

Leaders are intelligent and confident because they believe in the values,

believe in themselves, and develop personal power to lead themselves.

Followers are ignorant and cowardly because they follow their feelings, are filled with self-doubt, refuse to learn, and let other people or things control them.

Leaders Are Trustworthy, Followers Are Unreliable

Leaders are trustworthy because they follow and believe in values, so they are honest, responsible, full of integrity and personal leadership ability.

Followers are unreliable because they follow their feelings, so they are dishonest, irresponsible, lacking integrity and personal leadership ability.

Leaders Follow Values, Followers Follow Feelings

Leaders follow others based on that person's values.

Followers follow others based on their feelings, normally pursuing the wrong interests, and letting other things control their destiny. Let me explain:

- ❖ If you let food control your mind, then you become a follower. However, if you control what and how much you eat, you will be a leader.
- ❖ If you let drugs control your mind, then you will be a follower, but if you control your mind and avoid drugs, you are a leader.
- ❖ If you let nicotine control your mind, then you will be a follower, but if you control your mind and avoid cigarettes, you are a leader.

Most importantly, leaders always lead themselves.

The primary difference between leaders and followers comes down to the amount of leadership ability they have. Leaders have great leadership ability while followers have none. Only you can develop your personal leadership to become a leader, not a follower.

Now that you know what defines leaders and followers, you can begin to develop the leader within you by learning more about what it takes to be a leader: personal leadership.

HOW TO DEVELOP THE LEADER WITHIN YOU

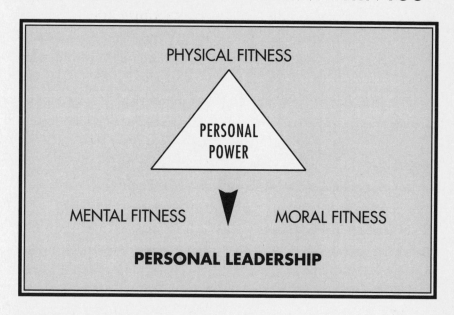

We all have a great leader within us, ready to be developed.

Your personal leadership comes from your personal power. If you want to develop or improve your personal leadership, you must increase your personal power. Your personal power comes from three sources, which are like the three corners of a triangle: physical fitness, mental fitness, and moral fitness.

Physical fitness bestows physical power, physical toughness, and physical courage; mental fitness bestows mental power, mental toughness, and mental courage; moral fitness bestows moral power, moral toughness, and moral courage. Physical, mental, and moral fitness create personal power, and personal power is personal leadership, which gives you personal freedom.

You need to develop personal leadership so you can lead yourself. When you can lead yourself, you can change your life. When you can change your life, you can change the world.

1% of leadership is innate
99% of leadership is developed

The 1% comes from the fact that we all have bodies, minds, and hearts.

The 99% comes from our personal power, which is developed through training. 33% of our personal power comes from our physical fitness, 33% comes from our mental fitness, and 33% comes from our moral fitness.

Build personal leadership so you can lead yourself.

1% of leadership is innate

Our bodies give us the innate ability to take action. Our minds give us the innate ability to think, learn, and make rational decisions. Our hearts give us the innate ability to feel and have a conscience. However, these innate abilities only represent 1% of leadership.

99% of leadership is developed

33% OF LEADERSHIP COMES FROM PHYSICAL FITNESS

Physical fitness is having good internal health (healthy organs) and external health (strong muscles), which gives you physical power, toughness, and strength. In order to build physical fitness, you have to get rid of physical fat and build physical muscle. Physical fat will make you obese. It will also make you lethargic, stressed, ill, weak, and tired all the time. It's difficult to lead yourself, let alone others, when you have physical fat. Physical muscle will give you energy, speed, agility, and endurance, which will make it easier to lead yourself and others.

Remember: a sound body creates a sound mind, providing you support in taking the right action. If you are physically fit, you can better lead yourself and others. A leader must exercise daily and eat wisely for health and energy; hence physical fitness is a constant necessity in maintaining physical power, toughness and strength. Without the foundation of physical fitness, you cannot have personal power.

33% OF LEADERSHIP COMES FROM MENTAL FITNESS

Mental fitness is the balance of positive thinking and knowledge, which gives you mental power, toughness, and strength. To build your mental fitness, you have to eliminate any mental fat you have and build mental muscle.

Mental fat is made up of negativity, laziness, ignorance, and fear, which will make you indecisive, weak-minded, stupid, cowardly, and dysfunctional. Mental fat makes it impossible for you to lead yourself and others.

Mental muscle is made up of positivity, wisdom, and vision, all of which give you intelligence, optimism, constructive thinking, communication skills, and the foundation of an indomitable spirit. Mental muscle makes it easier to lead yourself and others.

To build mental muscle, you have to exercise your mind by learning, using that knowledge, and thinking positively. To do so, first, cleanse your mind and eliminate mental fat through positive thinking. Second, open your mind as you seek out more knowledge. Knowledge is important because it provides direction and leads to fulfillment. Keep your mental cool in order to make sharp judgments and come to the right decision. Without mental fitness, you can't have personal power; therefore, it is crucial that you develop your mental fitness.

33% OF LEADERSHIP COMES FROM MORAL FITNESS

Moral fitness is the balance of emotion (warm heart) with reason (cold mind); this balance is known as conscience, which gives you moral power, toughness, and strength. This balance of emotion and reason is the key that guides you when deciding what is right or wrong. In order to build your moral fitness, you must throw away your moral fat and build moral muscle.

Moral fat consists of a lack of control over emotions, dishonesty, irresponsibility, a severe lack of integrity, and a warped sense of right and wrong. Having moral fat will make you angry with yourself and others, hate yourself and others, doubt yourself and others, and become jealous of others. When you have moral fat, you become weak, insecure, and immoral, taking you and others in the wrong direction

Moral muscle consists of the control over emotions, honesty, integrity, responsibility, and a strong sense of right and wrong. Moral muscle will help in building a strong character and in leading yourself and others in the right direction.

Without moral fitness, physical and mental fitness is meaningless, even dangerous to you and society, because neither can teach you right from wrong. For example, Adolf Hitler had physical and mental fitness but no moral fitness, which made him one of the most diabolical leaders ever. Therefore, you must be morally fit to do the right thing and follow the right direction in life.

The balance of emotion and reason also acts as a counterbalance. For example, a warm-hearted (emotional) person must have firm reasoning (cold mind) in order to be an effective leader. If a leader shows great compassion but is indecisive, then chaos results. If a leader demonstrates great reasoning but is cold-hearted, the result is inflexibility, which causes irreparable personal and professional damage. Balance is the key to moral fitness, and from this balance; a leader gains influence and conviction. Consequently everyone, including the leader, is led in the right direction. By having a conscience, a leader follows his or her principles and heart for the good of the people.

Moral fitness is a matter of inner discipline. To stay morally fit, you have to have a warm heart to understand others emotionally (emotional fitness) and reason (a cold mind) to make sharp judgments and stay grounded in reality. As a morally fit leader, you will lead others and

yourself in the right direction. To achieve personal power, you must build physical, mental, and moral fitness through exercise, education, and discipline.

Now that you understand what it takes to build personal leadership, the next step to becoming a leader lies in learning how to lead yourself and then learning to lead others.

Lead Yourself

You have the amazing power to control your destiny by leading yourself. In order to lead yourself, you must develop your personal leadership. The stronger your personal leadership is, the bigger and brighter your destiny becomes.

However, leading yourself is your own responsibility. You should never hand your life over to anyone because the consequences of not leading yourself can be fatal. If you don't lead yourself, someone or something will take advantage and seize control of your life; he, she, or it will become your puppet master, making you a follower. In order to have personal freedom, you have to lead yourself; personal leadership has the power to change your life.

THERE ARE TWO MEN who were perfect examples of how personal leadership can forever change lives: Thomas Edison and Elvis Presley. These men used the power of personal leadership to break free from their impoverished backgrounds and become two of the most influential and famous people ever. However, Edison and Presley's lives went in opposite directions because of their different levels of

> The most important step to being a leader is leading yourself.

leadership. Let's take a closer look at the lives of these two men to better understand the importance of leading yourself.

Lighting up the World with Leadership

Thomas Alva Edison was one of the most brilliant inventors ever, producing many inventions that changed the world. His biggest contribution to society brought light, literally, to a world of darkness.

Edison's early years of experimentation with electric lighting were marked with disappointment, but he refused to give up. He remained resilient through hundreds, even thousands, of attempts at establishing a reliable form of the electrical light bulb. Edison's failures were so numerous the media and his colleagues mocked his efforts, doubting Edison's ability to bring his vision to fruition.

While Edison was in the midst of his struggles, a young reporter asked him why he continued to waste time and money developing the right carbon filament for the light bulb, which appeared to be a pointless task. Edison told the reporter that he did not consider himself a failure. Despite failing more than 5,000 times to invent electrical lighting, he thought of his failures as 5,000 ways not to create electrical lighting and 5,000 times of coming closer to his dream.

Motivated by the criticism and the countless near misses, Edison led himself to believe that he could finish the task. Despite more than 10,000 efforts of creating the right carbon filament and 1,073 failures at creating the light bulb, his persistence and personal leadership paid off.

When he finally perfected the light bulb, he installed electrical lighting in half-a-square-mile area of New York City. In addition to that, Edison invented the phonograph and the first ever motion picture projector and created an improved version of the telephone. He also founded General Electric, which made him a millionaire. By the end of his life, Edison had registered an impressive 1,093 inventions with the U.S. Patent office, making him one of the greatest inventors in history.

How did Edison accomplish all of these things? He led himself to success because he had personal leadership, even when the odds were against him. Edison believed that he could do anything he put his mind to, and allowed no one to control him.

THE KING OF ROCK 'N ROLL

When the phrase "the King of Rock 'N Roll" is mentioned, only one name comes to mind: Elvis Presley. The late entertainer had remarkable talent and a strong burning desire to succeed; his unwavering determination to be a rock star in the 1950s was a testament to his desire. With his personal leadership Presley went from driving a truck in Memphis, Tennessee for $40 a week, to making millions as one of the nation's top music and movie stars.

As quickly as Elvis rose to stardom, he came crashing down under his destructive vices. His weight eventually ballooned, as he became addicted to pain killers, liquid Demerol, and heavy-duty depressants. Rhythm guitarist Jon Wilkinson couldn't believe Elvis's freefall:

> **"It seemed like the enthusiasm had just left. No matter how hard we tried to pump him up, Elvis would stand there with his thumb hooked in his belt. It was like he was just there to sing a few songs and pass out a few scarves, but all the thrill had gone."**

During his 1976 tour in Charlotte, North Carolina, he forgot lyrics. In Cincinnati, Ohio, Elvis appeared "confused," as some media outlets put it, and in St. Louis, Missouri, he was so overmedicated that his personal physician could barely get him on stage. "Elvis seems weak," St. Louis Post-Dispatch columnist Harper Barnes wrote of the perfunctory 50-minute show. The comment was an understatement considering Elvis collapsed midway through the performance and was unable to wake up.

On August 17, 1977, at around 1:30 p.m., Elvis's girlfriend entered his bathroom and discovered him lying on the floor with his gold pajama bottoms down around his ankles, his face buried in a pool of vomit on the carpet. His friend Joe Esposito came and worked desperately on the body, but there was little doubt in his or anyone else's mind that Elvis was gone just like that, at the age of 42.

> Do you want to hold your own strings, or be a puppet?

Using his personal leadership, Elvis Presley had everything he ever dreamed of: fame, wealth, and success. Once Elvis became a success, he no longer led himself. Elvis fell just as fast as he rose to stardom because he let himself go physically, mentally, and morally, costing him the most important thing, his very life. Elvis Presley illustrates that success truly begins or ends with personal leadership.

Thomas Edison and Elvis Presley weren't born into a position of leadership. They developed their leadership abilities, turning their visions and dreams into a reality. However, as Elvis illustrated, even successful people can destroy themselves once they give up leading themselves. The key to survival and success is leadership.

Now, I will show you how to develop your own personal leadership so you can lead yourself through action philosophy, influence, and discipline.

How to Build Personal Leadership

In order to develop and strengthen physical, mental, and moral fitness, all crucial parts of personal leadership, you have to have action, influence, and discipline. Having one or two of these things are not enough;

you must use all three. Without action, nothing works. Without influence, you have nothing to discipline; without discipline, action becomes meaningless.

- ❖ **ACTION:** Action is the core of personal leadership.
- ❖ **DISCIPLINE:** Discipline is a key to developing personal leadership.
- ❖ **INFLUENCE:** Influence is crucial to personal leadership.

ACTION

What is the most powerful thing on earth? Is it knowledge? Ideas? Wealth? Fame? Weapons of mass destruction? Personal or national resources are all power, but remain just potential power until they are put into action. If potential power isn't put into action, it becomes meaningless. In order to put potential power into action, an action philosophy must be followed. An action philosophy is a philosophy that states action makes things happen, inaction doesn't. True leadership begins with an action philosophy, not from a position or title; positions and titles need leadership to validate them.

IN ORDER TO UTILIZE THIS ACTION philosophy, you must desire and decide to do so.

> Action is the electricity that empowers us to change.

For example, you want to get in shape, you want that perfect job, or you want to build a relationship with a certain person. Unless you decide to act on these desires, your dreams won't come true. Using action philosophy led me to the happiest moment of my life: Meeting my wife.

From the moment I saw Sonja, I knew I wanted to marry her because I couldn't bear the thought of living without her. Action philosophy helped me realize that the only way this was going to happen was if I asked her out on a date. I knew that if I never asked her out, I wouldn't have developed a relationship with Sonja and had such a loving companion. I am very privileged she has stood by my side for 19 years and is the mother of our two lovely children.

Seeing the fruits of action philosophy has helped every day in every way—with my family, my business, and in my personal relationships.

Ideas + action = the most powerful thing on earth.

Without action, you can't develop physical, mental, and moral fitness, you can't tap into potential power and transform it into actual power; without action, nothing works. Develop personal leadership through action to change your life, and make your dreams come true! Action philosophy is the core of leadership.

DISCIPLINE

When people think of discipline, most associate it with punishment, like being grounded for doing something bad when you're a child. Discipline is inner training, which gives you internal strength. This internal strength gives you the ability to continually apply your knowledge, skills, and action to improve yourself.

Look back at Teddy Roosevelt. He was frail and weak until he disciplined himself to train and make his body stronger. Without discipline, no one can continue training him or herself physically, mentally, and even morally.

Discipline also changes bad habits to good habits; builds new good habits, and maintains all good habits. The foundations of discipline are honesty, integrity, patience, and responsibility, which teach us the difference between right and wrong. The benefits of continued discipline in life are self-improvement, inner strength, a profound sense of self-confidence, inner peace, and the development of a strong personal character. All of these benefits will shape anyone into a strong leader.

NELSON MANDELA SURVIVED 27 years of imprisonment in South Africa because he disciplined himself to stick with what he believed in. Mandela never allowed anyone to control him, even after being imprisoned by his government and put in constant mental and physical anguish. His discipline gave him the power to lead himself to freedom, even when he was behind bars. Once finally freed from prison, Mandela secured freedom for the black citizens of South Africa, and later became president of South Africa. Nelson Mandela is regarded as one of the greatest leaders in modern history.

> Discipline is the joy of self-improvement, not punishment.

The natural result of discipline is self-improvement. Through discipline, leaders improve themselves personally, professionally, and socially, making them better leaders. Discipline is one of the best ways not only to maintain strong leadership, but also to improve it.

Without discipline, the actions you take become meaningless because you won't know if what you are doing is right or wrong. Discipline is crucial in maintaining and strengthening physical, mental, and moral fitness. By making self-discipline a habit, you will become a true leader.

The faithful practice of self-discipline has an amazing trickle-down effect for true leaders, whose habits inspire discipline and self-improve-

ment in others. Leading others to improve themselves shows you have personal power. Discipline is the backbone of leadership.

INFLUENCE

Influence is a major factor that determines whether you become a good leader or a bad follower. Who you associate with changes your life.

Think about a child's upbringing. For example, an American child who grows up in a Korean family will speak Korean more fluently than English and be attentive to Eastern culture. Similarly, a Korean child who grows up in an American family will speak English more fluently than Korean and be attentive to Western culture.

Now that you know how influence works, I'd like to show you how important it actually is in shaping who you are as a person.

> No one is an island, everyone is human.

CONSIDER THE YOUNG MAN who drops out of high school to associate with a thief. The thief will likely influence the young man to become a criminal. If the young man instead sticks with a politician, most likely he will also become a politician. His future is shaped by with the person he associates with. All types of influences ultimately shape us in one way or another.

You have the choice to associate with whomever you want; these choices will change your life so always choose the right influences not only to learn from them, but also to build strong relationships with them. Influence is crucial to leadership.

Now that you know how to build personal leadership and lead yourself, you can learn how to lead others.

Lead Others

When it comes to leadership, there are those who push others around through a position of power and those who lead others with personal leadership.

If there were two different managers, and you had to work with one of them, which one would you choose: Manager A leads using only his position of power pushing people around, pressuring, intimidating, merely monitoring his employees, and wastes everyone's time. Manager B leads with personal leadership in his position motivating, energizing, and empowering his employees to maximize their potential.

More than likely you would choose to work with Manager B because Manager A's kind of leadership makes work unproductive and makes employees miserable. Manager B's leadership makes work productive and employees feel proud and wonderful.

As the above examples illustrate, truly leading others does not lie in just giving orders; you must recognize, trust, respect, and motivate them. You especially must lead yourself so you can lead others with personal leadership. Once you can lead others, you can build good relationships, lead organizations, nations, and even change the world.

However, in order to lead others well, you have to understand the nature of leadership: Why you follow other people, and what does it take to lead others?

WHY DO YOU FOLLOW OTHER PEOPLE?

- ❖ You have to. For example, in a country run by a dictator, if you don't follow the dictator, you will go to jail or get executed because he has the power of dictatorship. If you don't do what your boss says, you could lose your job; you follow him because he has the power of money. You obey the police because they enforce the laws; they have the power of law.

- ❖ You like to. When you like following someone that means you believe in that person's vision or ideas for personal, professional, or social improvement. This person leads through the power of value. When you love others and follow them, you are following your emotions; this person leads through the power of love. When you love a song and follow that singer, this person leads

through the power of feelings. When you follow celebrities, they lead through the power of fame.

❖ You follow others out of courtesy. For example, if someone were helping you, you would follow that person out of appreciation.

WHAT DOES IT TAKE TO LEAD OTHER PEOPLE?

People don't follow someone who is weaker than they are; they usually follow those who are stronger. The foundation of this strength is power, and there are several different types of power:

DICTATORSHIP POWER comes from fear, intimidation, and/or violence. Examples of those who have used only dictatorship power without personal power include Adolf Hitler, Joseph Stalin, and Saddam Hussein.

POSITIONAL POWER comes from a title or position of power. Jobs, businesses, even politics contain examples of arrogant or ignorant people who use only their positional power without personal power to show off or oppress others.

FINANCIAL POWER comes from having a lot of money. Many businesses contain examples of people who use only financial power to gain control.

SPIRITUAL POWER comes from spirituality. Examples of those who use spiritual power without personal power to gain control include cults who use religion for selfish purposes.

KNOWLEDGE POWER comes from intellect and knowledge. An example of someone who uses knowledge power without personal power to gain control over others is a con artist.

EMOTIONAL POWER comes from emotion. Examples of those who use emotional power without personal power to manipulate and control others include some celebrities.

PHYSICAL POWER comes from physical ability or strength. The best example of someone who uses physical power without personal power to control others is a bully.

PERSONAL POWER comes from personal leadership, which includes physical fitness, mental fitness, and moral fitness. When a person combines personal power with the other powers, even dictatorship power, he or she leads always thinking of the benefit of others in mind. It is the moral fitness aspect that makes the difference between a dictator leading with only his own benefit in mind, or the benefit of his people in mind. For example, to reform a corrupt government or even a corrupt company you may have to threaten and/or intimidate others. Although the person being threatened doesn't feel good, it could be for his own good and the good of others. Personal leadership includes a strong belief in values and the need to respect, care, understand, and motivate others. Some examples of leaders who used personal power include Mohandis K. Gandhi, Dr. Martin Luther King, Jr., Thomas Edison, Teddy Roosevelt, Billy Graham, and Abraham Lincoln.

In order to be a good, strong leader, you must follow values, not feelings. You must also develop and use personal power for personal leadership. If you follow feelings, you will become a weak, positional leader and will be forced to rely on dictatorship power, positional power, financial power, spiritual power, knowledge power, emotional power or physical power alone. You will be a bad leader. Always remember that positional, financial, knowledge, physical, emotional, even dictatorship power must be used for the good of others, not for personal gain.

Now that you know what it takes to lead others, you must know how to build, maintain, and improve your leadership abilities through influence, communication, and action so you can lead others better.

Three Leadership Keys for Leading Others

1. **INFLUENCE:** With influence comes power, and power is leadership.
2. **COMMUNICATION:** Communication is the most effective tool in leading others.
3. **ACTION:** Action is a key in leading others.

INFLUENCE

There are two ways that influence works. Earlier, I discussed that being influenced by the right people was key to your development as a leader. Now you must learn influence's application in leading others.

Influence is the power that affects a person's thinking, which can leave a lasting positive or negative impact. Not only are you influenced by others in shaping who you are as a leader, you can use influence to accomplish many objectives personally and professionally, some of which can include self-improvement, creating win-win relationships,

> The power of influence is life-shaping, creating heroes or villains.

even strengthening businesses and nations. The only way you can earn influence is by gaining trust and respect. You gain trust and respect from others by being honest, being responsible, having integrity, and proving your abilities. From influence, you gain cooperation, which builds strength and unity. Unity leads to power. Without trust and respect no one will follow you, making you an ineffective leader.

Gandhi used his influence to rally the people of India into a national movement of non-violent independence from Great Britain. He gained influence by earning respect and trust from his countrymen.

Through Gandhi's leadership and influence, Indians participated in ongoing, non-violent resistance against the British and ultimately gained their independence.

To gain influence, you have to earn trust and respect from others by being honest, responsible, consistent, developing your personal abilities, and having integrity. Leaders are able to earn respect, trust, and influence from others because of these traits. You always need to earn trust and respect from others in order to maintain your influence.

If you have influence, you will have the power to change your life and the lives of others. Influence is a key element of leadership.

COMMUNICATION

In our lives, we use internal and external communication to communicate with others. Internal communication is talking within yourself and listening to your body and mind. Through self-observation and self-discovery, internal communication strengthens inner understanding and assists in forming powerful relationships with others, because once we understand ourselves, we can better understand others. Examples of external communication are social interactions such as talking, listening, and observing, which promote understanding of others. By learning and practicing external communication skills such as choosing the right words to say, controlling your voice, expressing yourself through pleasing facial expressions such as smiling, understanding others, and acting positively, you will not only get others to like you, but you will like yourself even more. You gain more self-control, self-confidence, and positive energy.

Without communication, people can't understand each other. If you can't understand what someone is saying, can you honestly follow him or her? If people can't understand you, can you honestly lead them? You can't follow or lead anyone

> Communication skills and leadership go hand in hand.

without being able to understand what others are saying, and you can't be understood if people don't know what you are saying. All of these things make communication so crucial to leadership. In fact, communication is the best tool for leading yourself and others towards personal and professional success.

ACTION

Action philosophy is very important to personal leadership. However, action philosophy is also very important in leading others. You must take action to be more effective as a leader. Allow me to explain.

Aside from my friends, family, and business associates, no one knows who Y.K. Kim is. But people may recognize what I've done, what I am doing, and what I will do. If Bill Gates hadn't created Microsoft Windows and become the richest man in the world, would anyone listen when he talks about health issues in Africa? Who would recognize Michael Jordan if he weren't the world's greatest basketball player? Who would pay attention to George W. Bush if he weren't President? People talk about Bill Gates, Michael Jordan, and George W. Bush because of what they have done, what they are doing, and what they will do; people pay attention and talk about their actions, and that makes them leaders.

Remember that no one knows or cares about you if you don't do anything. Once you start something, people start to take notice and talk about what you are doing.

> The greater the act, the greater the results.

No one can lead if he doesn't take action. No one will follow someone who does not take action. Without action, nothing happens and nothing works. Maintain and improve your leadership by taking action. Action is critical when leading others.

With these keys, you can now unlock even more ways to lead others.

Ways to Lead Others

In the real world, you can lead others directly, indirectly, or through a combination of both.

Direct leaders lead others through face-to-face contact. They can be members of a family, the military, friends, teachers, coaches, co-workers or bosses. Direct leaders exercise real action philosophy.

Indirect leaders lead others through a medium—books, tapes, newspapers, radio or television—relying on the polish of their communication skills.

Great leaders use direct and indirect leadership to lead others. The President of the United States, for instance, directly influences the people around him, but most of us are indirectly influenced through his broadcasted and printed speeches.

When you know how to lead yourself and others, you can build great relationships, lead organizations, lead in the real world, and lead yourself to succeed in life.

> Being a leader is your choice! Maximize your life!

SUMMARY
Be a Leader, Not a Follower

There are two different types of people in our society, leaders and followers, and we all have the potential to be either. It is entirely up to you to what you become. In order for you to become a leader, you must choose to lead yourself.

How to Develop the Leader Within You

Develop leadership by using your innate abilities to become physically, mentally, and morally fit, thus gaining personal power.

- ❖ **LEAD YOURSELF.** To lead yourself you must follow action philosophy, learn from the right influences, and discipline yourself.
- ❖ **LEAD OTHERS.** You follow other people because you have to, like to, or out of courtesy.

People don't follow someone who is weaker than them; they usually follow those that are stronger. The foundation of this strength is power.

Three Leadership Keys for Leading Others

Influence, communication, and actions.

WAYS TO LEAD OTHERS
- ❖ Direct leaders lead through face-to-face contact.
- ❖ Indirect leaders lead through a medium such as TV, books, newspapers, or the Internet.
- ❖ Great leaders use direct and indirect leadership to lead others.

REVIEW OF "BE A LEADER, NOT A FOLLOWER"

Are you a leader or a follower? _____
_____
_____

What are the differences between leaders and followers?
_____
_____

What is personal leadership? How can you build personal leadership?
_____
_____
_____

What is physical fitness and why is it critically important in building personal leadership?
_____
_____

What is mental fitness and why is it crucial in building personal leadership?
_____
_____

What is moral fitness and why is it vital to building personal leadership?
_____
_____

What three building blocks make your personal leadership stronger?
_____
_____

There are three reasons why people follow other people. Please identify what they are.

_____

_____

In order to lead others, you have to have power. What kind of power should you use to lead others?

_____

_____

What are the three leadership keys for leading others?

_____

_____

_____

How do direct leaders lead? Please name one example of a direct leader in your life.

_____

_____

How do indirect leaders lead? Please name one example of an indirect leader in your life.

_____

_____

How do great leaders lead? Please name one example of a great leader in your life.

_____

_____

Develop Personal Power

CHAPTER three

Discover how powerful you really are

W E ARE ALL SPECIAL. We have such amazing qualities and awesome potential, and we all deserve to succeed. In fact, all of us have a tremendous power lying within, begging to be discovered. This power is so incredible that it can transform you into the person you have always wanted to be. This is *personal power*.

Personal power will revolutionize your life on so many levels, handing you the reins of personal freedom. Personal power makes the negative positive, the lethargic passionate, and the weak strong; but this power will remain just potential power until you dig deep and break it free. Once unleashed, personal power will maximize your life.

THE BEST WAY TO TAP your personal power so you can fully maximize your life is through the following seven steps.

> Personal power is the light within the lantern of leadership.

THE SEVEN STEPS TO BUILD PERSONAL POWER

1. **DISCOVER YOURSELF:** Unleash your potential with the power of self-discovery.

2. **BUILD PHYSICAL FITNESS:** Shape up with the Four Wheels of Health.

3. **DEVELOP MENTAL FITNESS:** Expand your mind through education and positive thinking.

4. **BUILD MORAL FITNESS:** Discipline your personal freedom, discipline your instincts, and follow principles.

5. **MANAGE YOUR TIME & MONEY PRODUCTIVELY:** Take control of your time and money to fully enjoy life.

6. **CREATE A POSITIVE SELF-IMAGE:** Become more valuable to yourself and to others by having a positive appearance and a positive attitude.

7. **LOVE YOURSELF UNCONDITIONALLY:** Build self-esteem by loving yourself.

STEP ONE: DISCOVER YOURSELF

Germany's Adolf Hitler is notorious for committing one of the greatest atrocities in modern history: murdering six million Jews during World War II. Sadly, he was not the only oppressive ruler to commit such heinous acts. More than three centuries before Hitler's time, Japan's Pung Sin Sukil inflicted genocide against the Korean people during the War of Im Jin Ohi Ran.

On April 15, 1592, Japan suddenly attacked Korea with 200,000 soldiers and over 1,000 warships. The Korean military found they were greatly outmatched by the Japanese fighting force as they tried defending their country. After the collapse of Bu San, Korea's second-biggest city and the biggest bay near Japan, the Korean military lost control of most of Korea. With its control of Bu San, Japan occupied almost all of Korea, except the state of Jun La.

However, it wasn't just the Japanese's near-total occupation that frightened the Koreans. It was also their merciless tactics. As part of Japan's agenda to crush the spirit of the Korean people, Japanese soldiers attacked towns, trying to capture every single civilian, including women and children, and cut off their noses with a sharp knife. However, strong young men were not mutilated. Instead they were captured to be sold as slaves. If the soldiers presented a bag full of noses to the Japanese government, the soldier had the right to keep the money from the sale of one of the slaves.

Having watched Japan sack almost all of his country, Korean Admiral Sun-Shin Lee waited for orders from his government to fight and protect the nation's last state, Jun La. Admiral Lee's navy was the country's last line of defense. Armed with only 24 warships, Admiral Lee devised a clever strategy in the face of a superior Japanese military. In fighting that began in May 1592 and stretched through September of the same year, Lee's navy fought 17 battles against the Japanese. Using the first ironclad warship ever invented; Admiral Lee's forces captured 207 warships and destroyed another 152. The Japanese suffered 33,780 casualties while the Koreans lost no warships and sustained only 243 casualties.

With the momentum of the war swinging towards Korea's favor, Admiral Lee severed the Japanese military's supply route on the ocean, cutting their armies off from supplies, food, and weapons. With the Korean forces gaining the upper hand, the Japanese changed their strategy to regain the advantage in their quest to completely conquer Korea. Their new focus: Eliminate Admiral Lee through political channels.

Japan's change in strategy couldn't have been timelier. At the time, Korea was politically divided between two parties: one supporting Admiral Lee, and the other supporting Admiral Kyun Won. Jealous of Admiral Lee's victories and his appointment as Commander-in-Chief of the Korean Navy, Admiral Won gained political power through bribery by using his wealth to smear Admiral Lee. A Japanese spy learned of Won's plan and conspired with him to rid Korea of Admiral Lee. Korea's king, Youn Lee, became enamored with Admiral Won and imprisoned

Admiral Lee in February of 1597. Once Admiral Lee was incarcerated, King Lee appointed Admiral Won as the new Commander-in-Chief of the Navy.

The government began torturing Admiral Lee in prison, a punishment which only got worse when he refused to admit that he did anything wrong. Finally, a longtime friend of Lee's, a prime minister, led a special campaign that freed him. Upon leaving jail, Sun-Shin Lee was given probation and permitted to reenlist in the army with no rank. Despite being disgraced and dishonored, the former Commander-in-Chief accepted his plight and made the most of his situation.

During his probation, Sun-Shin Lee's mother died. According to the rules of his probation, he was not allowed to travel to pay his respects. Lee loved and admired his mother more than anyone, and he was devastated that he was unable to attend her funeral. He wrote in his diary that his absence from his mother's funeral was the saddest day of his life. To this day, Lee's diary, in which he wrote about his fighting tactics and strategies as well as his personal feelings and philosophies, is used by many Korean people as a guide to overcoming obstacles in daily life. Korean President Jung Hee Park, who modernized Korea, said Sun-Shin Lee's diary was a major influence in constructing modern Korea.

With Admiral Won in power, the Japanese seized their opportunity and almost entirely destroyed Won's fleet. Only 13 warships remained. Swallowing his pride, King Lee asked Sun-Shin Lee to help the country again. Despite being tormented and disgraced by his government, Sun-Shin Lee accepted and was reappointed the Commander in Chief of the Navy; the past was the past to him. Admiral Lee now worried about protecting Korea's people and rebuilding the nation's navy.

In the wake of Admiral Lee's reappointment, the King saw the pathetic state of Korea's naval power and ordered him to give up the ocean. Only 13 warships remained, none of which were ironclad. Their navy appeared to be greatly outmatched by the Japanese. Admiral Lee refused to concede the waters and begged his government's permis-

sion to fight the Japanese. Lee began rebuilding the navy from scratch, aided by the support of the Korean people.

As soon as he began rebuilding the navy, Admiral Lee received an urgent report from his guards;

> "When you go to war, if you think of only survival and fighting, you will die. Forget survival and death, and try your best to fight and win."
> —Admiral Sun-Shin Lee

they spotted 200 Japanese warships gathering at Aha Ran Jin, just outside of the Yuol Dol Mok channel that led right into the state of Jun La. Lee realized that he needed to devise a strategy to destroy a superior Japanese fighting force or else Korea's hope for freedom would be crushed.

Years earlier, he had observed that when high tide occurred in the Yuol Dol Mok channel, the sea level would rise 100 feet and hide the coastal rocks. Because it was a very narrow and long channel, he believed he could lure the Japanese Navy into the channel and cause many ships to crash into the rocks once the tide went out. With that in mind, Admiral Lee and his small fleet set out to Yuol Dol Mok to fight. However, the admiral's team leaders lacked faith in Admiral Lee's strategy, letting their warships hang back one to two miles from the adverse tide conditions and the battle, waiting for Admiral Lee's orders; only the admiral's own warship stayed in the high tide at Yuol Dol Mok. Lee and his crew fought gallantly against 10 of the strongest Japanese warships for one hour. Acting alone, Admiral Lee's warship successfully blocked the Japanese from moving through the channel. He knew that they could not lose this battle because the moment the Japanese gained the advantage, Korea would be truly doomed.

Holding his ground, Admiral Lee decided to finish off the Japanese

DEVELOP PERSONAL POWER

once the tide was low. He signaled the remaining 12 warships to join the fight, and together they destroyed 133 Japanese warships in one of the most stunning military victories ever. The victory at Yuol Dol Mok strengthened the spirit of the Koreans, who went on to win the war—a victory that led to 300 years of peace throughout Asia.

During the six-year war, the Koreans destroyed 935 Japanese warships while only sustaining 1,002 causalities. The Japanese managed to destroy only one warship under Admiral Lee, while sustaining 126,380 causalities. Admiral Lee was undefeated in all 23 of his battles.

> "If you know the enemy troops and your own military forces, you can fight 100 times, and win 100 times."
> —Son Ja
> war strategy

LIFE IS JUST LIKE WAR: You will meet insurmountable obstacles through out your life, and you will need personal power to beat them. How do you get personal power? By developing the right strategy to build the personal power needed to overcome any obstacle and win in life. How do you develop such a strategy? The same way Admiral Lee developed a strategy to build the military power needed to overcome many insurmountable obstacles and win the war: through the power of self-discovery.

Self-Discovery

Like you and I, Admiral Lee was nothing special until he used self-discovery to build the military power needed to win the war. To understand how he was able to accomplish such tremendous feats, we need to know who Admiral Lee was and how he used the power of self-discovery.

Born March 8, 1545 in Seoul, Korea, Sun-Shin Lee was the third of four sons from a military man. Growing up, Lee studied with his brothers and excelled in school. Although Lee had a natural gift for writing, he wanted to be a martial artist. In 1566 at the age of 21, he began his martial arts training.

When he first tried to enlist in the army, he failed the government martial arts exam after falling from a horse and breaking his leg. Undeterred, Lee took the test again in 1576 and passed, entering the military as a low-ranking soldier. At the age of 31, he was much older than the average soldier (most were about 20 years old).

Despite beginning his military career at the lowest rank, Lee was promoted very quickly. In 1582, he was discharged dishonorably for insubordination after refusing to follow an illegal order from a superior. Readmitted four months later, Lee continued rising through the ranks, gaining a prominent position at the Jun La state security office. In February 1591, at the age of 46, Lee was appointed County Chairman, a position that preceded his promotion to the Commander-in-Chief of the Navy post for the state of Jun La.

It was as an admiral that **Lee used the power of self-discovery** and proved his mastery in tactics and strategy. According to his diary, as Commander-in-Chief of the Navy, Admiral Lee accomplished seven things that proved pivotal to Korea's victory against Japan in the War of Im Jin Ohi Ran:

1. He researched Japanese and Korean war histories and analyzed current Japanese military conditions for their strengths and weaknesses. Lee discovered the Japanese were more proficient with the sword than the Koreans, so he decided not to fight in that fashion. Admiral Lee also discovered that the Japanese preferred using shotguns in battles instead of cannons. He took advantage of this by choosing to use Korean cannon-bearing warships to fight the Japanese from a distance.

2. Admiral Lee assessed his navy's strengths and weaknesses. Admiral Lee considered institutional control to be extremely important in the military and instituted standard rules of conduct and discipline. Lee also inspected the navy's weaponry and facilities, determining

most were in disrepair. Maintenance of these facilities and warships were so poor that Lee found them practically unusable. He set out to fix this problem as well.

3. He compensated for his navy's weaknesses by building the world's first ironclad warship in 1592, which proved pivotal in destroying numerous Japanese warships.

4. He weakened his enemy's attacks by building obstacles in the ocean to block Japanese warships from easy passage to Korea.

5. Admiral Lee encouraged a more aggressive training approach with soldiers to increase their strengths and reduce their weaknesses, helping them learn new fighting skills and the advantages of teamwork.

6. Lee further strengthened his navy by infusing discipline through fair leadership. Good soldiers were rewarded with awards and promotions, while insubordinate soldiers were punished severely, which built unity and eliminated mutiny.

7. By being fully prepared, Lee and his men had full confidence whenever they entered battle, feeling like that they would do their best to win. This confidence was seen throughout all of their successes during the War of Im Jin Ohi Ran.

In the same way Admiral Lee used the Son Ja war strategy to win the war, you must use it to win in life. If you know your own worst enemy and your own best friend, you can fight a hundred times and win each time. If you know your strengths and weaknesses and improve yourself to fight for yourself, you will successfully win in life. Now, let me show you how you can discover your strengths and weaknesses.

Some people are very successful and happy at their job, while others are successful but not happy, or unhappy and unsuccessful at their job. Why?

Those who are happy and successful in their job have three things in common: They love what they do, they always know what they are doing, and they do their job well. Those who are successful but unhappy are capable of doing their job well but hate it. Those who are unhappy and unsuccessful in their job hate what they are doing and are incapable of doing their job.

In order to be happy and successful in your job (and in anything else you do), three things are required. First, you have to love whatever you do. Second, you must know what you are doing. Third, you need to know how to do whatever you have set out to do well.

With these things in mind, you must reach deep within yourself to discover who you really are and what you like to do so you can not only choose what you want to do in life but improve your weaknesses and fortify your strengths. Once you do these things, you will change into a better person and live a truly happy and successful life.

However, to do all of these things, you must pierce the layers of self-perception.

The Layers of Self-Perception

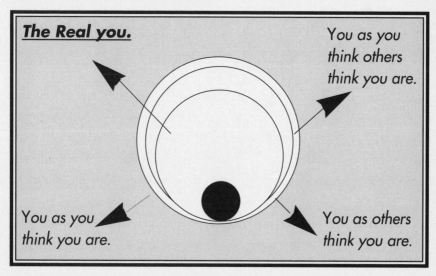

There are four layers of self-perception: you as you think others think you are, you as others think you are, you as you think you are, and the

core, the real you. Through self-discovery, you will pierce all of these layers in order to truly understand who you really are.

The best way to discover who you really are, your strengths and weaknesses, so you can increase your strengths and improve your weaknesses and make a better you, is through the power of self-discovery. There are twelve aspects of self-discovery. In the following exercise, you will examine each of these aspects and define what they are for you. Space is provided so that you may write down each of your self-discovery findings in this section, or you may take a separate sheet of paper and write down your findings on there instead.

But first, here is an example. This is the way I perceive myself.

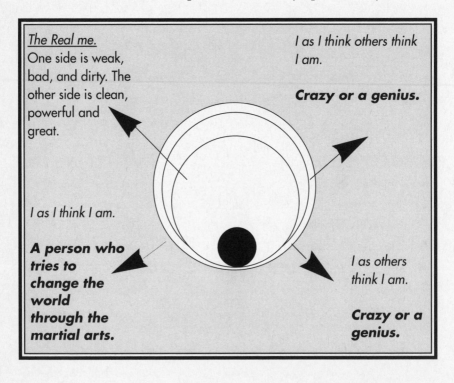

Now, take a moment and assess your own layers of self-perception to get a better idea of who you really are and fill in the following diagram.

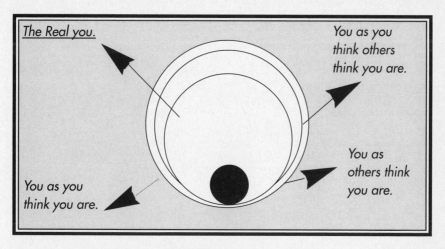

The Real you.

You as you
think others
think you are.

You as
others think
you are.

*You as you
think you are.*

The Twelve Aspects of Self-Discovery

1. **PURPOSE OF LIFE:** Finding your purpose of life gives your life meaning.

2. **IMPORTANT VALUES OF LIFE:** Prioritize your life by discovering your personally important values.

3. **TALENTS:** Unearth the tools that will lead you to success.

4. **SKILLS:** Discover the skills you need to achieve your goals.

5. **FACTORS OF ENERGY AND JOY:** Reveal what generates the most energy and joy in life to empower you.

6. **PREVENTING FRUSTRATION:** Stop frustration at its source to live a peaceful life.

7. **PEOPLE WHO BRING YOU THE MOST HAPPINESS:** Seek out those who make you happy.

8. **AREAS OF SELF-IMPROVEMENT:** Expose your weaknesses to strengthen them.

9. **MOST VALUABLE PERSONAL ASSETS:** Identify which assets are most valuable to you and harvest their rewards.

10. **PERSONAL ROLE MODELS:** Who inspires you, creates who you will become.

11. **PERSONS MOST NEEDED AND RESPECTED:** Through these people, you gain many advantages in life.

12. **LIFE'S MOST IMPORTANT THINGS:** Discover your life's most important priorities.

ASPECT 1: PURPOSE OF LIFE

When we know our purpose in life, we are able to find our life's true destination, which makes having purpose vital for all of us. Purpose is not a goal, but rather why you have that goal. Here are my purposes in life:

1. **HAPPINESS:** Everyone wants to be happy and stay happy; nobody likes being unhappy. Happiness is the ultimate achievement. Happiness is a great motivator in whatever we do in our lives, but it can't be stolen or bought; happiness must be earned.

2. **MAKE THE WORLD A BETTER PLACE TO LIVE:** I want to make the world a better place so our children can enjoy the future because I feel indebted to society and this planet for all it has done for me. I am repaying this debt by promoting and teaching the martial arts so more people can receive its benefits: self-improvement towards a healthier, stronger, smarter, richer, happier, and successful life.

3. **LIVE LIFE TO THE FULLEST:** My other purpose is to maximize my life to the fullest through various projects, including the building of a martial arts university to provide leaders for the future that promote physical, mental, moral, financial, and life fitness so they can change the world's lifestyle. By ensuring the success of the martial arts community, students will carry priceless knowledge with them forever. They will also feel that they have lived their lives to the fullest.

Now, it's your turn. Identify your thoughts on this subject and discover the power of having purpose in your life. By knowing your life's purpose, you will find direction and meaning.

What are the purposes of your life and why?

```
1. _____
   _____
   _____
2. _____
   _____
   _____
3. _____
   _____
   _____
```

ASPECT 2: IMPORTANT VALUES OF LIFE

We believe in values and constantly seek them out because they bestow personal power, aiding in our quest to discover who we truly are. By knowing what we value the most, we have a mental picture of what we should be working towards to gain personal power. Here is what I value the most:

1. **PEACE OF MIND:** Having peace of mind means having a mind that is clear, content, and worry-free. I especially like having peace of mind before going to bed at night, and when I wake up in the morning. With peace of mind, I feel energized in the morning and tranquil at night. Without it, my achievements mean nothing.

2. **HEALTH:** Health is vital to me. Without health, I could not have the energy I need to achieve all my hopes and dreams. Even if I became the richest and most successful person in the world, it would all be meaningless without my health.

3. **PERSONAL LEADERSHIP:** Personal leadership gives me the power to set positive goals, which guide me in a positive direction that creates hope and energy in my daily life. Personal leadership also gives me personal power, which is personal freedom, allowing me to control my own destiny.

4. **RELATIONSHIPS:** Though I value all of the relationships in my life, the one I value the most is the relationship I have with my family. My family is everything to me; without them, I wouldn't be here. My life is more meaningful because of my family.

5. **FINANCIAL FREEDOM:** Money can't buy happiness or healthy relationships, but it can easily destroy them. Financial freedom is very important to me since it relieves my stress, gives me personal freedom, and is an excellent tool for achieving personal and professional goals.

Now, please write down what values are the most important to you and why they are so important.

1. _____
   _____
   _____

2. _____
   _____
   _____

3. _____
   _____
   _____

4. _____
   _____
   _____

5. _____
   _____
   _____

ASPECT 3: TALENTS

You discover your tremendous potential through your natural talents. For example, if you write or talk well, then you have linguistic talent. If you can solve problems easily, then you have a talent for logic. If you know how to sing or play an instrument, then you have musical talent. If you can draw or design well, then you have visual talent. If you can make friends quickly, then you are socially talented. If you can do a physical activity well without ever practicing it, then you have natural physical talent. If you can solve mathematic equations easily, then you have a talent for numbers. If you understand others and lead them well, then you have a talent for leadership. There are so many different talents. Look at what you do best in life and you'll figure out your talents right away, but remember that a talent is raw. It must be developed into a skill so it can be used to its maximum potential. I've learned to appreciate and use the talents I've been blessed with.

What are my five greatest talents?

1. **LEADERSHIP:** My leadership talent enabled me to develop wisdom, vision, an indomitable spirit, and an open mind. Being able to develop this natural talent changed my personal and professional life; I have personal freedom and success because of my leadership.

2. **INTELLIGENCE:** I was able to use my intelligence to become a better communicator internally and externally. Internally, I used this improved communication not only to discover who I really am and what I truly feel in all situations, but also to discover the answers to winning that changed my life. Externally, I developed into a better instructor, writer, and public speaker in my field. All of these things made me a more effective communicator on all levels.

3. **INTUITION:** Having strong intuition has helped me make a lot of right choices that improved my life personally and professionally.

4. **STRONG SENSE OF ORGANIZATION:** My strong sense of organization really helped me in building a strong martial arts organization.

5. **ACUTE SENSITIVITY:** My acute sensitivity helped me understand others and myself. Not only did this talent give me the power to build strong personal and professional relationships, it helped me become an excellent promoter of the martial arts to the public so many people would want to practice and become healthier, stronger, smarter, richer, and happier.

Now, it's your turn. Write down your thoughts on what your five greatest talents are, and how they have affected your life.

1.

2.

3.

4.

5.

ASPECT 4: SKILLS

Even if you have a talent to do something, if it is not developed into a skill, that talent remains raw and unrefined. If you don't have a specific

talent to do something, you can develop your skill level to the point that a skill will become second nature, just like a talent.

What are my five most valuable skills?

1. **LEADERSHIP SKILLS:** My leadership skills have gotten me where I am today. I will continue to improve my leadership skills so I can help others become leaders, too.

2. **COMMUNICATION SKILLS:** By disciplining my communication skills, I have not only been able to build great relationships with my family, but with others, giving me great hope for the future. The more I discipline and improve my communication skills, the closer I am to reaching my personal and professional dream, being the best speaker and promoter of the martial arts.

3. **PEOPLE SKILLS:** Thanks to improving my people skills, I have built unbreakable bridges to success in my life.

4. **ORGANIZING SKILLS:** By developing my organizing skills, my dream of building a martial arts university is slowly becoming a reality.

5. **PROMOTIONAL SKILLS:** It is by improving my promotional skills every day that I am able to promote Martial arts World.

Now, it's your turn. Write down what your five most valuable skills are, and how they have affected your life.

1.

_____

_____

2.

_____

_____

```
3. _____
   _____
4. _____
   _____
5. _____
   _____
```

ASPECT 5: FACTORS OF ENERGY AND JOY

Discovering what brings us great energy and joy is vital to the self-discovery process. By finding out what brings us both energy and joy in our lives, we put much more effort in achieving these factors. When we do something that we enjoy, it empowers us even more. I have received great energy and joy from each of the things below.

What are five things that bring me energy and joy?

1. **TAKING ACTION:** Taking action is good for my well-being, whether it's practicing martial arts, walking, speaking, writing, organizing, or teaching. Such activities encourage and energize me, making me feel alive.
2. **HAVING A POSITIVE ATTITUDE:** Having a positive attitude generates positive energy, allowing me to maximize my life.
3. **DOING MEANINGFUL THINGS:** Doing meaningful things, including making meaningful plans, taking meaningful action, and having meaningful conversations, revitalizes my mind and lifts my spirits.
4. **ACHIEVING GOALS:** When I have achieved a goal, I feel like I've conquered a gigantic mountain. Achievement gives me great pride.

5. **SHARING WITH OTHERS:** I love sharing my experiences, knowledge, heart, and wealth with others because it motivates me to improve myself.

Now it's time for you to reflect on what brings you energy and joy in life, and why.

1. _____
   _____
   _____

2. _____
   _____
   _____

3. _____
   _____
   _____

4. _____
   _____
   _____

5. _____
   _____
   _____

ASPECT 6: PREVENTING FRUSTRATION

Figuring out what frustrates us, and why, is important because when we understand what these frustrations are, we can strive to prevent them from interfering with our lives. Here's what frustrates me the most:

1. **UNFAIRNESS:** Unfairness is unbalanced, unjust, biased, hurtful, and problematic. When unfairness is unavoidable, it depresses and angers me because I feel powerless to change the situation.

2. **NEGATIVITY:** Negativity creates an uncomfortable atmosphere, crippling the potential to succeed. Dealing with negativity makes me unhappy for three reasons: it thwarts teamwork, disrupts thinking, and drags me down.

3. **LAZINESS:** Laziness is your enemy, my enemy, success's enemy, and failure's best friend. When I'm forced to deal with laziness, time becomes an adversary instead of a friend because being lazy means not being productive.

4. **IGNORANCE:** Ignorance is the choice to be ill-informed, rather than being educated or informed. It reflects a closed mind that refuses to embrace common sense and self-improvement. The choice to be ignorant is crippling. It is all of these things that make ignorance so frustrating to me.

5. **LYING:** When I'm forced to deal with liars, I get incredibly frustrated because they can't be depended on, personally or professionally. You can't work or build relationships with liars because of their unreliability.

Now, write down your thoughts on what frustrates you the most and why.

1. _____
   _____

2. _____
   _____

3. _____
   _____

4.

_____

_____

5.

_____

_____

ASPECT 7: PEOPLE WHO BRING YOU THE MOST HAPPINESS

Interacting with people who bring us happiness makes our lives meaningful and productive because these people enrich and strengthen our lives. In fact, we normally forge lifelong bonds with those who make us happy. Here are some of the people who have brought me great happiness:

1. **MY FAMILY:** I'm privileged that my wife is my best friend, business partner, and advisor as I keep reaching for my dreams. My mother and brother bring me great happiness in unique and special ways. My children are an extension of me, and I enjoy teaching them important family values and how to win in life. My in-laws keep me grounded in reality.

2. **WORLD MARTIAL ARTS RESEARCH FOUNDATION EXECUTIVES:** I am fortunate to have Master Tim McCarthy as my business partner. We can talk about any subject and be very productive. I also have great hopes for the future when I talk to Master Winkle and Master Pelt, and I feel relaxed, yet energized, in my conversations with Master Mike Bugg.

3. **MARTIAL ARTS WORLD INSTRUCTORS AND STAFF:** I enjoy the meaningful time I share with my instructors and my company's staff everyday.

4. **LEADERS OF THE MARTIAL ARTS COMMUNITY AND OF THE REAL
    WORLD:** I receive much joy from being around leaders of the mar-
    tial arts community because we share our thoughts and ideas
    about the current and future state of the martial arts. I feel enor-
    mously satisfied after talking to leaders who lead the real world be-
    cause it gives me the opportunity to exchange ideas about the
    martial arts and share its benefits.

5. **MY STUDENTS AND SEMINAR AUDIENCES:** I become invigorated
    when interacting with my students and seminar audiences. I often
    learn lots of surprising things, making my time with them even
    more enjoyable.

Now, reflect for a moment about the people who bring you happiness,
and write down your thoughts. Who brings you the most happiness,
and why?

1.

2.

3.

4.

5.

ASPECT 8: AREAS OF SELF-IMPROVEMENT

Without the urge to continually improve, we become stagnant. There-fore, we must constantly seek out ways to better ourselves so that we can reach our highest possible potential and attain personal power.

Here are the areas in my life I continually strive to improve:

1. **LEADERSHIP ABILITY:** I know I have room to grow in terms of lead-ership. By always striving to have the right leadership, I build self-confidence, earn respect and trust, and improve relationships with myself and with others. I become a more effective leader.

2. **ATTITUDE:** I continually make the effort to deal better with nega-tivity, laziness, ignorance, unfairness, and even dishonesty prop-erly. By handling these situations correctly, I really can maintain a positive mental attitude, make my days less stressful, and enjoy my daily life.

3. **BUILDING GOOD RELATIONSHIPS:** Also, I constantly improve the way I build good relationships. I understand I must make myself a necessary and useful person to strengthen my relationships. I realize that the responsibility of building and maintaining good re-lationships is a lifelong task.

4. **COMMUNICATION SKILLS:** I'm a native Korean, and English is my second language. I understand that I always need to be more pro-ficient in English as it is America's primary language. By improv-ing my command of the English language, I become more effective as a communicator and public speaker.

5. **PROBLEM-SOLVING:** One of my biggest needs as a leader is solv-ing problems with tact. I must improve my diplomatic skills when questioning others. As a leader, the need to figure out why things are happening is very important to me. I have the responsibility to find answers for problems, but I need to handle these situa-tions with tact.

Now, it's your turn. Pause a moment to reflect on the five areas in your life you would like to improve on and why.

```
┌─────────────────────────────────────────────┐
│  1.                                         │
│     _____     │
│     _____     │
│  2.                                         │
│     _____     │
│     _____     │
│  3.                                         │
│     _____     │
│     _____     │
│  4.                                         │
│     _____     │
│     _____     │
│  5.                                         │
│     _____     │
│     _____     │
└─────────────────────────────────────────────┘
```

ASPECT 9: MOST VALUABLE PERSONAL ASSETS

In establishing goals in our lives, we gain purpose and direction. With purpose, we attain personal rewards with the accomplishment of our goals. We then reap our personal rewards through tangible and intangible assets. Here are my most valuable personal assets:

1. **LEADERSHIP ABILITY:** Leadership is personal power and personal power means I have physical fitness, mental fitness, moral fitness, financial fitness, and life fitness. Leadership is my best asset because it makes my life healthier, stronger, smarter, richer, happier, and successful.

2. **MY FAMILY:** My family means everything to me. They give me the strength I need for my personal and professional life.

3. **EARNING THE TITLE OF GRANDMASTER:** None of my achievements would have been possible if it hadn't been for my decision to learn the martial arts and eventually become a Grandmaster.

4. **MARTIAL ARTS WORLD:** Martial Arts World is an extension of who I am and what I've done in the martial arts. It has allowed me to impart the values and physical, mental, moral, and even financial benefits of the martial arts to hundreds of millions of people.

5. **U.S. CITIZENSHIP:** I am honored to be an American citizen. I think being an American citizen is a great privilege because of the United States' positive impact on other nations around the globe. Being an American citizen feels like being a citizen of the world.

Now, it's your turn. Write down what your most valuable personal assets are, and why you are glad to have them.

1. _____

_____

2. _____

_____

3. _____

_____

4. _____

_____

```
5.
_____
_____
```

ASPECT 10: PERSONAL ROLE MODELS

Role models are key to forming an individual's identity. People often copy a role model's actions, so the need to select the correct role model is significant to personal and social development. Good role models inspire good behavior, while bad role models encourage bad behavior. I have learned the value of having good role models. They gave me direction and helped me find my purpose in life. Here are my role models:

1. **FROM A PERSONAL STANDPOINT, MY MOTHER, HYUNG SOOK KANG, MY LATE FATHER, WON SOO KIM, AND MY LATE MASTER, CHUNG HYUP LEE:** My mother is my personal role model. Despite losing her husband, daughter, and home to the Korean War, she forged on with her unbreakable spirit and strong leadership, molding me into the person I am today. My late father is my true spirit. He selflessly enlisted in the army in 1950 to defend our native homeland in the Korean War. His last words before going into battle, "If everyone thought about their families and not about protecting their country, who would defend our country? We would all be dead," still have an impact on my life, even to this day. My late Master was a truly great leader in my life and a hero to me; his teachings changed my life.

2. **FROM A KOREAN NATIONAL LEADERSHIP STANDPOINT, SAE JONG, THE KING WHO CREATED KOREAN ALPHABET, ADMIRAL SUN SHIN LEE, AND CHUNG HEE PARK, THE 3RD PRESIDENT OF KOREA:** King Sae Jong created the Korean alphabet so Koreans would have a lasting, written form of communication. He indirectly taught me the importance of education in life. Admiral Lee

is a great role model because he indirectly encouraged me to discover myself so I could lead myself and lead others more effectively. President Park personified courage, inspiring me to have a "Yes, I can" positive mental attitude and to take care of others and myself through leadership.

3. **FROM AN AMERICAN LEADERSHIP STANDPOINT, GEORGE WASHINGTON AND ABRAHAM LINCOLN:** Presidents Washington and Lincoln are true American leadership role models because of their undying quest for democracy and belief in happiness as well as equality for all.

4. **FROM A BUSINESS STANDPOINT, INVENTOR OF ELECTRICAL LIGHTING THOMAS EDISON, FORMER CHAIRMAN OF GE JACK WELCH, AND FOUNDER OF HYUNDAI CHU YOUNG CHUNG:** Edison and Welch are American business role models because of their strong spirit and approach to their goals. Edison never buckled under stress in his pursuit of inventing electrical lighting. Welch's experiences taught me the practicality and efficiency of organizational leadership by building a winning team. Mr. Chung influenced me with his fighting spirit and relentless determination to win.

5. **FROM AN INSPIRATIONAL STANDPOINT, 26TH U.S. PRESIDENT TEDDY ROOSEVELT AND EVANGELIST BILLY GRAHAM:** Roosevelt and Graham are inspirational role models. Roosevelt inspired me with his winning spirit and leadership qualities, while Graham's work taught me the value of honesty and integrity, making me a better leader and a better person.

Now, it's your turn. Write down your role models and the impact they have had on your life.

1.

_____

_____

2.

_____

_____

3.

_____

_____

4.

_____

_____

5.

_____

_____

ASPECT 11: PERSONS MOST NEEDED AND RESPECTED

We all need specific people for their talents and skills. However, it's their personality and character that inspires respect for them within us; need and respect must work harmoniously for relationships to survive. I have come to realize the importance of needing and respecting people in my own life today.

1. **MY WIFE, SONJA KIM:** I need Sonja Kim more than anyone. In addition to being my wife, Sonja is my advisor, coach, supporter, and best friend. I respect her because of her great character and willingness to share herself with me.

2. **MY PARTNER, MASTER TIM McCARTHY:** I need Master Mc-Carthy for his self-management skills and attention to structure and detail. I respect his integrity and strong sense of responsibility.

Master McCarthy's leadership qualities have personally and professionally strengthened me.

3. **MY PARTNER, MASTER KEITH WINKLE:** I need Master Winkle for his loyalty, contribution, and commitment to making Martial Arts World a success. I respect him for his fighting spirit and his ability to triumph over adversity.

4. **MY PARTNER, MASTER KIRK PELT:** I need Master Pelt because of his commitment, vision, and work ethic. His keen intelligence, dedication, and tireless effort helped make Martial Arts World what it is today. I respect him for his dynamic leadership ability and character.

5. **MY PARTNER, MASTER MIKE BUGG:** I really need Master Bugg in order to finish my projections, and I respect him because of his openness, his willingness to give everything an honest effort, his excellent sense of teamwork, endless creativity, and positive attitude.

Now, it's your turn. Take the time to note the people you most need and respect in your life.

```
1.
   _____

2.
   _____

3.
   _____

4.
   _____
```

> 5.
> _____
> _____

ASPECT 12: LIFE'S MOST IMPORTANT THINGS

Understanding the most important things in our lives is instrumental to our pursuit of happiness. Often, we don't really know what they are until we face our mortality. To convey the importance of knowing what really means the most to us, I have posed the hypothetical question below. Please answer it thoughtfully so you can see what is most important to you in your life. I learned a lot from the exercise. I hope you do, too.

If I only had six months to live, what five things would I do?

1. **COMPLETE OUR MARTIAL ARTS CURRICULUM, INCLUDING THE BOOK *WINNING IS A CHOICE*, TO SECURE THE PROPER EDUCATIONAL TOOLS FOR STUDENTS, PROSPECTIVE MARTIAL ARTS LEADERS, AND MARTIAL ARTS SCHOOLS IN THE FUTURE:** Much like completing a martial arts curriculum, finishing *Winning Is a Choice* would enable me to provide lifelong guidance for people around the world. It would be a small token of appreciation to the planet Earth for giving me life.

2. **SECURE MY FAMILY'S FUTURE AND SPEND AS MUCH TIME WITH THEM AS POSSIBLE:** I have a responsibility to secure my family's future. I also would enjoy spending time with them because I love my family more than anything.

3. **SHARE MY KNOWLEDGE, EXPERIENCES, AND COMPASSION WITH MARTIAL ARTS WORLD LEADERS:** I would share myself completely with Martial Arts World leaders so they could pass my lifetime studies, extensive research, experiences, and knowledge to

their students. By doing all of these things, it will help the instructors and their students.

4. **GO ON A SPEAKING TOUR TO RAISE FUNDS AND ESTABLISH THE FOUNDATION OF THE MARTIAL ARTS UNIVERSITY SO THE EDUCATION OF OUR WORLD'S FUTURE LEADERS CAN BE ASSURED:** I would dedicate as much time and energy as possible to go on a speaking tour and raise funds that would properly establish the foundation for the Martial Arts University, a school that would emphasize martial arts education as the key to the future.

5. **PROMOTE THE BENEFITS OF THE MARTIAL ARTS TO THE PUBLIC UNTIL MY LAST BREATH:** I strongly believe martial arts can change the world, and I would promote its physical, mental, moral, financial, and life benefits until my last breath. Practicing martial arts helps people become healthier, stronger, smarter, richer, happier, and more confident, ingredients that build an indomitable spirit, which allows everyone to lead a successful life.

Now, it's your turn. Think about the five things you would do if you had six months to live and write them down. By doing so, you will discover what really means the most to you.

1. _____
   _____

2. _____
   _____

3. _____
   _____

```
4.
_____
_____
5.
_____
_____
```

ASPIRATIONS: YOURS AND MINE

❖ ***WHAT IS MY DREAM?** To build a martial arts university that promotes physical, mental, moral, financial and life fitness, creating the future leaders of the new millennium who will carry on martial arts values to the world.

❖ ***WHAT IS MY PERSONAL GOAL?** To become the greatest speaker ever in the martial arts on the subject of self-improvement.

❖ ***WHAT IS MY PROFESSIONAL GOAL?** To build a martial arts school on every street corner in the world so everyone can practice and enjoy the benefits.

❖ ***WHAT ARE MY FAMILY GOALS?** To support education 100%, encouraging my children to earn at least a master's degree in the field of their choice, travel around the world with my wife to discover the world, and learn more about other cultures while spending lots of meaningful time with her.

❖ What is your dream?
❖ What is your personal goal?
❖ What is your professional goal?
❖ What are your family goals?

Every month, review the results of your Power of Self-Discovery and your Personal Aspirations. Every once in a while, re-evaluate the results of your Power of Self-Discovery and your Personal Aspirations. Remember that you are very special and unique. You possess the potential to succeed in life.

STEP TWO: BUILD PHYSICAL FITNESS

What is the most important thing in your life? Is it money? Power? Fame? Love? Education? Family? Ideas? Health? I had to pay an almost fatal price to find the right answer to this question.

"Why am I going to the emergency room again?" I asked myself as the ambulance sped towards the hospital. I lay on a gurney as the paramedics watched over me, making sure I wasn't going to shift and bang on the insides of the ambulance. I had done this before, six other times, and I was going for the same reason: every muscle in my body screamed in agony. Stress coiled around my body, choking the life out of it.

"But why should I be worried?" I thought to myself. "This is nothing new, and this can be fixed again. The doctor will x-ray me, tell me there's nothing wrong inside my body but suggest I need a few days of rest; he'll give me some painkillers, and he'll send me home, just like that. I'll be in the hospital three to five hours tops. Nothing to worry about here."

Once we got to the hospital, I was rushed to the x-ray room. I could hear the squeak of the wheels on the hospital floor and smell the disinfectant rising from the floor tiles. The sounds and the smells made me very uncomfortable; I didn't like being here.

When we finally got to the x-ray room, the orderlies tried lifting my body off the gurney, but it was hopeless. With each tiny movement I howled, frightening everyone around me. I was in sheer agony when just an inch of my body was moved because my neck, upper body, and lower back were stiff, stiffer than a rock. More nurses and orderlies had to help lift my body off the gurney and onto the x-ray table because I couldn't stop screaming. Finally, I got my x-rays done and was taken to a quiet room by one of the nurses.

The doctor came in shortly after and informed me even though the x-rays showed nothing was wrong, my condition was still very serious. He said that he could offer muscle relaxants but at the same time told me the best way to recover from this was just to relax. The doctor also said that if I didn't recover properly, my condition eventually would become irreversibly crippling. He gave me the prescription, and I was released again.

When I got home, I took the muscle relaxants prescribed to me and was ready to get back to work. I tried moving. Nothing except excruciating pain coursed through my body. "Why isn't this working?" I angrily asked myself. "This worked the last six times. Why isn't it working now?" I was getting so frustrated. I had so much to do and couldn't do it because my body chained me to this bed. I couldn't do anything for myself. My wife had to feed me, wash me, and change my bedpans. I no longer was Y. K. Kim, a Master Instructor of the Martial arts. I was a baby.

However, I refused to panic. I thought I would be o.k. after a few days, just like before, and while I rested I could do some paperwork, just like before. My only worry was that my wife had to take care of me while she worked a full-time job. I was so sorry that I was putting her through this ordeal.

But after a week, my body still refused to move. Now, I got worried, very worried. I wondered if I would ever be able to move again.

This thought made me take stock in the things I've done in my life. At first I was proud of my accomplishments, but then it dawned on me that I was doing way too much. I wondered if I was going anywhere at all. I realized if I stayed bedridden for the rest of my life, all my achievements would become meaningless: none of my dreams would come true if I didn't make the effort to recover. I told myself I would do whatever it took to be healthy again.

AT FIRST, even the smallest movement of my body was excruciating. Pain weighed my body down, but I kept fighting through it to move in any way that I could. I started by turning my body from side to side in bed. It was incredibly painful at first, but I slowly saw and felt the improvements.

Health is the foundation of everything we do in life.

Once I was able to move my body, I started getting myself out of bed to move around the house. My upper body and lower back were still unable to support my entire weight so I had to crawl to get anywhere. One of my greatest accomplishments was the fact I could actually go to the bathroom in the bathroom and not in a bedpan: a sign of being one step closer to being independent again.

Eventually, I carefully forced myself to stand upright, using whatever I had to support me at first. Once I finally got used to standing again, I had to re-teach myself how to walk. Right off the bat, each step was excruciating because my body wanted to give up and get back into that bed so badly, but my mind wouldn't allow me to give into the pain, and my spirit gave me the strength to keep going. I had to walk again. At the same time, I looked at how I lived to determine what needed to be done to stop my body from ever doing this to me again. After extensive research, I realized that my lifestyle was totally wrong and unbalanced because of the ways I abused my body.

Whenever I had a headache, a stomachache, or my muscles were stiff or sore, I took medicine to relieve them, instead of taking the time to discover the causes of these aches and pains and prevent them. One day, all my small aches and pains ganged up on my body, paralyzing it. The next thing I knew, I was being rushed to the emergency room in an ambulance for the first time.

My sleeping habits didn't make my health any better. With my schedule, I only slept two to three hours a night. I felt guilty if I slept more than that. I wanted to work as much as possible, even if I had to catch a nap briefly on my office floor in the wee hours of the morning.

However, I sometimes dozed off while teaching and even while driving. I was incredibly lucky that I didn't get into a car accident. Despite these warnings, I was proud that I was an iron man, working harder, faster, longer than anyone else was. I completely ignored one of the body's most important natural healing mechanisms: Rest, which included a minimum of six to eight hours of sleep every night.

Plus, I abused my body terribly with the wrong diet. I had a voracious appetite, largely because of my aggressive martial arts regimen, but I didn't know how to satisfy it properly. I ate and drank anything and everything including fast food, candy, and fried foods, savoring every meal regardless of its nutritional value. All I saw was that it was food, and I had to have it. I thought since I practiced martial arts that my body could handle a few transgressions.

So I learned nothing from the last six times I was hospitalized. I just worried about my students, the school, and my martial arts reputation being ruined if people learned of my repeated hospital visits, meanwhile constantly making the same mistakes over and over. If it weren't for practicing the martial arts, my unhealthy lifestyle would have paralyzed me permanently. The martial arts gave my body the strength to fight against my bad habits.

However, I was my own worst enemy because I did what I thought was right and never followed any other advice. Ignoring the body is a recipe for disaster. Prevention is always better than any cure.

After months and months of rehabilitation, I was finally able to walk normally again, and I felt very lucky to be able do the things we all take for granted like standing, walking in the park, playing with my kids, even just going up and down staircases.

> Health transcends wealth, fame, education, and power.

I HAD TO LEARN the hard way that **health is the most important thing in my life**. It is much more important than money, power, fame, love, education, ideas, or family. Without my health, money, power, fame and love were meaningless. Education and ideas are very important, but without health I could not use them at all. My family is even more important to me, and that is why my health is the most important thing in my life. If I am healthy, I can take care of them; if I am not healthy, I can not take care of them and may even hurt them.

However, health problems aren't just harming us as individuals. In fact, health problems are hurting our entire nation. Here are some startling statistics (all statistics are U.S. only):

❖ 64% of the population is overweight.
❖ 30% of the population is obese.
❖ 39 million workdays of productivity are lost because of obesity.
❖ In 2000, the cost of obesity in the U.S. was more than $117 billion.
❖ Stress is linked to the six leading causes of death: heart disease, cancer, lung ailments, accidents, cirrhosis of the liver, and suicide.
❖ The Occupational Safety and Health Administration (OSHA) declared stress a hazard of the workplace, costing American industry more than $300 billion annually.
❖ 19 million people suffer from depression yearly.
❖ $69 billion is spent annually on mental health.
❖ 30 million people suffer from drug & alcohol addiction annually.
❖ $245.7 billion is annually spent on combating drug & alcohol addiction.
❖ In 2002, America spent $1.6 trillion on health care (around $5,440 per person).

These numbers are jarring, but there is hope. I realized that we could change all of these statistics through **The Four Wheels of Health**. Allow me to show you how this change can be made possible by utilizing this new concept of physical, mental, and moral fitness so that we can all lead rich and healthy lives.

The Four Wheels of Health

1. EAT & DRINK WISELY.   2. EXERECISE DAILY.

RIDE THE FOUR WHEELS OF HEALTH
TO LIVE A HEALTHY LIFESTYLE.

3. REST PROPERLY.   4. THINK POSITIVELY.

1. **EAT & DRINK WISELY:** Lead a healthy lifestyle through a healthy diet.
2. **EXERCISE DAILY:** Energize your life by losing weight, releasing stress, and getting in shape.
3. **REST PROPERLY:** Recharge your energy with proper rest.
4. **THINK POSITIVELY:** Focus on the positive to generate passion in your life.

By changing your lifestyle through The Four Wheels of Health, you will be healthier, stronger, smarter, richer, happier, and have a successful life.

99% of our personal health is dependent on the kind of lifestyle we lead. When we have an unhealthy lifestyle, we become weakened, tired, and are more vulnerable to illness. When we lead a healthy lifestyle, we live stronger, happier, more energetic, and healthier lives. So what is a healthy and unhealthy lifestyle?

A healthy lifestyle is the balance of *eating and drinking wisely, exercising daily, resting properly* and *thinking positively,* which are **The Four Wheels of Health**. By applying all four habits in unison, you gain a single-minded purpose: being healthy. An unhealthy lifestyle is a lifestyle that ignores one or more of the above-mentioned habits, allowing yourself to be poisoned by the toxins of physical fat, mental fat, and even moral fat. These toxins will destroy your body, mind, and heart, and lead to the total unbalancing and destruction of your health.

So why are **The Four Wheels of Health** so important to health? First off, you are what you eat and drink. The healthier your diet, the healthier you will be. If eating wisely is essential to maintaining good health, then why do some vegetarians look sickly and weak? Because eating and drinking wisely alone doesn't maximize health.

Then there is exercise, which is the best way to get in shape, building physical muscle, burning physical fat, releasing mental fat such as stress, tension, and building mental muscle; exercise is very important to health. However, why do some of the fittest athletes in the world get terminal illnesses, including cancer? Exercise alone doesn't guarantee good health: You need more than that to be truly healthy.

Next, there's recharging your energy, which is done through proper sleep and rest. Even though properly recharging the body is critical to achieving and maintaining good health, why do retired people get sick more often if this is the case? Rest alone cannot make anyone healthy: you need to do more than recharge your energy to be truly healthy.

Eating and drinking wisely, exercising daily, and recharging your energy are very important to health. At the same time, you can't be healthy if you have just these three elements working together. There's a fourth and final element needed to build and maintain good health. Someone could have a great diet, a great exercise routine, and always look very well rested yet be depressed, anxious, worried, nasty, or angry all the time. With that kind of attitude, do you think that person could be considered truly healthy or maintain good health for long? Absolutely not! Positive thinking is the key to eating and drinking wisely, exercising daily, and recharging energy properly, which creates good habits and eliminates bad ones. Without positive thinking, which is mental muscle,

you cannot maintain good health because negative thinking creates stress, and stress is the stem of sickness. It is because of all of these things that positive thinking is the most important wheel in **The Four Wheels of Health**.

These four habits are like the four wheels of a car. If all four wheels don't work together, then the car will crash. If you don't discipline all four habits simultaneously, you will crash as well. Therefore, balance is the key to achieving great health.

NOW, HOP IN AND BUCKLE UP. We are about to take a life-changing ride on **The Four Wheels of Health**.

EAT AND DRINK WISELY

I learned of the effects of good nutrition when I visited my native country of Korea in 1996, 20 years after I had emigrated. As I waded through the crowds of Seoul, I was stunned to see so many teenagers taller than the teenagers of my generation (the 1960's). I strained to find teenagers who were my height, 5'5", and found very few who were. Growing up in Korea, I knew of few tall people like those in the West so it was quite a shock to see such an abundance of tall Koreans. I wondered what led to the change in physical stature. I learned that a better economy led to improved diets. Nutrition impacted Koreans in a gigantic way; I realized that you really are what you eat.

I make it a point to eat more vegetables, fruit, and fish for these foods curb fatigue and disease. I stay away from junk food (processed food, greasy and white sugar-based items) and red meat. I find red meat is heavier, harder to digest, and it gives me fatigue. If I know I am about to have a long practice or about to do lots of physical work, I eat lots of good carbohydrates for energy. If I am going to have a light workout, I eat fewer carbohydrates. When I want to work out and build muscles, I eat lots of protein. I also drink seven cups of water a day, both for hydration and purification. I discovered that water actually conserves energy. I also enjoy drinking cranberry, orange, and apple juices, and herbal tea. Herbal tea is harmless and it relaxes me. I don't drink soft drinks, coffee, or alcohol because they offer no healthy benefits.

ONE OF THE DIRTIEST habits I quit was smoking. I hated the emotional, physical, and financial control cigarettes had over me. So much of my money and health was wasted on this disgusting habit. I only smoked out of insecurity, believing that smoking made me an adult. When I finally gave up smoking, I stopped smelling like cigarettes, more money stayed in my pocket, I could go anywhere I wanted to, and my body stopped craving nicotine. Nicotine no longer controlled me; my life totally changed.

> Wisdom begins and ends with what you eat and drink.

I quit drinking for almost the same reasons I gave up smoking. I hated how alcohol controlled me. When I drank, I felt invincible, but once it left my body, I felt empty and weak. I soon realized those physical symptoms stemmed from withdrawal. I also recognized that I couldn't practice martial arts or write when I was inebriated. I decided to take charge of myself and quit drinking permanently.

The benefits or consequences from our eating and drinking habits are determined by whether we are proactive or reactive eaters and drinkers. What are the differences between proactive and reactive eaters and drinkers?

- ❖ Proactive eaters and drinkers take responsibility for their own health by watching what they eat and drink.
- ❖ Reactive eaters and drinkers eat and/or drink in reaction to a specific situation, such as anger or stress, allowing their emotions to control their diets.

❖ Proactive eaters and drinkers consume foods that are beneficial to their health.

❖ Reactive eaters and drinkers consume things that are harmful to their health because what they put in their bodies makes them think that they feel good. Some of the consequences of reactive eating and drinking include alcoholism and obesity, both detrimental to health.

When we have proactive eating and drinking habits, we will eat and drink wisely to maintain our good health. Eating wisely, drinking wisely, quitting smoking and drinking made a profound difference in my life. I especially noticed the tremendous improvements in my performance in the martial arts and in the speeches I gave at seminars.

What you eat can make you stronger or weaker, energetic or lethargic, even determine what kind of mood you will be in for the day; you truly are what you eat. Always eat and drink wisely to energize your life.

Exercise Daily

The best way to understand how vital exercise is to health is to think of it as necessary maintenance.

Imagine you have just washed and dried a shirt and you smell it to make sure it is clean. It smells clean, doesn't it? Now imagine you've been wearing that same shirt for ten days and you smelled the sleeves. It smells awful, doesn't it? That shirt can be washed and it will be clean again. However, if you wear that same shirt for three or even six months and not wash it, it will be so foul that when you finally wash the shirt, it will tear into a million pieces. You can always go and buy a new shirt, right?

Now think of your body like a shirt. Exercise is what cleanses your body. If you exercise, your body will be just like a clean shirt, but if you don't exercise, it will be just like a filthy shirt. You can buy a new shirt when it becomes filthy, but you only have one body. Once you throw away your body, you have thrown away your life, literally. You cannot be brought back; that's why exercise is incredibly important.

EXERCISE IS AN empowering and transforming habit that anyone can take advantage of. Exercise will burn physical fat, rid the body of toxins, improve circulation, develop coordination, tone muscles, and strengthen the immune system. Exercise also burns mental fat, which releases stress and tension, making you more positive, and burns moral fat, which will exorcise your insecurities and build high self-esteem.

> Exercise is the best vaccine against illness.

You cleanse, maintain your body, and increase your longevity through exercise. Neglecting exercise causes the body to be unmaintained and lazy, decreasing the chances of you living a long and full life. The effects of exercise or a lack thereof are far-reaching and indiscriminate. The failure to govern your body will shorten your life regardless of how strong or powerful you are. On the other hand, there is also no discrimination in terms of who benefits from exercise.

Exercise can also generate mental strength. It helps me immensely when I'm writing. There are days when I feel like that my fingers can't type or that I'm blocked so I get out of the office and exercise. Once I work up a sweat, I often come up with new ideas and the thoughts just gush out of me.

Exercise's greatest advantage is its ability to assist in managing, reducing, and eliminating stress. Stress is part of our everyday lives, and, for some of us, a part of being successful. However, studies repeatedly have shown that stress must be released in order to maintain good health. In fact, stress is linked to six of the leading causes of death: heart disease, cancer, lung ailments, accidents, cirrhosis of the liver, and suicide. Thus, releasing stress is critical for survival, and exercise is one way to do it.

I realize there are some who say they're too busy to exercise. Some exercises don't need any equipment, much time, or a special place. All you need is your body and mind to practice anywhere, anytime, and anyplace. For example, smile and laugh, meditate, or move your body a little. You can do exercises such as these in your house, office, outside, in an airplane, or while driving (except meditation). You can choose any exercise based on your physical condition: walking, jogging, weightlifting, cleaning up at home, doing yard work, aerobic exercises, biking, power breathing, power exercises, or the martial arts. Kick out stress and tension, lose weight, get in shape, and change your life through exercise. The bottom line is make the time to exercise.

REST PROPERLY

I mentioned at the beginning of this chapter that I used to only sleep two to three hours a night at a time for fifteen years, thinking I could work harder and longer than anyone else; I was proud of that. I believed that if I worked more, then my dreams would be achieved faster. Eventually, my bad sleeping habits caught up with me to the point where I became so exhausted that one time I slept for 54 hours, waking up only to eat and go to the bathroom.

I didn't realize that my body, performance, and productivity would suffer the next day without sufficient rest. I fell behind instead of staying ahead of my workload. My work habits were wrong.

Through research and experience, I've since determined that the majority of people's bodies are designed for eight hours of work; eight hours of recreational activities, which can include eating, exercising, hanging out with friends, having fun; and eight hours of peaceful sleep to recharge the body's energy for work and recreation. (This allotment of time varies from person to person or job to job. Some people may work ten or even twelve hours a day; some only need six hours of sleep; while others sometimes spend more than eight hours doing fun, recreational things as well.)

Another way to recharge your energy is setting time aside for you during the weekend so you can be refreshed for the workweek ahead. This may include spending time with family, going fishing, cleaning the house, etc.

You also need a personal break every day during work to recharge your energy as well, and the length of the break depends on the profession you are in; some professions require more rest than others. A personal break allows the body and mind to rest as you recharge yourself.

How to recharge your energy

- ❖ Use time wisely by proper time management.
- ❖ Develop good sleeping habits by sleeping peacefully for 6 to 8 hours a night (This allotment of time doesn't apply to everyone. You can sleep less or more, depending on your body's condition. Normally, babies and small children require more than 8 hours of sleep.) Those who use sleeping pills might find it interesting to know that avoiding caffeine, intensively exercising, even taking a shower can aid sleep, thus eliminating the need for sleep-inducing drugs.
- ❖ You can take a personal break simply by smiling, showing appreciation towards someone, stretching your neck and shoulders, thinking about something enjoyable, or taking a moment to meditate. How do you meditate? Visualize you are sitting near the ocean, a mountain, a garden, or any other nice place. Just taking the time to relax can be the perfect way to get recharged.
- ❖ Listen to your body, find out what it wants and needs, and give your body what it desires.

You need good sleeping habits and personal breaks to properly recharge your energy.

Think Positively

Eating and drinking wisely, exercising daily, and recharging energy are very important to creating and maintaining a healthy lifestyle, but they are totally ineffective without positive thinking. By thinking negatively instead of positively, you hurt yourself mentally and physically, making it too difficult to start or even make a habit out of practicing the other three wheels in **The Four Wheels of Health**; positive thinking is the foundation of health.

Once you understand what it takes to develop and maintain positive thinking, you attain and appreciate good health.

How to think positively:

- ❖ Always focus on the positive.
- ❖ Set positive goals.
- ❖ Think, talk, look, listen, and act positively.
- ❖ Eat wisely, exercise daily, and recharge your energy.
- ❖ Follow your principles by pursuing the truth.
- ❖ Believe in yourself to build self-confidence.
- ❖ Exorcise your mental fat to be worry-free.

Being worry-free is vital to developing a positive frame of mind. If you are not worry-free, then you have negative emotions that make it impossible to think positively, thus blocking the other ways to build positive thinking. It is through my personal experience that all it takes to be free of irrational fear, anger, illogical hatred, jealousy, guilt, anxiety, and depression is to make the choice to be so.

Be Free of Irrational Fear. We experience two types of fear in our lives, rational and irrational. **Rational fear** is the cornerstone of our self-preservation instinct. **Irrational fear** can hinder or even hurt us. Also, fear raises its head when we face risks. How we respond to those risks determines if fear is a positive or negative thing. Think about what our society would be like if everybody lived in fear. There would be no progress. No airplanes, computers, electricity, phones, or medicine. We probably still would be living in the Stone Age. The handling of fear, therefore, is far-reaching in our lives.

You must have self-confidence to have courage so it is totally necessary that you always believe in yourself and be positive. By believing in yourself, you will have strong self-confidence and the courage needed to eliminate irrational fear.

BE FREE OF ANGER. Anger is a feeling of extreme hostility that has harmful consequences on many levels. Physically, anger can wreck your health; mentally, it can strain your brain; emotionally, anger generates negativity; and socially, it can destroy friendships. Therefore, it is extremely important and beneficial to control, release, and, if possible, prevent anger.

Where does anger come from? Anger is created when someone is inflexible in their difference in personal rules or opinions with another person. Anger can also occur from a failure to understand others, being hateful, jealous or lacking self-confidence.

The key to preventing, controlling, and being free of anger is flexibility, which means you must be understanding and open-minded and compromise when resolving your differences with others. However, the control of anger is not one-dimensional. Self-control not only applies to how you handle your opinions, but how you react to others as well. If someone is rude to you, it's smart not to be rude back. Staying in control during these kinds of situations reflects maturity and understanding.

BE FREE OF ILLOGICAL HATRED. If you hate somebody, you actually hurt yourself in the long run because harboring hatred is toxic to your body and mind. By exorcising hatred from your heart, you successfully achieve inner peace.

It's critical to determine the difference between logical and illogical hate. Hate is logical when it applies to the hatred of immoral or illegal actions such as crime and drugs. However, most forms of hatred are illogical and negative. Hating someone just because of the color of his or her skin is illogical. Hating someone just because he or she doesn't practice the same religion is illogical. Hating someone just because of his or her opinions is illogical. When you hold on to illogical hatred, that hatred becomes a time bomb in your heart; it will only be a matter of time until it explodes and destroys you.

The key to eradicating illogical hatred is flexibility and unconditional love. We must embrace our differences instead of fighting against them.

BE FREE OF JEALOUSY. When you are jealous, you want things that others have that you don't have, or you can't do something that others can do. Insecurity or low self-confidence is the defining element of jealousy. In most cases, jealousy is a negative emotion that creates conflict, making positive thinking almost impossible.

However, jealousy can be transformed into something positive: motivation. For example, when you see a friend succeed after all of his hard work, and you decide that you want have as much success, you are motivated to change your life. On the other hand, if you were in the same situation and reacted with jealousy, you would try to pull the other person down just to make yourself look more successful, or you would get depressed and do nothing to change the situation.

Set positive goals and work towards them to be free of jealousy. By focusing on your goals, you won't have any time to be jealous of others. You can also think big, believe in yourself, and love yourself unconditionally to be free of jealousy. By converting jealousy into motivation, you will think positively.

BE FREE OF GUILT. Guilt is the feeling of remorse, shame, or the realization of personal blame over a past action. Guilt occurs when someone becomes aware of a mistake or wrong that he or she has made, whether the mistake or wrong was an unintentional or intentional act of irresponsibility. When a person admits a wrong and regrets it, guilt becomes a character-building experience. In fact, the recognition of guilt when a wrong is committed is crucial to a person's ethical growth.

But when guilt is not recognized, the guilty party can become numb to the differences between right and wrong, potentially following the wrong path in life. Conversely, harboring guilt can limit your potential in life, leaving you paralyzed with doubt, depression, and negativity. Guilt can also be a waste of time and energy.

In learning how to eliminate guilt, it's wise to remember that you can't change the past. Therefore, remaining guilty because of a mistake is unnecessary; holding onto guilt will not get rid of it. What you *can* do to get rid of guilt is acknowledge your mistake and be regretful over it. At the same time, if you can fix your mistake, do so. Making amends can go a long way toward helping you feel guilt-free. If you can't make amends, learn from your mistake and move on.

BE FREE OF ANXIETY. Many people confuse anxiety with fear. For example, if you said that you were anxious over facing an opponent at an upcoming tournament, you actually weren't anxious, you were afraid. Now, if you said you were uneasy about traveling, but you did not know why, you were anxious. With anxiety, there is an element of uncertainty, while with fear you know what you are afraid of, and why.

Anxiety is an uncomfortable feeling of fear, uneasiness, or concern about something that is going to happen, or that you think is going to happen. Anxiety can strike anyone. It can work like an alarm, warning us when we are in danger. Negatively, anxiety can have both physical and emotional symptoms, which can be mild or severe. When anxiety is severe, people may not be able to do their usual daily activities. Continued anxiety can lead to physical and mental breakdowns.

Find the cause of your anxiety attacks by examining every aspect of your life: past, present, and future. After you've discovered the cause of your anxiety, you can handle it easily. Prevent anxiety attacks by loving yourself unconditionally, so that you gain self-esteem and can ferret out the cause of your anxiety. Once you throw away your anxiety, you will eventually gain peace of mind, and peace of mind creates positive thinking.

BE FREE OF DEPRESSION. Depression is the condition of feeling sad or despondent. One cause of depression is a past event, which can include a break-up or struggle of a relationship, job related problems, losing a competition, or failing a test. Another cause of depression is a lack of self-esteem. The symptoms of depression include an inability to concentrate, insomnia, loss of appetite, and feelings of extreme sadness, dejection, and/or hopelessness.

The key to being free of depression is to find its cause and understand it. Also, be physically active. When you are physically active on a constant basis, you will energize yourself and drive depression away. Think positively and love yourself unconditionally to build self-confidence. With positive thinking and self-confidence, you will block depression from coming anywhere near you.

Stress for Success!

To completely free ourselves of worry and negativity, we must rid ourselves of stress. Stress is a sign of responsibility. Even though stress is a very necessary tool of survival and success in life, too much stress is dangerous. Stress is like the air in a balloon: Too much air will pop the balloon. Too much stress will make you go "pop," too. Remember that stress is linked to six of the leading causes of death, including heart disease and cancer, and costs American industry more than $300 billion annually.

Stress drained me physically, mentally, and emotionally, corrupting me with negativity and nasty habits. In fact, stress was the main cause of my seven emergency room visits. I suffered because I had no clue what stress was, how to prevent it, or release it properly. Once I learned all of these things, I became relaxed and productive, making me physically, mentally, and emotionally healthier and stronger. The good news is that you will be okay, too, once you know how to release stress and shape up.

So how do you figure out if you have too much stress? Symptoms of stress start with a headache, then stiffness, beginning from the neck, moving to the shoulders, then to the upper back, and finally to the lower back. Internally, the heart is heavy as a stone, breathing becomes harder, you can't think and hear clearly, you feel very tired and moody, you lose your appetite, and get stomachaches. Eventually, you will reach the point where someone says the wrong thing to you, and you will explode.

The three things you need to do in order to prevent stress are:

1. Be flexible.
2. Develop a habit of preparation.
3. Lead a healthy lifestyle by practicing **The Four Wheels of Health**.

However, there are times that stress can't be prevented. In these cases, it is absolutely crucial that you know how to handle stress. Keep in mind that there are right and wrong ways to handle stress. When you handle stress properly, life becomes more manageable. If you release stress in the wrong way, you will receive twice as much stress back, pos-

---

MANAGING STRESS:
THE RIGHT AND WRONG WAYS

Stress for success with the best ways to beat stress:	Stress for failure with the worst ways to beat stress:
1. Smile and laugh.	1. Internalize stress.
2. Meditate.	2. Take out your anger on others.
3. Have positive conversations.	3. Eat junk food.
4. Organize your house, office or yard.	4. Smoke.
5. Play with a pet.	5. Abuse drugs.
6. Shower or bathe.	6. Drink alcohol.
7. Exercise.	7. Fight.

VS.

sibly ruining your life. Once you achieve balance through correct stress maintenance, you will be filled with positive energy. With that in mind, I would love to share with you how I learned the right and wrong ways to manage stress.

Without stress, you can't have a successful life; yet if you don't know how to release it, stress will destroy you. Prevent stress and release it correctly so you can have a successful life.

Lose Weight and Get in Shape

America's struggle with weight is fast becoming a dangerous epidemic with 64% of its population, including 9 million children, suffering from being overweight or obese. The United States is the only nation in the world in which the majority of the population is overweight. Being overweight or obese can be potentially damaging in a variety of ways:

- ❖ Causing back, knee, and ankle problems that severely limit their mobility.
- ❖ Damaging the cardiovascular and respiratory system, which can cause fatigue, lethargy, and make them more likely to suffer potentially fatal heart attacks.
- ❖ Creating physical difficulty in taking care of their loved ones.
- ❖ Inflicting a professional and social disadvantage due to their appearance, making them more vulnerable to depression and low self-esteem.

We have to lose weight (physical fat) and get in shape (build physical muscle). In this case, building physical muscle doesn't just give physical strength, but also more speed, agility, and endurance. When we have a lot of physical muscle, we will have great health, greater energy, and the personal freedom to do the things we want to do in our everyday lives.

However, in order to lose weight you must do more than diet. You must involve your mind, your body, and your emotions. The following are the best ways to lose weight and feel great.

1. Set positive goals.
2. Change your lifestyle.
3. Execute your plan.

Special note: Before you begin any diet or exercise program, consult your physician.

Once you have made these plans, execute them and never, ever give up, even after you've achieved all of your goals, because you don't want to gain back the weight you have fought so hard to lose. The best way to maintain your weight after you've lost it is by teaching others to reach the same positive goals. That way you are reminding yourself why what you have done was totally necessary while helping so many others reach their ideal weight and live healthier lives in the process.

Preventing bad health is always better than trying to cure it. Take care of yourself by eating and drinking wisely, exercising daily, resting properly, and thinking positively. Follow **The Four Wheels of Health** to change your life for the better. Take care of your health when you are healthy. Don't wait until it's too late.

STEP THREE: DEVELOP MENTAL FITNESS

In Chapter 2, we briefly touched on mental fitness, which is the balance of knowledge and positive thinking. From this balance comes mental muscle. The more mental muscle you have, the more fit and rational your mind will be. In fact, mental muscle will help you develop and maintain a positive personality. How? You feed your mind with education while you clean it with positive thinking.

However, you don't want mental fat, which consists of negativity, laziness, ignorance, and fear. When you have mental fat, you become cowardly and mentally weak, allowing your brain to get so clogged that learning anything new at all will be impossible.

Mental fitness is also vital to self-improvement and adaptability, especially in our rapidly changing world. Mental fitness allows us to be well informed in making the correct decisions, increasing wisdom, improving our lives, leading ourselves, and gaining personal power. Ceasing the pursuit of knowledge is irreparably damaging on a personal, social, and a professional level.

Education makes us more mentally fit and can be regarded with the same importance as food for the body. Without food, you die. Without education, your mind dies too. In short, education is invaluable, offering unlimited power and endless freedom. Anyone can benefit from education in four different ways.

The Four Educational Systems
These systems of education will empower you:
1. **ACADEMIC EDUCATION:** Learning in schools.
2. **SOCIAL EDUCATION:** Learning from society.
3. **FAMILIAL EDUCATION:** Learning from family or those regarded as such.
4. **SELF-EDUCATION:** Teaching oneself.

Develop mental fitness to enlighten yourself and tap into your enormous potential.

> You are what you learn.

ACADEMIC EDUCATION. An academic education is the learning of knowledge through a combination of teachers and textbooks. Higher levels of education, such as college, are incredibly valuable because they train us to become professionals in the real world. An academic education is also beneficial because it creates real world opportunities, with many people finding work in a profession out of their field. People with a substantial amount of academic education are appreciated for their skills and are rewarded accordingly. Society could never have been civilized without an academic educational system.

By embracing and participating in the academic education system, you make an investment in your life from which you never stop reaping the benefits.

SOCIAL EDUCATION. Social education is the accumulation of practical knowledge from the real world, acting as a guide in personal situations. Essentially, a social education is the possession of common sense, the know-how to handle a variety of day-to-day occurrences. For example, a social education teaches us appropriate behavior for various situations: such as going to church, going out on a date, working, talking with friends, etc. Keeping an open-mind, being understanding, and listening to others are all important people skills that are part of a social education. In many ways, a social education gives us the bulk of our knowledge.

A social education also guides us in who we choose to associate with, acting as an aide when making an intelligent decision about whom to associate with for self-improvement. For example, associating with successful or working with successful people helps you be successful. On the other hand, associating with unsuccessful or lazy people leads you nowhere. With a social education, you can build great, lasting relationships.

FAMILIAL EDUCATION. Familial education is the foundation of academic, social, and self-education. We accumulate our first bits of knowledge from our family, which include discipline, honesty, integrity, responsibility, morals, values, and the most important thing in life, the difference between right and wrong. These bits of knowledge not only are the foundation of wisdom with common sense, but the foundation of the development of our self-confidence as well.

Because of its fundamental values, familial education also is the most simplified and enduring form of education. When family members care about each other, they create a need for the sharing of knowledge. It is these acts of caring and sharing that make familial education the foundation of learning.

SELF-EDUCATION. Self-education is the accumulation of knowledge through the discipline of teaching oneself. It is the most multi-faceted of the four educational systems and an extension of academic, social, and familial education. Examples of self-education include reading books, listening to educational tapes, doing research, and learning from our own mistakes and successes.

Many people believe that education only occurs in elementary schools, high schools, or colleges, but this belief couldn't be further from the truth. Look at some of the greatest people in history to see the importance of self-education. Thomas Edison's endless self-education paid off big time when he brightened the whole world. Lincoln's endless self-education paid off when he became President of the United States.

The following are seven methods with which you too can educate yourself:

1. Read books.
2. Be inquisitive.
3. Open your mind and learn from your failures and successes.
4. Develop a writing habit, including keeping a diary of your experiences.
5. Listen to educational, inspirational and motivational materials while driving (cassettes, CDs).
6. Attend seminars and associate with great teachers, great learners, and all the right people.
7. Learn from communicating within yourself.

Remember: self-education means you discipline yourself to continue your education. If you stop educating yourself, that means you limit yourself. Without education, the mind becomes stagnant, limitations are created, and self-improvement grinds to a halt. Therefore, education is not only enlightening, but also a self-sustaining part of the human process that allows you to enjoy life to the fullest. **A great leader is a great learner.**

STEP FOUR: BUILD MORAL FITNESS

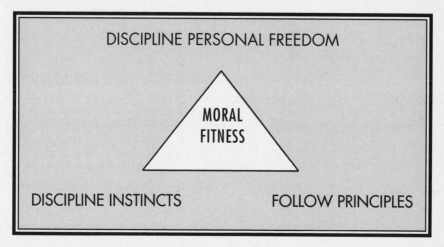

1. Know the difference between freedom and indulgence, and why personal freedom needs to be disciplined.
2. Understand the meaning of instinct and discipline, and why instincts need discipline.
3. Learn what principles are so they can be followed.

In Chapter 2, it was mentioned that moral fitness is conscience, which is the balance of emotion (warm heart) with reason (cold mind). In order to build up your moral fitness, you must use moral muscle, which is honesty, integrity, responsibility, and a strong sense of right and wrong.

Without moral muscle, you have moral fat, which replaces your conscience with dishonesty, irresponsibility, a severe lack of integrity, and a warped sense of right and wrong, making you immoral. By having moral fat, you become weak and insecure, causing you to doubt yourself and doubt others, hate yourself and hate others, and become jealous of others. Also, when you have moral fat, you easily get angry with yourself and others.

In order to further build moral fitness so it can be exercised and maintained, you must *discipline personal freedom, discipline your instincts,* and *follow principles.* These three things will prevent you from becoming immoral and will make your fight successful.

Discipline Personal Freedom

Freedom is one of the most powerful gifts we all have. What we do with it shows if we are moral or immoral.

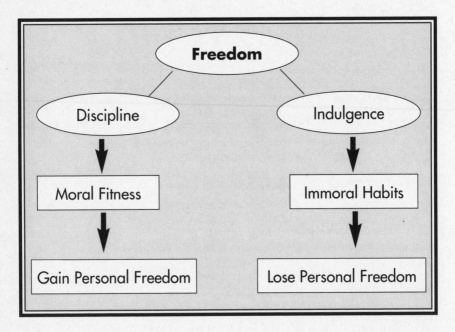

To better understand the true meaning of freedom and why it must be disciplined, the following questions must be answered: What does the phrase **"Give me liberty or give me death"** mean to you? Would you choose liberty or death?

Even without knowing why or when this phrase was stated, everyone would choose liberty over death without hesitation. It's safe to say we all want freedom, and we certainly don't want to be dead. The problem is that we must know when and why this statement was made so we can understand its true meaning.

It was during the American Revolutionary War that Patrick Henry made this famous statement. This statement addressed the feelings of the American colonists while the British controlled the American colonies. The colonists were so angry with their unfair government that they took up arms and risked their lives for the freedom of their nation, not for the good of an individual or for the sake of greed.

Therefore, the true meaning behind Patrick Henry's statement is that we must fight for our own freedom and take responsibility for our actions in order to earn true personal freedom.

However, there are so many people who think that freedom means they are 'free' to do whatever they want, disregarding the consequences. These people aren't being responsible; they are being indulgent.

It is wise to choose responsibility over indulgence because when we make indulgence a priority in our lives, we become tainted with immoral habits, which corrupt us and sometimes others as well, eventually taking away our personal freedoms. You still missed the point, here. For instance, indulging in junk foods can make you fat, and being fat may take away your personal freedom to wear certain clothes or participate in some physical activities - and extreme indulgence, could result in early death due to coronary disease. Sexual indulgence may lead to diseases, and even death in the case of venereal diseases and AIDS. Teenagers are especially vulnerable because they completely misinterpret personal freedom to be indulgence, not responsibility, suffering the emotional, physical, moral, and sometimes legal consequences for their misunderstanding.

True personal freedom is not indulgence. In order to earn and maintain it, you need both responsibility and discipline. By controlling ourselves, we will eventually earn true personal freedom. If we do whatever we want without discipline and responsibility, we lose personal freedom. Indulgence is immorality, not freedom. Consider our right of free speech. We can speak out against injustices and our government, but we can't call in a bomb threat or threaten someone's life without the risk of imprisonment. Thus, there is responsibility in free speech.

We also must take responsibility in our use of freedom of the press. We can print truthful information about someone, or even state a controversial opinion about something. However, we can't publish slanderous or libelous statements without the threat of a lawsuit.

Like America's forefathers fought for the freedoms of all Americans, you have to fight for your own personal freedom to develop moral fitness, not for the sake of indulgence. Once it is earned, personal freedom requires discipline and responsibility to maintain it so you do not lapse into immorality.

Discipline Instincts

There are five primary instincts that we must discipline if we are to attain true personal freedom: *appetite for food, sexual desire, honorable recognition, material possessions,* and the *desire to win.* Let's look at each instinct and the impact discipline has on them in greater detail.

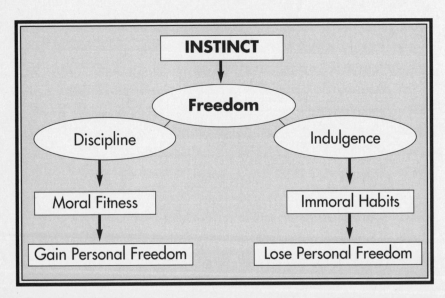

APPETITE FOR FOOD

Our appetite for food is the most important instinct in our lives, for without it, we would not know when to eat and drink to refuel our bodies. Without food, we can't survive.

However, if we don't discipline our appetite, we become indulgent, gaining too much weight by eating too much of the wrong kinds of food. Such a lack of discipline and responsibility can afflict us with fatigue, sickness, and loss of self-esteem. This immoral habit makes us more likely to suffer from obesity, which is a common problem in our society. The end result of this indulgence is the loss of our personal freedom. Only by disciplining our appetite for food will we energize our bodies and minds, and gain true personal freedom.

The bottom line is to either control our appetite or let it control our lives. Here are some suggestions you should try that will help you discipline this instinct:

- ❖ Drink seven to eight cups of water everyday to stay hydrated and feel energetic.
- ❖ Eat healthy foods such as fruit, fish, vegetables, etc.
- ❖ Avoid junk food, red meat, white-sugar products and caffeinated drinks.
- ❖ Eat slowly by chewing food more thoroughly. Doing so will help prevent weight problems and indigestion.
- ❖ Do not drink alcohol excessively for too much of it destroys the mind and body.
- ❖ If you are trying to lose weight, avoid carbohydrates, sugar-rich food, and drinks such as bread, rice, pasta, fruits, juice, and soft drinks.
- ❖ If you work a lot physically, eat a sufficient amount of carbohydrates, fruits, and juices to generate energy.
- ❖ If you are building muscles, eat sufficient amounts of protein.
- ❖ Avoid eating right before going to sleep at night.

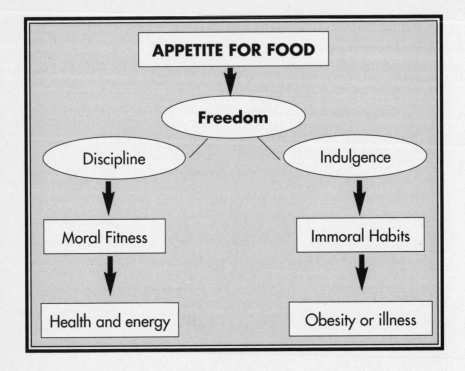

❖ Fight for yourself until discipline of your appetite becomes a
   habit.

Control your appetite and enjoy your meals; don't let your appetite
control you.

SEXUAL DESIRE

Sexual desire drives the human race to procreate, prolong, and bond our
species; it is actually productive energy. Without it, humanity would not
exist. However, if we don't discipline and take responsibility for our sexual desire, we become indulgent and immoral, to which the consequences can include guilt, shame, the destruction of relationships,
receiving sexually transmitted diseases, imprisonment, and even death.
With discipline, we will be able to enjoy our sexual desire properly, build
strong personal relationships, and gain true personal freedom.

Here are some ways to control this instinct:

❖ Use your energy productively. Don't let your craving for physical contact take precedence over other important things in life.

❖ Clear your mind. Take your mind off your temptations by focusing on worthwhile activities.

❖ Think of the consequences of your actions. Imagine your worst fear happening because of your lack of self-control.

❖ Fight within until control of your sexual desire is a habit.

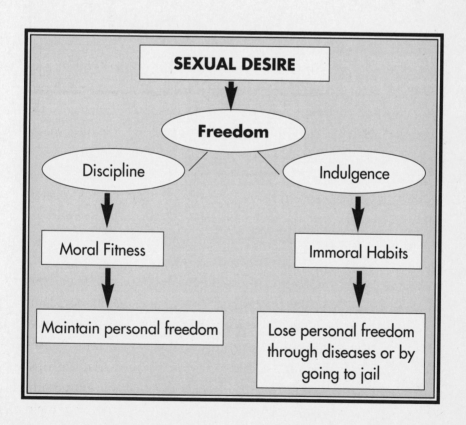

It's important to remember sexual desire stays with us for most of our lives. Disciplining ourselves in this area strengthens our character and increases personal power. Never stop disciplining your sexual desire.

HONORABLE RECOGNITION

We strive to attain honorable recognition because of our instinctual need to be recognized by others. If we aren't consistently recognized for our honorable actions, we lose our sense of right and wrong, doing anything we want regardless of how harmful or shameful it may be. The end result of a lack of honorable recognition is that we become apathetic, chaotic, and animalistic, no longer caring about what we do or how our decisions affect others.

This instinct can generate personal power, develop good character, leadership ability, and create an excellent work ethic. However, none of these positive qualities can exist without discipline. When our need for honorable recognition is left unchecked, we will take inappropriate actions for this recognition, and the consequences can be grave to us and to others.

One example of this instinct gone unchecked was John Hinkley's attempted assassination of former President Ronald Reagan and the subsequent crippling of the President's press secretary, Jim Brady. Hinkley committed this crime because he believed that actress Jodie Foster would finally take notice of him. Hinkley earned notoriety for his heinous act, leaving a negative impact on society. This tragic incident is just a mere demonstration of how lethal the instinct of honorable recognition can be without discipline.

The desire to be honorably recognized is an instinct most of us appreciate for its value. It's important to remember that honorable recognition and respect are earned, and only we can choose to earn them. Here are some ways to discipline our instinctual need for honorable recognition:

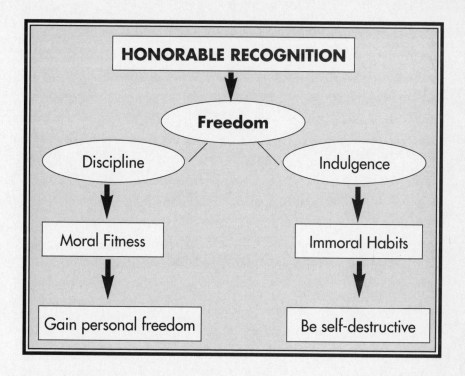

- Build your personal leadership ability to always be a necessary person.
- Recognize, respect, appreciate, motivate, help, and share with others.
- Always be honest, responsible, and have integrity.
- Never stop improving yourself by keeping an open mind and constantly educating yourself.
- Fight for yourself until you make disciplining your need for honorable recognition a habit.

When we never stop improving ourselves, people will recognize us.

MATERIAL POSSESSIONS

The need for material possessions serves multiple purposes, including serving as a need for shelter and self-preservation. For example, housing shelters us from the elements and helps keep us safe. Likewise, clothing covers our bodies and protects us, as well as making us feel secure. Also, the need for material possessions drives us to be successful because we want them to make life more comfortable and secure. In fact this instinct drives societies to improve themselves. Without material possessions, we would live like animals.

However, if our instinct for material possessions isn't disciplined, we become indulgent, thus creating immoral habits. Once we discipline our need for material possessions, success will be ours.

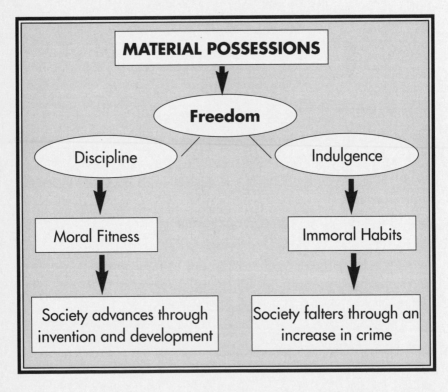

The bottom line for all of us is choice. We can choose between being enslaved by material possessions or control our worldly impulses, enjoying what we have along with enjoying earning material possessions.

Here are some ways to discipline this instinct:

- ❖ Look at those less fortunate than yourself and take stock in what you have.
- ❖ Visualize an uncontrollable lifestyle of greed that could wreck your life.
- ❖ Imagine someone stealing something that you *really* need.
- ❖ Remember that in death you cannot take anything with you except your name.
- ❖ Fight within yourself until you make disciplining your need for material possessions a habit.

By developing discipline in the need for material possessions, we successfully fight within ourselves.

DESIRE TO WIN

The desire to win energizes all walks of life, ensures progress on an individual and societal level, and creates leaders. Without the instinctual desire to win, personal, professional, and global progress would be impossible. However, if this desire isn't disciplined, we will become indulgent and immoral, turning us into losers. Hence, the wise handling of this instinct is paramount to success.

Competition is everywhere. Actors compete with each other for starring roles, bigger paychecks, and awards. CEOs drive their businesses to compete with other businesses in order to survive and succeed. Politicians compete with each other to win elections.

The instinctual desire to win is the catalyst of progress. Without it, our society would be plagued by stagnation. However, the need to win must be acted on in a controlled manner, otherwise society would de-evolve into a savage state, creating a constant state of warfare. When uncontrolled, our competitive instinct becomes dangerous.

For example, in 1994 Tonya Harding admitted knowledge of an attack on Nancy Kerrigan at the U.S. Ice Skating Championship in Detroit.

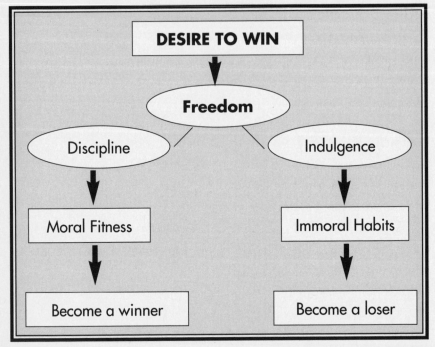

Kerrigan was clubbed in the knee by an accomplice of Harding's ex-husband Jeff Gillooly, and was unable to compete. Despite this, Kerrigan was awarded a spot on the U.S. Olympic team. The U.S. Figure Skating Association subsequently banned Harding for life, and ex-husband Jeff Gillooly received two years in prison.

Here are two ways to discipline this winning desire:

- ❖ Compete within yourself.
- ❖ In your fight to win, always fight fairly.

It's imperative to remember that you can be your own worst enemy through indulgence. Therefore, it is prudent to compete within yourself to maintain control over your winning instinct as you build moral fitness.

Without instinct, we can't survive or succeed. Without discipline, instinct produces self-defeating immoral habits. Only when instinct and discipline work together will the roads of instinct and discipline lead to moral fitness.

Follow Principles

What are principles? Principles are the rule of nature that represents the three most important things in our lives: harmony, truth, and survival of the fittest. Since we are part of nature, we have to follow these principles in order to survive and succeed.

HARMONY is duality in life, which is "yin" and "yang," positive and negative, female and male, night and day, hot and cold, water and fire, etc. Without a negative and positive charge, electrical light could not exist. Without a male and a female, we could not exist.

Harmony demands that for us to survive and succeed, we must cooperate with each other, showing mutual appreciation and respect in the process; no one is an island. People need people to survive and succeed. Following harmony builds moral habits; ignoring it makes you immoral.

TRUTH. Nature never lies. You plant corn and corn stalks grow. You plant an apple seed and an apple tree will grow. It's impossible to plant an orange seed and have it grow into a banana tree.

In order to build moral habits, you must follow the truth, which means you should be honest, responsible, and always do the right thing. If you don't, you will become immoral.

SURVIVAL OF THE FITTEST. In the jungle, the lion chases after the wildebeest and kills it; the human world is no different. If you are strong, you will survive, but if you are weak, you will die.

However if you merely focus on your survival, then you will be uncaring and ruthless, becoming immoral in the long run. Supporting and helping others in the real world builds moral fitness. It is important to discipline your survival instinct so you are not only able to survive, but able to create harmony and follow truth.

Remember that following principles is morally right. Fighting against them is immoral.

STEP FIVE: MANAGE YOUR TIME & MONEY PRODUCTIVELY

I dreaded sitting in front of a computer, always looking at it like it was some sort of evil monster. I knew so little about computers that I didn't even know where the 'ON' button was. Most of the time, I asked my secretary or another member of my staff to type up my work for me. When I wanted my Korean notes transcribed onto the computer, I turned to my father-in law, Mr. Dong Il Yun. Mr. Yun was and still is a computer programmer with an excellent command of both the English and Korean languages. He helped me immensely in transcribing my Korean writings onto the computer. I was so grateful to him for all of his help. Little did I know what was about to happen.

One day, I asked my father-in-law for his help and he replied, "I'm not helping you anymore. You have got to learn on your own."

"But…but…please I need your help," I pleaded. "I can't do this by myself. I don't even know how to turn on a computer. Don't do this to me; I need you, please." We stood there for a moment, looking at each other in silence. He extended his right hand, and in it was a card.

"What's this," I asked.

"Instructions on how to turn on and use your computer. This is the last bit of help I'm offering you. From now on, you're on your own. Best of luck to you."

After he left, I worried because I needed to transcribe my writings to the computer soon. "I have a business to run," I thought to myself, "I don't have the time to learn how to type, much less learn the operation of a computer." I tried one last time to get my father-in-law to take care of my work for me, but he wouldn't budge. I finally realized I had no choice but to learn.

My knowledge came in baby steps. First, I learned how to turn the computer on and off. Then I did some basic typing exercises for a week. When it came time for me to write, it took three days to write one page—work I ended up losing because I didn't know how to save my files properly.

For a month frustration gripped me. I was still irked at my father-in-law for forcing me to do this by myself. "I've done nothing to anger him," I thought. "Why is he punishing me like this? Why is he forcing me to learn? I'm just wasting time doing this stuff."

With all the trouble I had, I thought about asking my secretary to transcribe my Korean notes into English. I was about to leave my office and give her my notes when it hit me; she didn't know Korean. I had no choice but to learn how to type in Korean.

Eventually after weeks of toiling, I learned how to type both in Korean and English. Typing was no longer a great trouble; it was finally a great tool.

To this day, I'm thankful that my father-in-law used some tough love because I can't even begin to figure out how much time and money I saved. Before I learned how to type, it would take me anywhere from half an hour to an hour just to write a page by hand. Then I asked somebody to type and edit the copy for me. Now, I could do the same task in just five to ten minutes. I could work whenever I needed to, even use the Internet.

Saving time and money weren't the only benefits I gained. Knowing how to type reduced my stress and boosted my confidence because I no longer had to depend on others to get my work done.

To paraphrase an old Eastern proverb, "Mr. Yun taught me how to fish, instead of giving me the fish." My father-in-law helped me save time and money, which relieved my stress and opened a whole new world for me as a writer. I've always loved writing, but I knew that having to depend on someone to type was time-consuming and frustrating. Now, with all of this new knowledge, I can write whenever my heart desires.

> The hands
> of time can
> push your
> life forward
> or keep it
> grounded.

LEARNING HOW TO TYPE taught me the three most important things about how time management maximizes the value of time.

1. How important setting priorities is to good time management. For example, learning how to use my computer and to type became a priority, once no other alternative was available to me.

2. How crucial preparation is to time management. For example, practicing basic typing exercises saved me time in the long run when I began writing this book.

3. The importance of time management itself, whose benefits include saving money, reducing stress, and making life productive and enjoyable.

The most important thing I realized was that time is not just money, time is life. In order to manage my life productively, I must manage my time productively. Without proper time management, I won't just waste time and money, but waste my life. Effective time management revolutionized my life.

Manage your life with all the right habits

1. Prioritize Your Daily Activities: Determine what is extremely urgent, urgent, important, necessary, or unnecessary in your daily life.

2. Make preparation a habit: Plan, organize, practice, and put into action everything that you do.

3. Organize your life: Learn to manage time on a short and long-term scale.

4. Discipline yourself to follow a daily plan: Planning daily is the best way to develop a habit of good time management.

5. Use time wisely: Using time wisely is necessary for good time management.

6. Achieve financial fitness: Control your money; don't let money control you.

Prioritize Your Daily Activities

Prioritization is essential to time management because it allows you to determine what is an extremely urgent, urgent, important, necessary, or unnecessary priority, enabling you to group priorities in order of importance so time can fully be utilized.

An **Extremely Urgent** priority is one that needs the most attention among multiple simultaneously occurring **Urgent** events or just a singular priority that needs instant attention. For example, let's say you are at home right now and three urgent priorities pop up at the same time: 1) your kitchen has accidentally set on fire while you are cooking dinner; 2) your baby is crying in the next room; and 3) you have diarrhea. Which of these is extremely urgent? In this case, you would deal with the kitchen fire first because the house could burn down with you and the baby in it if you don't put it out.

An **Urgent** priority is one that is in need of immediate attention. For example, the need to go to the bathroom, answer a ringing phone or doorbell, attend to a crying baby, extinguish a fire in the kitchen, or catch a flight could all be classified as urgent.

An **Important** priority is one that needs a great deal of attention, but not immediate attention, such as personal health, education, safety, family, or business.

A **Necessary** priority is one that is essential to achieving a task or goal, but does not require immediate attention. Mowing the grass and cleaning the house can be considered necessary.

An **Unnecessary** priority is one that isn't urgent, important, or necessary. During working hours, this may include watching TV, going to the beach, and chatting on the Internet.

Keep in mind prioritization is not absolute. Things of importance vary from person to person and circumstance to circumstance.

To better understand the importance of prioritization, try your hand at prioritizing the following activities. Please circle the number to the right of each activity based how you would prioritize it:

PRIORITIZATION KEY
1. Extremely Urgent. 2. Urgent. 3. Important. 4. Necessary. 5. Unnecessary.

ACTIVITIES

Going to the bathroom.	1.	2.	3.	4.	5.
Answering a telephone call.	1.	2.	3.	4.	5.
Watching TV.	1.	2.	3.	4.	5.
Eating dinner.	1.	2.	3.	4.	5.
Doing homework.	1.	2.	3.	4.	5.
Cooking food.	1.	2.	3.	4.	5.
Going to a business meeting.	1.	2.	3.	4.	5.
Spending time with family.	1.	2.	3.	4.	5.
Exercising.	1.	2.	3.	4.	5.
Cleaning house.	1.	2.	3.	4.	5.

This is how I prioritized these activities. *However, keep in mind that priorities can change based on the situation.*

❖ Going to the bathroom: 1. It is **Extremely Urgent** because it allows the body to continue functioning properly.

❖ Answering a telephone call: 2. This is **Urgent** because if we don't answer the phone right away, the caller will hang up and we will miss the call. **Note:** Though answering the phone itself is an urgent priority, staying on the phone after you've answered it is another matter. If the call is informative, then the call is also **Important** (3) or even **Urgent** (2). If the call is from a salesperson wanting to sell you something you don't need, then the call is **Unnecessary** (5).

* Watching TV: 5 or 2. Watching TV for fun is **Unnecessary**, but watching it for important information such as a hurricane watch is **Urgent**.
* Eating dinner: 3. It is **Important** to eat.
* Doing homework: 3. It is **Important** for achieving academic success.
* Cooking food: 3 or 2. It is **Important**. However, if guests are coming to your home, then cooking becomes **Urgent**.
* Going to a business meeting: 3 or 2. It is **Important** and depending on meeting, can be **Urgent**.
* Family activity: 3. It is **Important**.
* Exercising: 3. It is extremely **Important** in maintaining good health.
* Cleaning house: 4. It is **Necessary**.

With this knowledge of prioritization in mind, you now can **organize** your priorities to properly utilize time.

Take the time to organize the following eight responsibilities related to the home using numbers 1 through 8 in putting them in order. After putting these responsibilities in order, explain your choices.

RESPONSIBILITIES	ORDER
Cutting the grass.	
Answering a the phone.	
Answering the doorbell.	
Cooking dinner.	
Cleaning the house.	
Watching T.V.	
Attending a family meeting.	
Helping a child with homework.	

1._____

2._____

3._____

4._____

5._____

6._____

7._____

8._____

This is how I organized these responsibilities:
However, priorities can change based on the situation.

1. **Answering the doorbell** is urgent.
2. **Answering the phone** is urgent.
3. **Cooking dinner** is important.
4. **Helping a child with homework** is important.
5. **Attending a family meeting** is important.
6. **Cleaning the house** is necessary.
7. **Cutting the grass** is necessary.

Now, take the time to organize the following seven responsibilities related to work using numbers 1 through 7 in putting them in order. After putting these responsibilities in order, explain your choices.

RESPONSIBILITIES	ORDER	REASON
Attending a meeting.		
Answering a phone call.		
Assisting a customer.		
Reading the mail.		
Chatting with a co-worker.		
Analyzing a report.		
Chatting with a friend on the Internet or over the phone.		

1._____

_____

2._____

_____

3._____

_____

4._____

_____

5._____

_____

6._____

_____

7._____

_____

This is how I organized these responsibilities. However, keep in mind that priorities can changes based on the situation.

1. **Assisting a customer** is urgent.
2. **Answering a phone call** is urgent.
3. **Attending a meeting** is important.
4. **Reading the mail** is necessary, but it can be important depending on the mail.
5. **Analyzing a report** is necessary, but it can be urgent or important depending on the nature of the report.
6. **Chatting with a co-worker** is unnecessary.
7. **Chatting with a friend on the Internet or over the phone** is unnecessary.

If you disagree with the way I prioritize things, that's ok. My main intention is that you think about your priorities. I'd rather you disagree with me for good reason than agree with me without thought.

Make Preparation a Habit

Preparation is the process of planning, organizing, and/or practicing a task in order to execute it successfully. Preparation can be as simple as writing a grocery list or as complex as building your own house. In fact you'll notice that you are less stressed, less tense, and you will save more time, money, and energy when you are prepared. Most important of all, preparation will give you a clear method of achieving your goals.

Now, let's check out your preparation know-how. Take a few minutes to check one or more of the boxes that apply to each task below. For example, if you think a task needs only to be planned, put a check in the "plan" box. If you think a task needs more than one element of preparation, check all the boxes that apply.

TASK	PLAN	ORGANIZE	PRACTICE
Grocery shopping			
Going on a trip			
Making a speech			
Building a house			
Competing at a tournament			

Done? Great. Let's look at each task in greater detail.

Grocery shopping requires only simple planning. Make a grocery list before you leave the house so you know what your shopping needs are. The list doesn't have to be organized, and you don't really need to practice running up and down supermarket aisles before you start shopping.

The first thing everyone does before **going on a trip** is plan. The questions we usually ask ourselves when planning include: "What is my destination? How will I get to my destination? Where am I staying? What is the purpose of my trip? What will the weather be like at my destination? What will I do once I get to my destination?" so you know how to pack your luggage accordingly. You organize your trip by making travel and hotel reservations. You can't practice going on a vacation, although it sounds like fun.

Making a speech requires all three elements of preparation to ensure its successful execution. You plan for a speech by getting details about your audience, the subject of the speech, and where and when it will be made. As you write the speech, you organize it so it touches on that subject and its related topics in the correct order. You practice it over and over to make sure that when you execute it, it should be one of the best speeches you've ever given.

Before you can even think of **building a house,** you have to have building plans so you know what kind of house you are building, how big it will be, what materials it will take, etc. You have to make sure the building process is organized so you can gather all of the necessary materials and laborers and the house can be built correctly. Then, you execute those plans. However, you must remember that building a house requires constant organizing as its being built so you are prepared for any unexpected events that may happen during the building process.

In order to **win a tournament,** you have to prepare very well before participating in it. First, you have to plan how you will win the tournament. Second, you have to organize the additional details needed to make your plan work. Finally, you must practice physically and mentally to be ready to win.

ORGANIZING YOUR LIFE

Organization is the systematic arrangement of something to achieve order. It is one of the most pivotal necessities in time management, making it important on both a personal and professional level. The foundations of organization are prioritization, preparation, and self-discipline. After mastering these foundations, we can schedule and even delegate responsibilities to further organize our lives

Here are some ways to organize your life:

1. **ORGANIZE YOURSELF: First,** list your ultimate goals and plans. **Second,** list your yearly goals and plans. **Third,** make a list of your monthly goals and plans. **Fourth,** list your weekly goals and plans. Finally, list your daily goals and plans, which will be explained in the next section. By listing all of these things you can clearly see your goals, giving you direction and motivation to accomplish them.

2. **ORGANIZE YOUR HOME OR OFFICE:** Write down a "to do" list for your office or home. By making this list, you, your family, and/or your co-workers will see what needs to be done in a set timeframe, making you and them more likely to take the initiative, be more productive, and more efficient in completing tasks.

3. **ORGANIZE MASSIVE PROJECTS:** You can't do massive projects by yourself. The key to doing massive projects is to break them down into smaller, manageable tasks and to delegate these tasks accordingly to the right people for maximum effectiveness. To keep things flowing smoothly, review your decisions from time to time. By extending your body and mind, you can accomplish many things in a short period of time.

DISCIPLINE YOURSELF TO A DAILY PLAN

When you plan your day on a regular basis, you develop a strong time management habit, helping you to be more productive on a conscious and subconscious level. In fact, most leaders in any field make daily plans.

Every day, you need to make a daily plan. You can make it when you wake up in the morning or you can plan for tomorrow before going to sleep at night.

The following is an example of a daily plan I use when planning my day. If you like, feel free to make copies and use it for yourself, or you can design your own daily plan format.

I AM RESPONSIBLE FOR MY OWN LIFE!
Thursday, 10 / 16 / 2003

THINGS TO DO	DONE?
1. Edit editorial for magazine.	
2. Prepare for convention in detail.	
3. Reserve airline ticket for L.A. seminar.	
4. Call and confirm with CNN for TV interview.	
5. Send an e-mail to all regional directors about project.	
6. Organize new office.	
7. Buy new computer.	
8.	
9.	
10.	

SUCCEED THROUGH EXECUTION!
Appointments

TIME	PLACE	CONTACT	FOR
7:00 am	NBC TV N.Y.C.	Jim Smith (212-354-1000)	Interview
12:00 pm	White Garden	Bill Bush (222-2000)	Business
3:00 pm	Afternoon staff meeting at the office	All staff	New project
7:00 pm	Kennedy Center	Richard Reagan (234-2300)	Speech

MAXIMIZE MY LIFE!

I AM RESPONSIBLE FOR MY OWN LIFE!

_____ , _____ / _____ / 20_____

THINGS TO DO	DONE?
1.	
2.	
3.	
4.	
5.	
6.	
7.	
8.	
9.	
10.	

SUCCEED THROUGH EXECUTION!

Appointments

TIME	PLACE	CONTACT	FOR

MAXIMIZE MY LIFE!

USING YOUR TIME WISELY

The one thing that the 6.3 billion people on this planet have in common is time. Everyone has only 24 hours a day to use, and no one can speed time up or slow it down to a standstill; how we use time determines who and what we are and will be in life.

Our level of success reflects whether we use our time effectively or ineffectively. Those who effectively manage their time show that they use time productively, and are successful in their lives. Those who manage their time ineffectively show that they waste their time, and are not as successful. Successful people control their time. Those who don't control time allow time to enslave them.

For example, if you enjoy your work and are productive, you control time. However, if you hate your job, you will throw productivity out the window and let time anchor you down.

Using time wisely is essential to good time management. Good time management should be utilized in everything from the smallest of actions to the most demanding tasks in the world. No matter how solid and detailed your preparations are, they will not be successful if you don't use time wisely.

Here are several ways to use and maximize your time to control it:

EATING WISELY will actually save time. Why? Eating wisely makes you faster, more efficient, and more productive in everything that you do. Poor eating habits will slow you down mentally and physically. You should eat and drink appropriately to ensure you are always thinking and performing at your maximum potential. For example, if you work in an office all day, don't eat too much. Because you don't use a lot of physical energy in an office environment, you don't need a lot of fuel. However, if you're a construction worker, you need plenty of food and drink because your body uses a lot of energy and needs fuel to replenish it.

RECHARGING YOUR ENERGY THROUGH EXERCISE AND PROPER REST allows you to maximize the time in your day. Exercising daily and doing mini-exercises such as laughing, meditation, and quick stretching, throughout the day to relieve stress leaves you more energetic and capable of handling time with increased efficiency. The simple act of smiling or relaxing for a few minutes can feel like a mini-vacation when you're stressed, allowing you to be more productive.

ACTING WISELY in your decision-making is another appropriate way to save time. On the job, or anywhere else, learn to say, "No," or, "Yes," to effectively use time. Remember, you only have 24 hours a day to work with, so by saying, "Yes," to top priorities, and, "No," to low priorities, you utilize the time in your day to its maximum potential.

MAKING USE OF SPARE TIME is yet another appropriate method of good time management. We often find ourselves with spare time when we are traveling or waiting for something. If not used properly, spare time becomes wasted time so use that spare time to your advantage. For example, if you're driving on a long road trip or just down the block, keep motivational or educational tapes or CDs handy so that you can listen to them. On an airplane (or while waiting for one) read a book, write one using paper, or work on your laptop computer.

THINKING POSITIVELY will help you enjoy whatever you do as you save lots of time and energy. If you focus on the negative instead, you can't concentrate, causing you to get stressed out and waste valuable time. Thinking positively is crucial to time management.

ACHIEVE FINANCIAL FITNESS

Money can't buy time, relationships, and happiness, but money can take our time away and destroy our relationships and our happiness.

However, you have no reason to be poor and tons of reasons to be rich. When you are rich, you know life will be easier for you. You can live in a beautiful house and drive a beautiful car. You can go wherever you want on vacation, even buy a beautiful vacation house. If you have elderly parents, you can take care of them. If you have children, you can put them through college. You can use your money to help others in many meaningful ways. Also, money is a very practical tool that can be used to accomplish your goals. You can make all of these things come true when you achieve financial fitness.

What is financial fitness? Financial fitness is the ability to control your money and not let money control you. In order to achieve financial fitness, you must have financial muscles, which are assets (income generators), and burn away financial fat, which are liabilities (unnecessary expenses). Once you have achieved financial fitness, you will gain financial freedom. Consider the following hypothetical scenarios regarding the importance of financial fitness.

Jack and John are best friends who went to high school together. Jack got sick of high school, dropped out, and got a full time job to support himself. Because Jack didn't have a complete high school education, he was paid barely above minimum wage at $6 an hour. Even with steady wage increases, ten years later, Jack still only made roughly $19,000 a year. What's even worse is that he spent $25,000 per year, $6,000 more than he makes. Because he is always short on money, Jack is always pre-occupied with paying the bills. Jack has to find a second job to make up the difference, thus allowing money to control him and his time.

However, John decided to go to college and work one part-time job while in school. Once he got his degree, John found a career. Though he made less money in the beginning, ten years later, John made about $45,000 a year. John also learned how to manage money properly so he only spent $20,000 per year and saved $25,000 a year. He controlled his time and money so he could maximize his life.

Because John made an early financial sacrifice to go to college, he used good time management and achieved financial freedom. By choosing to drop out of high school and spending all of his time working instead of enriching himself, Jack used bad time management and made himself financially fat.

HOW TO ACHIEVE financial fitness:

- ❖ Set realistic financial goals.
- ❖ Think big and spend wisely.
- ❖ Don't try shortcuts; don't be afraid to work harder and smarter instead.
- ❖ Build profitable investing habits (assets) and avoid unnecessary expenses (liabilities).
- ❖ Do not spend more than what you make unless you are making an investment.
- ❖ Take financial advice from people who have proven their financial management ability.
- ❖ Focus on your goal and manage your time productively.

> Money cannot buy time, but it can easily steal time away.

Financial fitness is not about how much money you have but how well you manage it. You have no reason to be poor. Achieve financial fitness and enjoy your life. If you can control your time and money, you can manage your life productively.

STEP SIX: CREATE A POSITIVE SELF-IMAGE

Years ago, I hired a manager named Kurt to run the daily operations of my school. Kurt was very impressive. He looked and talked like he was professional management material. I really thought that this was going to be the guy that would let me focus on teaching class and writing curriculum for my students; I was on top of the world, or at least I thought I was going to be.

After a short time, though, Kurt started coming to work late almost every day and fighting with the staff, destroying their teamwork dynamic.

DEVELOP PERSONAL POWER

There were many days where he chose not to show up at all, only adding to my worries. Things were so bad that I had to fire Kurt and clean up the mess he created.

I thought because of his positive appearance and excellent communication skills, Kurt would have an equally positive attitude. I was wrong, but despite this experience, I continued to judge people's attitudes by their appearances, until I met a woman named Ellen.

Ellen came into the school, asking about taking lessons. I saw that her hair was bright pink, she wore a tank top that didn't hide the tattoos on her arms and stomach, and she had piercings in her ears, nose, belly button, and in her tongue. When I looked at her, I thought, "Why would she do this to her body?" If she came into the school selling something, I would have thrown her out, but Ellen was interested in taking lessons so I had to treat her like any other prospective student.

As Ellen and I talked, I began feeling guilty. She was intelligent, had a great attitude, and seemed normal in every way. I only saw these things after looking at her with my third eye, the "eye" that we use to view someone's inner self. I realized that I had judged her only by her physical appearance. Ellen had a strange appearance but a great attitude.

My experiences with Kurt and Ellen taught me four important lessons in life about self-image:

1. Never judge people solely on their physical appearance.
2. A good external image can open other people's eyes, but can't open hearts.
3. A positive self-image *can* overcome a negative external image, but a positive external image *cannot* overcome a negative self-image. The key is to have balance. If you can maintain a positive self-image and a positive external image, you can open other people's eyes and hearts.
4. Always practice *third-eye observation*.

Now that the impact of a positive self-image has been established, we will now discover how it can unlock many doors of opportunity.

Unlocking Many Doors of Opportunity

Self-image is how you assess yourself, which influences how others assess you. Because almost everyone is attracted to positivity, a positive self-image is a tremendous personal asset that unlocks many doors of opportunity; this kind of self-image makes the possibilities of success endless. The two parts of self-image that need equal development are **appearance** and **attitude**.

APPEARANCE. What do you notice first about people when seeing them for the first time? Is it their face, hair, the clothes they wear, their body language? All of these things are part of appearance, which is how we initially judge people, forming a positive or negative first impression. These responses are a natural part of our observational abilities.

ATTITUDE. Once we get past appearances, we notice people's attitudes. Attitude is the direct reflection of the way a person thinks and acts. Communication skills are the external expression of attitude and consistency of actions is the internal expression of attitude. Most people are drawn to those who communicate positively because we are naturally attracted to positive people. However, if their actions are inconsistent with their speech, then they repel us. Once we get to their attitude, we truly know who they are.

Remember, appearance is always judged first. Having a pleasing and neat appearance for the appropriate occasion isn't just for the benefit of other people. A pleasing and neat appearance gives you self-esteem, earns you respect and trust from others, which makes you even more approachable and attractive. A positive attitude will increase your credibility, help you achieve your goals, and succeed in life. Let's examine the impact of appearance and attitude.

A good hairstyle is one of the best ways to improve or enhance your appearance; just changing your hairstyle can actually do wonders for your self-image. When Hilary Clinton became the nation's First Lady in 1993, the first thing I remembered about her appearance was her new hairstyle. Gone was the cheesy look, replaced by a hip, warmer one. In my opinion her new hairstyle changed her image overnight, helping to create a vision of friendliness and intellect—qualities that helped Mrs. Clinton become the first ever First Lady to be elected to the U.S. Senate.

Dressing for success also does wonders for your appearance and self-image. Consider the impeccable taste of television celebrity Regis Philbin, who displayed a visual duality that would have impressed even the most seasoned Hollywood wardrobe consultant. From his *Regis Live* morning show to his former place as the host of *Who Wants to be a Millionaire*, Philbin donned differing, but equally positive, attire. His morning suits were often lighter ensembles that featured visually striking ties while his evening suits were darker outfits that exuded professionalism. Philbin's choice of attire not only reflected his positive image, but also depicted his shift from daytime celebrity to nighttime star. Philbin's appearance undoubtedly helped both shows become hits, which generated revenue for their respective networks. His positive attitude also helped him become one of the most popular television personalities in America.

Companies pay millions of dollars to celebrities such as Michael Jordan, Tiger Woods, Britney Spears, and even Bob Dole to endorse their products in all forms of media. Why are these celebrities paid so much for their endorsements? It is because they have a positive self-image and companies want positive people to sell their products.

However, even if you were the most famous person in the world, when you have a negative self-image, not a single company in the world would have you endorse their products. Look at Mike Tyson and Michael Jackson. When they had a positive self-image, both men received lucrative endorsement deals. Once they let their self-image go, no company wanted them.

Remember that a positive self-image is a tremendous personal asset, leading you to a prosperous future. Now that you know the importance of a positive self-image, I will show you how you can have one of your own.

How to Build a Positive Self-image

❖ **APPEARANCE:** Develop a positive external image.

❖ **ATTITUDE:** Develop a positive external and internal image.

APPEARANCE

This *physical* aspect of self-image is conveyed positively through body language, proper hygiene, and dress. Here are some recommended guidelines for appearance:

1. Strive to be pleasant by smiling and laughing (except during inappropriate occasions).

2. Maintain proper hygiene. Maintaining proper hygiene includes bathing on a regular basis, brushing your teeth, and keeping a clean, neat appearance. If you're male, proper hygiene also means keeping your mustache or beard neat and trim, or staying clean-shaven. If you are female, this includes shaving unnecessary body hair such as legs and armpits. (Please keep in mind that these hygiene suggestions apply to American culture. Please adhere to the hygiene standards of your own culture.)

3. Keep up a professional hairstyle. (Do not try to cover your forehead with your hair, which implies sloppiness, uncleanliness, or that you might be hiding something.)

4. Dress appropriately for all occasions to always present a clean, attractive image. If you have a job interview, generally you would wear professional attire. If you have a formal event to attend, you'll wear formal attire. If you go to a friend's pool party, you'll wear a bathing suit. In whatever you wear, make sure that the colors of your clothes match.

5. Use positive body language when interacting with others. Keep your hands and arms open, not crossed or on your hips. Also; lean to-

ward people and not away from them to show interest.

A little bit of investment in your appearance can go a long way. Now, let's check out how to develop a great attitude.

ATTITUDE
There are two parts to attitude: character and personality. Character is the internal part of attitude, which reflects your level of honesty, integrity, and responsibility. Personality is the external part of attitude, seen and heard through communication. To have a positive attitude, you must have a positive personality and a good character.

To develop a great attitude:
1. Think, see, talk, listen, and act positively and with passion.
2. Always be honest, responsible, and show integrity.
3. Have an open mind.
4. Develop excellent communication skills.
5. Set positive goals.
6. Continue to educate yourself.
7. Continue building your personal leadership ability.

For all of their wonderful attributes, however, neither a positive attitude nor good appearance can singularly help you develop a positive self-image. They must be applied together to achieve the desired results.

STEP SEVEN: LOVE YOURSELF UNCONDITIONALLY

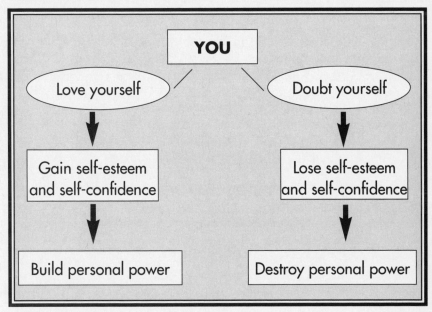

The most dangerous thing in the world isn't a weapon and it isn't a disease; it's self-doubt. Self-doubt is the most crippling feeling in the universe. When you are filled with self-doubt, your insecurities become so strong that you become a coward, afraid to do anything. This fear then turns into self-hatred, which makes you doubt, envy, and hate others as well. To prevent self-doubt from destroying you, you need to love yourself unconditionally.

The benefits of loving yourself unconditionally are priceless: you gain strong self-confidence, high self-esteem, and the ability not only to change yourself, but also to change the world. In fact, the most successful people in history were successful partly because they loved themselves. Those who failed, even after achieving great success, did so because they stopped loving themselves.

The greatest gift you can give to yourself is unconditional love because of its endless benefits. Without loving yourself, personal power would not exist. So embrace yourself and eradicate self-doubt.

DEVELOP PERSONAL POWER

Here are four ways to love yourself to build your self-esteem:

1. Love Yourself: To love yourself is to strengthen yourself.
2. Love your family: To love your family is to love yourself.
3. Love your job: To love your job is to energize yourself with passion.
4. Love other people: To love people is to show love for yourself.

*Love **creates**, love **unites**, love **energizes**, love **inspires**, love **motivates**; love generates **self-esteem**; love builds **self-confidence**; love **strengthens** body, mind, and spirit; love is the best **medicine for health**; love brings happiness; and love produces **success**.*

Love Yourself: "A Shoe Full of Holes"

There was once a young man named Lee who came from a very poor family. He was always reluctant to leave the house because of his shoes; they were riddled with holes. Having to wear these shoes squashed Lee's desire to change his life. He blamed his parents for being so poor.

One day, Lee was on a morning walk when he noticed lot of people gathering around a man that was talking. Lee was also drawn to the happy and well-spoken man. Lee tried to move in closer to get a better glimpse of this joyful speaker, but only saw his smiling face. When the man finally stopped talking, the group left. Once they left, Lee saw the speaker and was stunned; he had no legs beneath his knees.

"Here is this legless man who should feel devastated and miserable because he has no legs, yet he seems to be the happiest man on Earth," Lee thought.

Lee finally realized that all he did was complain about being poor and his tattered shoes. He was ashamed of his selfishness, but at the same time realized that the solution to his problems was not in new shoes, but learning to love himself for the way he was. By loving himself, Lee built his self-esteem and personal power, which forever changed his life.

Put yourself in Lee's shoes. Are you asking yourself why you aren't strong enough, aren't rich, aren't popular or beautiful, and aren't you good enough? If you are asking yourself these kinds of questions, you are poisoning your mind with insecurity, transforming your self-esteem into the ugly monster of self-doubt.

The good news is anyone can have self-esteem and self-confidence if they want them, and it's easier than you think to attain them. By loving yourself unconditionally, you gain high self-esteem, which generates positive energy, makes you more productive, and you gain more respect and understanding for others.

How do you learn to love yourself? You do so by believing in yourself, caring about yourself, and being proud of yourself.

BELIEVE IN YOURSELF

First and foremost, you must believe you are the most important person in the world to yourself because once you do, your belief in yourself will become so strong that no mountain will be too high to climb, no wall too tough to bust through, no goal ever impossible to reach. You will become unstoppable. So please try the following exercise that will help you believe that you are the most important person in the world to yourself.

> **Lay the book aside, stand up, and shout as loud as possible "I am the best in the world!" while thinking of your positive qualities. Do this, jumping up and down while pumping your arms in the air each time, for 10 times *(if you are in an airplane or in an office, just say it quietly)*. If you feel silly while and after you have done this, that's ok but don't stop. Keep trying until you feel that you really are the best in the world to yourself. Once you have finished all your stress, tension, and self-doubt will go away, you'll feel great,**

**that you are the best in the world, and that you are
unstoppable.**

The true meaning of the phrase "I am the best in the world" is that
you strongly believe in yourself, and that you are competing within
yourself, not competing with others, accepting that everyone has
strengths and weaknesses, positive and negative qualities, good and
bad characteristics. To say you are the best in the world is to also fight
against your weak points and negative qualities until you believe you are
strong, positive, and can do anything and everything. Most of all when
you say you are the best in the world; you believe that you are the most
important person to yourself in the world.

By acting with passion during this exercise, you begin feeling really good
about yourself; that's where believing in yourself begins.

If you don't believe that you are the best person in the world, you
can change what you believe and become the best person the world. You
are what you believe. As long as you believe you are the best in your
world, you compete within yourself to have strong self-confidence.
Remember: belief in yourself is the first step towards loving yourself
unconditionally.

Care for Yourself

When you care for yourself, you take responsibility for your body, mind,
and life, meaning that you respect your appearance and yourself. Caring
for yourself begins by showing appreciation for everything around you
and enjoying life. By appreciating what you have, you demonstrate that
you have strong self-confidence and good character.

However, it's important not to confuse self-care with vanity. When
you're vain, you may take responsibility for your appearance but you
don't consider how your conceited attitude affects others.

Self-care is a continual process. If you stop caring about yourself,
you lose everything. Elvis Presley stopped caring for himself once he fell

into a lifestyle of excess, indulging in food and drugs. Because of that, Elvis lost his wealth, fame, all of his achievements, dignity, and his life.

By caring for yourself, your high self-esteem shines to the world as you build your personal power. Strengthen yourself by caring for yourself.

BE PROUD OF YOURSELF

There's a difference between being proud of yourself and being arrogant. Arrogant people are arrogant because they have no self-confidence, thus putting on a show of false confidence as they try to fool everyone into thinking that they are really confident. Being proud of yourself shows you are honest and responsible, demonstrating that you are someone with integrity and ability. Having all these things means you have self-confidence.

Pride in yourself, not arrogance, is a positive attribute. Live and enjoy every day with passion and unbridled enthusiasm to make yourself proud. As long as you are proud of yourself, you will have personal power. When you take pride in yourself, you will achieve self-satisfaction. To be proud of yourself is to love yourself.

These are two quick tips on learning how to love yourself:

1. Think about your best qualities and begin your day by looking in the mirror and saying to yourself, 'I love myself,' with a smile between 10 to 30 times. Then, replace the phrases with 'I like me' with a smile; and 'I am the best in the world!' with a smile–all at least 10 to 30 times a day. If you stand in front of a mirror while doing these exercises, you will see and feel the fantastic results! Make your life fun, exciting, and meaningful.

2. Write down seven of your best qualities, your strong points, positive qualities, or good characteristics. Doing so will help you to naturally

love yourself as your sub-conscience will motivate, energize, and encourage you to continue loving yourself.

These are mine:
1. Leadership ability
2. Intelligence
3. Communication skills
4. People skills
5. Intuition
6. Passion
7. Physical, mental, and moral fitnes

What are yours?
1._____
2._____
3._____
4._____
5._____
6._____
7._____

Now that you know how to love yourself, you can learn the next way to build self-esteem, loving your family.

Love Your Family

Loving your family is key to the development of high self-esteem because loving your family teaches you the importance of open communication in building understanding, establishing reciprocal care, encouragement, and support.

Some people hate their family because of their family's faults or horrible actions, some of which include alcoholism, drug addiction, violence, and abandonment. You have no reason to like or support what your family has done wrong, but you should never hate them. Your hatred for your family could act as a poison, slowly eating away at you or as a time bomb, ready to explode in rage at any moment. We all make mistakes.

Love your family because they are your family, not for what they do or have done. Remember the power of forgiveness. You love your family, but you don't always love their choices in life. Always forgive their wrongs.

By accepting and loving your family for who they are, you motivate positive change within yourself and develop more trust and goodwill for your family at the same time. Don't forget that to love your family is to love yourself.

> **Now write down the three best things about your family. Remember: no one is perfect. Forgive the wrongs and focus on everything that is good and right about your family. You will only love your family more by doing so.**

These are mine:
1. My family cares for and loves each other.
2. My family understands and respects each other.
3. My family supports each other.

What are yours?
1._____
2._____
3._____

Now that you know how to love your family, you need to learn to love your job.

Love Your Job

While I lived in New York in 1977, I had a job cleaning stores, and that included cleaning their bathrooms. At first I hated cleaning bathrooms, but I eventually realized complaining about it wouldn't help make me or the job go any faster or feel any better. Instead, I started inventing ways to clean them faster, easier, and with better results, as I put these new ideas into action. I had no time to think negatively, work was much easier, and I finished earlier because of my new attitude towards my job. The quality of my work improved, too, because when I finished, the bathrooms looked immaculate, which made me look and feel good. I kept up a superb work ethic until I finally was able to do what I love, teach the martial arts full time. I learned something very valuable from these experiences; to love my job is to love myself.

We have the power to choose to love what we do and with this power, change our lives. Yet at the same time, some may feel change is impractical. Some feel trapped in their jobs, unable to leave because of financial constraints, a lack of education, or because of a limited job market. They feel that choice is not an option. Because of these things they constantly ask, "How can I love my job?" The answer is a simple one: You can choose. You can choose to love your job because that choice is always there.

Did you know most of us spend one third of our lives working eight or more hours per day, five days a week and at least a third of our day is spent at work? One third of our lives is work, so you had better enjoy it. If work isn't enjoyable, you lose valuable time forever. When you love your job, you work with passion, making yourself productive and valuable. Work doesn't feel like work; it feels like fun. Those who love their jobs exceed their potential and accomplish all of their objectives. Those who work solely out of obligation are typically mediocre in their productivity. Those who hate their jobs will be counterproductive. Therefore, the need to love your job is critical to success and happiness.

Anyone can love his or her job, but it's the commitment you show that makes a profound difference in your long-term potential as an employee or as an employer. Of course, it's best if you can find a job that you like. If you're in the right job, it's easy to develop passion for what you do. Then, set specific goals at your job and become a self-starter.

With these two things in mind, choose to love your job with unbridled passion, or find one that you can learn to love. If you're unable to find a new job now, learn how to love your current position; it will make the waiting bearable. To learn to love your current position, change your way of thinking. Compete with yourself; don't compete with others wrongfully. Focus on your boss' and your co-workers' strong points, and compliment them. Compromise with them to help them like you and create win/win relationships.

Once you've found the right job, make a continued effort to improve your job skills. Learn about all of your respective industry's latest technology and trends to better yourself. By loving your job, you build high self-esteem and generate personal power. To love your job is to love yourself.

> **Write down three of the best things about your job.**
> **Remember no job is perfect so focus on everything**
> **that is good and right about your job. You will only**
> **love your job more by doing so.**

These are mine:
1. I'm able to improve myself and help improve others.
2. I feel like I work with a second family.
3. My job is bigger than my life.

What are yours?
1._____
2._____
3._____

DEVELOP PERSONAL POWER

The final way to build self-esteem is to love other people.

Love Other People

When you love other people, you reflect your high self-esteem and self-confidence, and help to make your present and future very, very bright. However, if you don't love others, your present and future will be bleak because not loving other people makes it impossible to get dates, keep a family together, succeed at a job or as a business owner, or join social groups; you actually limit yourself.

For example, think of American politics. You've got right-wing Republican extremists who hate Democrats, and you've got left-wing Democrat extremists who hate Republicans. Because of their hatred and close-mindedness, neither side will ever achieve mainstream political success. In fact, each side, left- and right-wing, is not only hating the other side, but hating half of America, thus limiting themselves. You can disagree with or dislike the opinions of others, but you should never hate other people because that hatred only serves to hurt and limit you. Loving other people isn't just key to building your self-esteem, but essential to survival and success in the real world.

In fact, based on personal experience and studies, I found that 85% of our happiness comes from others, while the other 15% comes from within. The reason for these figures is that we have an instinctual need to make others feel happy and loved. When we make others feel happy and loved, we feel the same. For example, if you smile at someone, he or she will smile back.

The following examples illustrate the right and wrong attitudes we encounter in others and ourselves.

WEALTH

WRONG: I'm rich, so I only like rich people. I'm poor, so I hate rich people.

RIGHT: I like people regardless whether they are wealthy or not.

ETHNIC GROUPS

WRONG: I'm white, so I think I'm better than other races. I'm black, so I don't like other ethnicities. I am Asian, so I only like Asians.

RIGHT: I like to meet, talk, and befriend people of different ethnic groups because I love people.

RELIGION

WRONG: I believe in only my religion because all the other ones are wrong.

RIGHT: I am devoted to my religion, but I respect all other religions because I love people.

EDUCATION

WRONG: I have a Ph.D., so I am prestigious, and I ignore uneducated people. I am uneducated, and I hate educated people.

RIGHT: Even though I may be more or less educated than other people, I still respect them regardless of their education.

ORGANIZATION

WRONG: I am Republican, so I don't like Democrats. I am a Democrat, so I only like Democrats.

RIGHT: I may disagree with their opinions, but I like Democrats and Republicans regardless because I love people.

In order to love other people, eliminate negative thoughts, talk, and actions by changing them into positive thoughts, talk, and actions.

The ability to love others is powerful, but it wouldn't be possible if you didn't fight within yourself. By fighting within yourself, you learn to love yourself, your family, your job, and others.

By being a people person, people will love you, and you will have personal power. What goes around, comes around.

SUMMARY
The Seven Steps to Building Personal Power
Become the person you've always wanted to be.

1. **DISCOVER YOURSELF:** Unleash your potential power by discovering the real you.

2. **BUILD PHYSICAL FITNESS:** Eat and drink wisely, exercise daily, recharge your energy and think positively to become physically fit.

3. **BUILD MENTAL FITNESS:** Build mental muscle by exercising your mind with education and positive thinking.

4. **BUILD MORAL FITNESS:** Discipline your personal freedom, discipline your instincts and follow principles.

5. **MANAGE YOUR TIME & MONEY PRODUCTIVELY:** Manage your time and money to enjoy life. Don't let time and money control you.

6. **CREATE A POSITIVE SELF-IMAGE:** Create personal power by developing a positive internal and external self-image.

7. **LOVE YOURSELF UNCONDITIONALLY:** Loving yourself unconditionally creates self-esteem, allowing you to love your family, your job, and other people, giving you internal strength.

REVIEW OF "DEVELOP PERSONAL POWER"

What are the seven steps to building personal power?

_____

_____

Identify the four layers of self-perception.

_____

_____

What is the purpose of your life?

_____

_____

Based on what you have discovered about yourself, what would your personal, professional, and family goals be?

_____

_____

What are the Four Wheels of Health?

_____

_____

Why is positive thinking fundamental to achieving a truly healthy lifestyle? And how do you build, maintain, and improve positive thinking?

_____

_____

How do you free yourself from anger, illogical hatred, jealousy, guilt, anxiety, and depression?

_____

_____

What are the four systems of education?

_____

_____

What is moral fitness, and why is it important to have in your life?

_____

_____

What are the five primary instincts we must discipline so we can gain personal freedom?

_____

_____

What are the principles of life, and why is following these principles vital to successfully building moral fitness?

_____

_____

What are the six ways of managing your time and money productively?

_____

_____

Why should you create a positive self-image from the inside out?

_____

_____

Why should you love your family?

_____

_____

What benefits do you get by feeling passionate about your job?

_____

_____

How does loving others help you to succeed in life?

_____

_____

How do you make other people love you?

_____

_____

Build
WIN-WIN
Relationships

Enrich your life

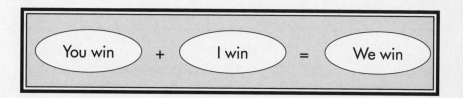

You win + I win = We win

I'VE NEVER BEEN ABLE TO understand how easily and unpredictably relationships fluctuate and change. I've witnessed people who almost violently hated each other one day become the best of friends the next. Then I saw people who were really really close suddenly at each other's throats. I've seen these changes happen between couples, siblings, families, and even nations.

Russia was a bitter enemy of the United States not too long ago. Now, they are allies. Germany and Japan fought viciously against America in World War II, and now they, too, are allies with America. I thought it was almost impossible to predict who would be friend or enemy because I saw them constantly change.

Then I saw families, siblings, and friends that had amazing relationships, celebrating the good and sticking together through the bad, always supporting each other. I saw this same kind of relationship between countries too, especially when England was the first to stand up and support the U.S. 100% after the attacks on September 11th. It seemed like these relationships would never end; I was envious. How could I have that kind of relationship?

For a long time, I couldn't figure out how these people and countries were able to accomplish such a feat until I realized the kind of relationship they had: a win-win relationship.

One of the best examples of a win-win relationship was that between Michael Jordan and Phil Jackson. Their extraordinary leadership built a win-win relationship that led the Chicago Bulls to unparalleled heights in the NBA, winning six NBA World Championship titles (1991-1993, 1996-1998). To better understand the importance of win-win relationships in the real world, we must look closer at the successful bond these two men forged.

Michael Jordan and Phil Jackson were individually talented and skilled from the start of their respective NBA careers. Both came into the NBA with tremendous potential and continued to be successful in their roles in the league. Once Jackson and Jordan made it a point to form a win-win relationship with each other and the Bulls, their potential increased exponentially.

With Jackson's guidance, Jordan combined the right attitude with his extraordinary skills and strong leadership to reap many rewards in Chicago, winning the NBA Finals' Most Valuable Player (MVP) award in each of the Bulls' championship seasons. *Time Magazine* named him the "The Best Athlete of All Time." In addition to all of these accolades, Jordan was the highest-paid player in the NBA and earned the most money from endorsements, more than any other athlete in the world. All of these things made him one of the most honored athletes in the world.

Jackson's supreme confidence in Jordan was never more evident than in 1997, when Jordan lost the regular season MVP Award to the Utah Jazz's Karl Malone. Jackson publicly denounced the decision. He believed Jordan deserved the award because of his character and skills.

Jordan respected Jackson equally, which became obvious following the 1996-1997 season when Chicago Bulls owner Jerry Krause threatened to break up the team for financial reasons. When Krause said he considered releasing Jackson, Jordan informed the management that he would leave the team if Jackson were released. Realizing his predicament, Krause re-signed both, and Chicago subsequently won its sixth NBA championship.

Michael Jordan's leadership proved vital to the team's fortunes. Not only had he been able to get management to re-sign Phil Jackson, Jordan was able to return to the team and win another championship.

PERHAPS OTHER NBA players were as talented or more talented than Michael Jordan was. If that's true, then how did he become one of the greatest NBA superstars of all time? If the NBA has lots of talented coaches, then how did Phil Jackson become a legendary NBA coach?

> Win-win relationships are the ropes that hold up the bridge to success.

Jordan and Jackson had dynamic leadership ability and knew that a win–win relationship was the only way to lead the Bulls to title after title. Their collective use of their leadership benefited themselves, their team, the fans, their sponsors, and the NBA. Michael Jordan and Phil Jackson illustrate the importance of win-win relationships in our lives.

Through the following Eight Steps to Building Win-Win Relationships, you, too, can build your own win-win relationships.

EIGHT STEPS TO BUILDING WIN-WIN RELATIONSHIPS

1. **DEVELOP THE PRINCIPLES OF WIN-WIN RELATIONSHIPS:** To truly be win-win, relationships need fairness, negotiation, and investment.

2. **HELP OTHER PEOPLE LIKE YOU:** People like positive attitudes so build a positive attitude.

3. **BE A NECESSARY PERSON:** People need people so be necessary.

4. **DEVELOP PROPER COMMUNICATION SKILLS:** Relationships begin or end with communication.

5. **EMBRACE THE FRIENDS OF WIN-WIN RELATIONSHIPS:** Embrace these friends to make others feel important in securing win-win relationships.

6. **AVOID THE ENEMIES OF WIN-WIN RELATIONSHIPS:** Prevention is better than a cure; avoid making others feel unimportant.

7. **STRENGTHEN YOUR SPECIAL RELATIONSHIPS:** Cherish the ones closest to you by tightening your bonds with them.

8. **MAKE INTERNATIONAL FRIENDS:** Open your heart and mind to the world.

STEP ONE: DEVELOP THE PRINCIPLES OF WIN-WIN RELATIONSHIPS

The principles of win-win relationships come from the belief that everything in the universe has balance, the "yin" and "yang," night and day, female and male, negative and positive, water and fire. This balance is known as natural dualism. Just as the human race needs a balance of both males and females to survive, relationships need a balance of the needs of each individual. There is no such thing as a one-time friend or enemy, or even a permanent enemy in win-win relationships because such an imbalance is against the nature of win-win relationships. If you can maintain balance, you can have good relationships, but if you can't maintain it, you will lose relationships.

Because people are beginning to realize that win-win relationships are necessary, they are becoming more and more common. Other relationship philosophies, "You lose, I win," or "I lose, you win," are unbalanced because one party ends up feeling good and the other feels bad. How do you maintain balance? By following the three principles of win-win relationships:

1. **FAIRNESS.** The balance of "you win" and "I win," so "we win."
2. **NEGOTIATION.** Communication is the key to negotiation. Relationships should never be dictatorships or a master and servant dynamic.
3. **INVESTMENT.** Care for your win-win relationships like you would a garden.

Fairness

Fairness is balance, illustrated by a "You win, I win, so we win" situation, unlike an "I win so you lose" or "you win so I lose" situation. Allow me to clarify why fairness is so important in building and maintaining win-win relationships.

Would you like it if your friend strives to make you a loser as he tries winning all the time, no matter what you do? I don't think so. Do you think if the roles were switched that your friend would like it, too? I don't think so.

Now, let's say you had an argument with your spouse: do you want to win or lose? If you say, "Win," you may win and then your spouse will be a loser. Do you like living with a loser? You would probably say, "No," which means if you continue to win arguments, you technically will eventually live with a loser. Do you think your spouse will be happy constantly losing argument after argument? I highly doubt it; that would make your spouse unhappy. If he or she is unhappy, do you think your spouse can make you happy? I don't think so. In order for both parties to be happy, you should develop a win-win relationship.

Always make sure that fairness is central to all of your relationships so that they become and stay win-win.

Negotiation

Negotiation is necessary to having and maintaining win-win relationships. If we do not learn to compromise, relationships will become one-sided, miserable, and eventually break apart, much like a master and servant or dictatorship relationship dynamic. Allow me to illustrate the need for compromise and negotiation in win-win relationships through the following scenarios.

Bob just got a big raise and wants to take his wife, Julie out to celebrate.

BOB: "Honey, I got a huge raise today."

JULIE: "Bob, that's awesome, congratulations! We should go out and celebrate. There's this movie I've been dying to see, and we should go to it."

BOB: "But, sweetie, I made 8 o'clock reservations to that fancy French restaurant you like so much. I want to spend this special night just with you."

JULIE: "I'm not hungry. We can do dinner anytime. According to the t.v. this movie is leaving theaters soon. I wanna go see it, tonight."

BOB: "But.... This is my night. I'm the one who got the raise."

JULIE: "Fine. You get some of your friends and take them out to dinner. I'm going with my girlfriends to see this movie." Julie grabs her purse and coat and walks out the door.

BOB: "But...but.... (The door slams.) Thanks a lot, Honey."

This is what can happen when you don't negotiate in a relationship. You end up doing either nothing for the night or something completely different from your spouse, just like Bob & Julie. Because they were unable to negotiate, their marriage will become miserable, and eventually fall apart.

Another couple, Jack and Mary, is in the same situation. Let's see how they handle it.

> **JACK:** (Rushing in the door) "Baby, I got a promotion at work today!"
>
> **MARY:** (Hugs Jack) "Jack, that's so wonderful. We should go out and celebrate. How about a movie?"
>
> **JACK:** "Honey, I have a better idea. How about dinner at a nice restaurant? We can get dressed up, have a great meal. There's that black dress of yours I really like."
>
> **MARY:** "But I've been wanting to see this movie for a long time and you promised you'd take me to it."
>
> **JACK:** "How about this: we get dressed, go out to a nice restaurant, and after we eat, we go to the movies. Fair enough?"
>
> **MARY:** "You are so wonderful! Thank you. (Kisses Jack on the cheek). I'm gonna go get dressed now."

Jack and Mary remembered that negotiation is part of the dualistic nature of relationships, so they communicated, compromised, and ended up doing what they both wanted. By doing all of these things, they continued having a win-win relationship, making both Jack and Mary incredibly happy.

Investment

Always invest in win-win relationships to help them grow and to maintain them, like you would invest care into your garden. If you cultivate plants and flowers, trim tree branches, and remove the weeds; your garden will look beautiful. However, if you do nothing with your garden or stop caring for it, it will be filled with weeds, eventually all the plants and flowers will be dead, and your garden will be ugly. You have to invest care in your win-win relationships as well so they don't become like an ugly garden.

Investment requires time, energy, patience, understanding, sacrifice, and especially care.

Applying the Principles of Win-Win Relationships

When I brought up the subject of win-win relationships to my students in class, one of them asked me how we could create a win-win situation in our next tournament because championships are win-lose situations. I told him that tournaments are tournaments, not relationships.

Then, I explained that in tournaments, you do your best, win or lose. Opponents are just opponents, not your enemy. After the tournament, you can build a good relationship with your tournament opponents. If you lose, you could get depressed or get angry and blame others for your loss. If you win, you could become conceited or arrogant, and others will ignore you. You aren't developing win-win relationships when you behave in these ways. If you lose, you should always show confidence and good manners as well as congratulate the winner because that opponent didn't defeat you in life. He or she only won the tournament. If you win, you should show appreciation to your coach and supporters, be very humble, and treat your opponents like winners. When you behave in this manner, you build win-win relationships—not just in tournaments, but in all aspects of life.

No matter what the circumstance, there is no alternative for a win-win relationship strategy. By working selflessly with others, you form the best relationships, ensure their success, and lead yourself to a successful life.

STEP TWO: HELP OTHER PEOPLE LIKE YOU

Why do you think other people like you? Is it because you're beautiful? Smart? Strong? Rich? Famous? Powerful? No. Though all of these things are nice to have or be; these aren't the real reasons why others like you. Other people will truly like you if, and only if, you have a **positive attitude**. Everyone naturally responds well to positivity. In fact, positivity is contagious.

What does attitude mean in the context of people liking you? Attitude is your habit; habit is your second nature, which is behaving almost without thinking. Behaving is an action informed by your way of thinking. Thinking and acting positively lead to positive results and are helpful to living a successful life.

What makes attitude even more interesting is that there are actually two parts to it. The first part is personality, which is seen by others, and the second part is character, which can be felt by others. The combination of personality and character determines whether a person has a positive or negative attitude, and how he or she is received. Thus, the ability to manage attitude is powerful, making it the most integral and important part of any relationship. Take at look at the following illustrations for a little more insight:

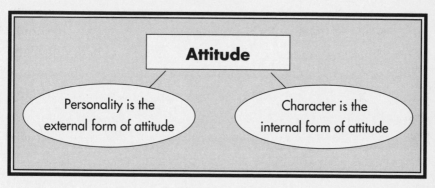

We must learn how to assess our personality (external form of attitude) and character (internal form of attitude) to determine their level so we not only know how to maintain and improve them, but assess others based on these factors as well. When we can accurately assess people's personalities and characters, we can better choose the right people to associate with in building win-win relationships.

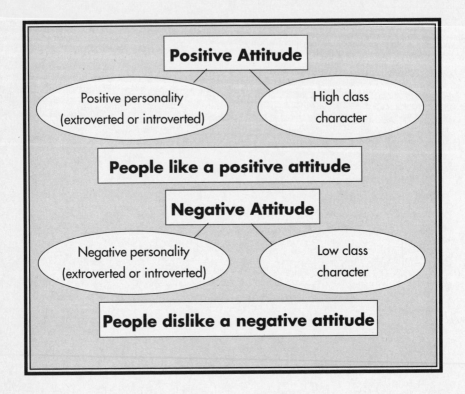

The Impact of Personality
Would you like to date or hang out with negative or positive people?
Misery loves company, but if you are a positive person, of course you would want to date or hang out with positive people because negative people pull you down, give you nothing but headaches, and make you miserable.

Personality is the way a person expresses himself or herself externally based on his or her emotions. Within this expression, people are extroverted or introverted. Extroverts are very outgoing and talkative, while introverts are quiet, mostly keeping to themselves. There are three types of personalities: positive, negative, or impersonal. The chart below illustrates what each personality is like when communicating and interacting with others.

Positive personality (Extroverted or introverted).	Conveys passion and optimism, is constructive, energetic and open-minded, which makes **people like them**.
Negative personality (Extroverted or introverted).	Conveys nastiness and jealousy; is critical, discouraging, angry, and close-minded, making **people dislike them**.
Impersonal personality (Introverted).	Conveys disinterest and is non-engaging, reflecting neither a positive or negative attitude, which **confuses others**.

Be a positive person so people will like you.

Probing the Depths of Character

Character is derived from conscience and inner strength, internal qualities we all possess. I classify character as high, middle, or low class; this classification has nothing to do with wealth, education, fame, skin color, religion, position, physical appearance or intelligence.

Low class Provokes dislike from others.	Traits include immoral thinking and action, selfishness, dishonesty, and irresponsibility, often hurtful towards others.
Middle class Commands no interest from others.	Traits are neither positive nor negative, while their moral compass and inner strength causes them to neither care about nor harm others.
High class Earns trust and respect from others.	Traits include moral thinking and action, honesty, integrity, responsibility, and generosity, and having an indomitable spirit.

Assessing Personal Character

The qualities that determine character come from thought and action. Our handling of these factors determines if our character is **low class, middle class,** or **high class.**

THINKING: What you think is what you will be.

CONVERSATION: Your conversational skills represent who you are.

TIME: Punctuality assesses your level of responsibility.

APPRECIATION: Recognizing someone for his or her positive qualities or actions shows how good you are.

CONSISTENCY: Following through with your own promises shows your reliability.

ETHICS: How ethical you are reflects the strength of your integrity.

GENEROSITY: Giving freely of yourself and caring about others shows how good you are.

Let's examine how each of these seven factors determines our character.

THINKING

Consider the following:

> **If you think big, you will be big.**
> **Think small, and you will be small.**

> **If you think good, you will be good.**
> **Think bad, and you will be bad.**

> **If you think positive, you will be positive.**
> **Think negative, and you will be negative.**

If you think the right way, you will act the right way.
Think the wrong way, and you will act the wrong way.
Energy in, energy out.
Garbage in, garbage out.

Your thoughts are truly the root of your habits.

Here is how thinking is divided in the formation of character:

LOW CLASS: People that have low class character always **think wrong and think small**. Their thoughts are always negative, pessimistic, selfish, and destructive. They think of ways to lie, steal from, corrupt, and con others with the intention of hurting, humiliating, antagonizing, horrifying, and/or destroying others. People with low class character wish for others to fail and enjoy watching them do so.

MIDDLE CLASS: People with middle class character **think only about themselves.**

HIGH CLASS: People who have a high class character always try to **think right and think big**. Their thoughts are positive, optimistic, selfless, and constructive. They think of ways to appreciate, recognize, help, support, motivate, and encourage others with the intention of sharing or accomplishing goals, ideas, and/or cooperation in order to improve the future. High class characters wish for everyone to succeed and encourage them to do so.

Do you think other people know what you are thinking? At first they don't unless you say what's on your mind, only you know what you are thinking. After a while, your actions will reflect what you are thinking, and other people will see what's on your mind.

Character, in terms of thought, is determined by a person's thinking over a period of time, or a habitual way of thinking. It also should be noted that a habitually bad way of thinking could be changed to a good way of thinking. By thinking positively, one can build a high-class character and form win-win relationships.

CONVERSATION

There is a saying that a person's heart can be known through conversation, which is a very wise statement, considering a lot can be determined about a person's character as well. Conversation can be uplifting and motivating, or demoralizing and degrading. All of us have the ability to choose our words carefully and powerfully affect others.

Here is how conversation is grouped in the formation of character:

LOW CLASS: People with low class character always have wrong or terrible intentions in mind when speaking with other people, often criticizing, complaining, discouraging, blaming, and generally talking bad about others without justification through negative, pessimistic, and/or destructive words.

MIDDLE CLASS: People with middle class character talk primarily about themselves or their self-interests.

HIGH CLASS: People with high class character always have the right intentions in mind when talking to other people, often talking about goals, dreams, ideas, and visions with others so that they can help to improve the future. These people are always energetic and cheerful as they motivate, encourage, acknowledge, and admire others. By doing these things, people with high class character make others feel excited, educated, valued, and proud.

Without conversation, relationships would be extremely difficult to build. Yet, it's important to have the right kind of conversation to establish win-win relationships. Positive conversation helps others to like you. Negative conversations make others dislike you. However, conversational miscues shouldn't be mistaken for lack of character. Perfection in communication is not possible for anyone, but establishing good communication habits is.

TIME

How we handle time shows how we value and appreciate it, not to mention our level of character. People can't trust those who lack time management but can trust and depend on those who have good time management skills. In fact, our mortality demands that we should sincerely care about time and use it wisely because time can't be captured or reused, so proper management of it is vital to success in life. By valuing time and developing punctuality as a habit, you honor it and reflect an outstanding character.

Here is how time management is divided in the formation of character:

LOW CLASS: People with low class character are irresponsible with their time, habitually 5, 10, or even 30 minutes late for work or appointments, offering no explanation or apology for their tardiness. They constantly look for opportunities to leave work early, ruining their reliability.

MIDDLE CLASS: People with middle class character strive to always arrive on time for work and always leave when they are supposed to.

HIGH CLASS: Those with high class character manage their time very well, always make the effort to arrive 5 to 30 minutes early to work or an appointment, stay late at work when there are necessary or important things to do. These people exhibit professional conduct when they are late, offering an apology. All of these things show that they are responsible with their time.

While time management is a key element in the development of character, it can't be effortlessly accomplished on a consistent basis. Humans make mistakes, so don't judge people based on one or two mistakes or situations that they have no control over. Understanding and flexibility are important in gauging time management as a character trait. When you manage your time productively, you develop win-win relationships, and you guarantee yourself a successful life.

APPRECIATION

Showing appreciation is one of the kindest forms of character one can display. If you show appreciation, people will always want to associate with you. In the following scenario, Bill, Jimmy, and Richard needed $20.00 for gas so they each could drive home. Charlie lent all of them $20.00.

Let's see how Bill, Jimmy, and Richard appreciate their friend's kindness.

LOW CLASS: Bill said he could pay back Charlie because he had money, but instead asked for more money later. When Charlie refused, Bill tried stealing the money he needed from him. Low class people never show any sort of appreciation, even when they're able to, let alone repay a simple debt, which is totally wrong. Furthermore, they show no appreciation for their friend's kindness. In some cases, this type of person has the nerve to ask for even more favors, insulting their friend's integrity in the process. Bill showed he was low class.

MIDDLE CLASS: Jimmy paid Charlie back and thanked him. These people always make an effort to repay a debt and show some appreciation. Jimmy is middle class.

HIGH CLASS: Richard tried paying back double what was lent to him, but Charlie refused the extra money. Instead, Richard took Charlie out to dinner. High class people always try to pay back their debt with twice as much as they borrowed and show sincere and deep appreciation for the gift that they received, which is totally right. They also remember to always reciprocate kindness. Richard showed he was truly high class.

Nobody likes feeling empty; showing appreciation will make others feel whole. Develop the habit of showing appreciation, beginning with yourself, then to your parents, and others. Once you do, you will have good relationships with others.

CONSISTENCY

Staying true to your word is extremely important in relationships. Trust is built through reliability. Consider the following scenario: John and George are very close friends who live in the same town. One Friday evening, John was looking for a buddy to accompany him to a bar.

GEORGE (hears a knocking door): "Who is it?"

JOHN: "It's me, John."

GEORGE (opening the door): "Hey man! Wassup!"

JOHN: "Nothin' much, bro. Just gonna go to a bar and grab a couple of drinks. Wanna come along?"

GEORGE: "No way, dude. I gotta ton of things to do before the big move tomorrow."

JOHN: "Oh Yeah! I forgot you were moving to your new house."

GEORGE: "Yeah, yeah. Um, John, I need a huge favor from you. I'm gonna need your help moving my stuff. I know we can do it in 3 or 4 trips with that truck of yours. I would so appreciate your help. Please?"

JOHN: "No problem man. What time do ya need me here?"

GEORGE: "11 o'clock in the mornin'."

JOHN: "That's do-able."

GEORGE: "Thanks so much. So I'll see you tomorrow, right?"

JOHN: "Yeah man, no worries. I'll see you at 11."

GEORGE: "Don't get too wasted."

JOHN: "I won't, I won't."

Upon arriving at a bar, John met two beautiful women, and they wanted to make a date to go on a picnic the next day, the same day George needed John's help in moving.

Let's look at John's possible responses, and how they correspond with the consistency of his actions compared to his speech:

Low class: *"Hey ladies. A picnic sounds like a great idea."* John forgot or ignored his promise to George, and his unreliability will hurt George. You couldn't depend on this kind of person and certainly would not call him a friend.

Middle class: *"I'd love to go on a picnic, but I promised a bud of mine that I would help him move. How about we all go out for dinner tomorrow night?"* He doesn't forget his commitment to George.

High class: *"Ladies, I would love to go on a picnic with you, but I made a promise to help a buddy of mine move out of his house. He's actually very intelligent, handsome, a great guy to be around, and very single. How would you two like to pitch in with the move tomorrow? We can all go out later that night on a double date."* John not only remembered his promise to George, but thought of a way to introduce George to his new lady friends; this kind of behavior is incredibly reliable.

Don't make a promise you can't keep. Remember: we aren't perfect. However, don't judge a person's character based on one or two mistakes. Always remember: Habits count.

ETHICS

The strength of your ethics reflects your level of integrity. Depending on your ethics, people will trust or distrust you. Ethics are especially important when you are put into a role where you are taking care of something, such as an organization or other people's money. A lack of ethics doesn't just harm you; it can harm others too. For example, when employees steal money or other items from their company and don't believe that what they have done is unethical, they not only hurt themselves (being reprimanded and possibly losing their jobs), but they hurt the company as well (more money spent on security). The more ethical you are, the more integrity and trust you will have from others.

Here is how ethics is divided in the formation of character:

LOW CLASS: People with low class character always lie, cheat, and steal from others, showing that they are dishonest in all aspects of life.
MIDDLE CLASS: People with middle class character don't lie, cheat or steal from others.
HIGH CLASS: People with high class character always show great integrity when dealing with and taking care of others, showing that they are honest in all aspects of life.

We should not judge people based on their mistakes, but we should judge them based on their habits. It's one thing if a person accidentally takes something once, but it's another when a person intentionally steals from others. When placed in a position where you are taking care of money or an organization, it is absolutely important that you have integrity, which will help you build good relationships with others. If you practice unethical behavior, you won't just destroy relationships, you may even go to jail. Always be ethical.

GENEROSITY

Being generous demonstrates personal leadership ability and that you are truly successful. Mother Teresa was the best example for generosity because she gave up her life to help unfortunate people. Ted Turner, founder of CNN, donated $1 billion to the UN in order to help out poverty stricken nations. Jerry Lewis uses his fame to promote and raise funds to fight against muscular dystrophy during his annual Labor Day telethons. Generosity is the best investment in filling your emotional tank of self-esteem.

Here is how generosity is divided in the formation of character:

LOW CLASS: People with this kind of character have an attitude of: **"Yours is mine, and mine is mine."** This type of person is self-centered, selfish, and wrong.

MIDDLE CLASS: Those with middle class character have an attitude of: **"Yours is yours, and mine is mine."**

HIGH CLASS: People with high-class character have an attitude of: **"What's mine is yours."** They will not only share their fame or money if they have it, those with this kind of character will also share their time, experience, and heart; this kind of behavior is right.

Remember: what goes around, comes around. When you are generous, people will be generous to you. Generosity will help create warm and meaningful relationships.

The Impact of Personality and Character on Relationships

With all of their variations, personality and character have a direct and powerful impact on how relationships form and work. Let's look at how personality and character influence different relationships.

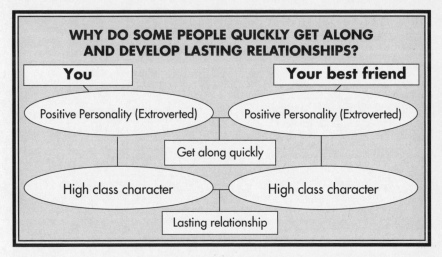

When two individuals with positive personalities and high-class characters meet for the first time, it is the beginning of an ideal relationship, a win-win association—the ultimate relationship. This kind of relationship begins with a bang, with the two parties acting like long-time friends in their first meeting. The immediate chemistry leads to a lasting relationship.

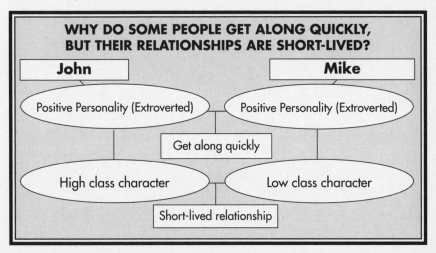

Equal personalities, but unequal character development results in a relationship that starts fast but sputters out over time. This kind of relationship is not unusual as similar personalities are often drawn to each other through their external expression. However, they often go their separate ways once their moral compasses conflict later on.

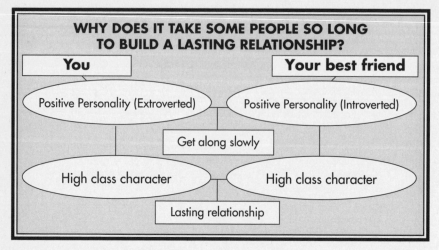

The difference in each person's nature (extroverted vs. introverted) causes the relationship to start slowly, but their conversation is still equal to that between long-time friends. Also, equal possession of high class character helps the relationship grow and strengthen over time.

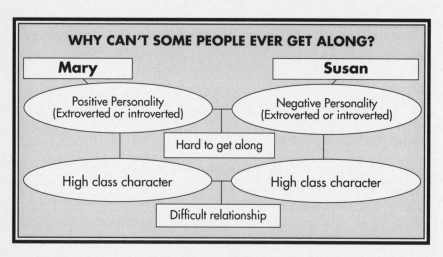

Opposing personalities and characters make for a grueling relationship. The two parties struggle to get along because one of them has negative conversational skills and unconvincing action. Though the other party has a positive personality and high class character, he or she will find it difficult ever getting along with a person of opposing qualities.

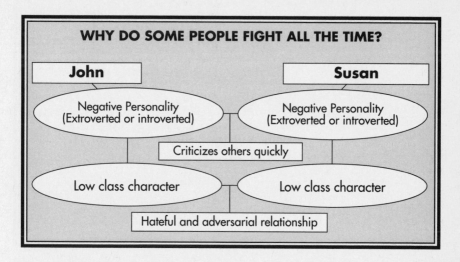

With equally negative personalities and low class characters, people in this relationship get off to a great start because both enjoy criticizing and mocking others. Eventually, they will conflict with each other and wind up enemies until the relationship is dissolved. Neither party can form a relationship with each other because of their incompatibility, which is the worst type of relationship to be in.

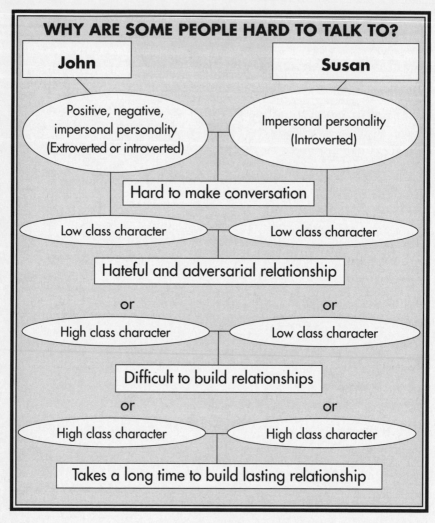

WHY ARE SOME PEOPLE HARD TO TALK TO?

John — Positive, negative, impersonal personality (Extroverted or introverted)

Susan — Impersonal personality (Introverted)

Hard to make conversation

Low class character — Low class character

Hateful and adversarial relationship

or — or

High class character — Low class character

Difficult to build relationships

or — or

High class character — High class character

Takes a long time to build lasting relationship

A person with an impersonal personality has no desire; is senseless and boring; doesn't pass judgment or display anger; and is emotionally detached. No amount of time can help these personalities to ever form a relationship.

However, there is an exception to this rule. If an impersonal personality has a high class character, he or she will eventually form a relationship with someone of equal character, regardless if she or he is positive, negative, or impersonal.

Now that you know how personality and character differences directly impact relationships, allow me to show you how to build a positive attitude so you can better form win-win relationships.

Build a Positive Mental Attitude

In relationships, attitude is more powerful than wealth, fame, education, or power. However, no one is born with a specific type of personality or character. Discipline develops and improves personality and character.

For instance, if an extroverted person with a positive personality doesn't discipline his character, he will offer you lip service when you ask him to do something ("Hey, I can do that. No problem.") but never get anything done ("Oops. I forgot. Sorry."). Also, if an introverted personality doesn't have discipline, at the very least she will be unable to properly release her feelings and emotions, keeping them all bottled up inside.

On the other hand, an introverted personality with high class character can discipline himself to become extroverted, keeping his character intact. Personality and character are made or broken based on discipline. Only you have the choice to discipline yourself to eliminate mental and moral fat, and build mental and moral fitness to have a positive personality and an outstanding character.

Let me show you how to develop, improve, and maintain a positive attitude, which is made up of positive personality and character.

START A SMILE CAMPAIGN WITH PASSION. A positive attitude begins with a smile. Start a smile campaign and always smile. Once you are more positive, it will be easier for you to live your life passionately. A smile campaign starts now and continues with passion.

SET POSITIVE GOALS. Setting positive goals produces positive thinking. Set positive goals now and pursue them.

FOCUS ON THE POSITIVE. There are five components to focusing on the positive.

1. Think positively. You are what you think. How you act becomes your habits, and your habits are your attitude, which defines your personality and character.
2. Look positively. Look at things with three eyes, instead of two (the third eye is the eye of the mind). Always look at the bright side, instead of the dark side. Looking positively will give you positive energy.
3. Talk positively. Choose positive words when communicating with others; doing so will give you positive results.
4. Listen positively. In order to always learn positive knowledge, listen to positive things and ignore negative things.
5. Act positively. Actions speak louder than words, so act positively.

EXERCISE DAILY. Anyone who wants to change his or her life for the better must change his or her body first; which will give him or her the strength to be positive. So start exercising today and exercise daily to get in shape to change your life for the better.

ASSOCIATE WITH POSITIVE PEOPLE. The old saying "Monkey see, monkey do" rings true when it comes to how people act in social groups. Choose to associate with positive people. Remember that negative people are always trying to pull down everyone around them, so avoid negative people.

FOLLOW THE PRINCIPLES OF LIFE WITH DISCIPLINE: The principles of life are harmony, truth, and survival of the fittest. By continuing to follow these principles with discipline, you gain honesty, integrity, a strong sense of responsibility, a willingness to work with others, compassion and indomitable spirit; these things are the foundation of character. In fact, your principles will help you to determine what is truly right and wrong. Always stand up for what you believe in and fight against opposing beliefs with an open mind.

EDUCATE YOURSELF. Be positive in seeking knowledge and truth for self-improvement.

STEP THREE: BE A NECESSARY PERSON

There are three types of people in our society: necessary, unnecessary, and invisible.

Necessary Person	**People need a necessary person.** This person has a positive attitude, personal leadership ability, and necessary skills.
Unnecessary Person	**Nobody needs an unnecessary person.** On a personal level, if a person lacks the right attitude or leadership ability, he or she becomes unnecessary to other people. On a professional level, if a person lacks the right attitude or skills, he or she becomes unnecessary to their profession.
Invisible Person	**Nobody is interested in an invisible person.** This person has an impersonal attitude, lacks leadership abilities, and is unskilled.

Let's take a closer look at each of these types of people to better understand them.

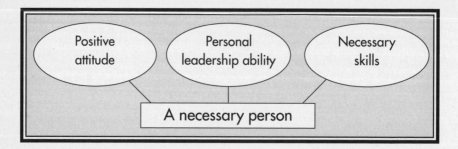

Though having a positive attitude is necessary to building win-win relationships, that alone is not enough to make your relationships strong. In order to strengthen your win-win relationships, you need personal leadership ability, and in some situations, even the right skills. Check out the examples below for more insight.

CHOOSE A LIFETIME PARTNER

Linda is interested in two men, Mike and Charley. Though both are incredibly attractive, positive, honest, and responsible, that's where the similarities end.

When things go as planned, Linda finds Mike and Charley a great joy to be with, but whenever an unexpected problem comes up during a date, they become completely different people. When Charley meets a problem, he doesn't know what to do; often looking confused, makes things worse, and ends up ruining the date. When Mike faces an unexpected problem, he stays cool and figures it out easily, no matter how difficult it is, making Linda very comfortable and at the same time avoiding potential catastrophe.

Now my question is who would Linda most likely end up marrying, Mike or Charley? Most likely, Linda would choose Mike **because fun alone does not help marriages stay together**. Mike would be a great personal coach and advisor when needed, and could help in any crisis. The two of them together will make life easier and successful. Though Charley is a good person, and she has lots of fun with him, he doesn't have personal leadership ability. Almost everyone would make the same choice that Linda would because everyone wants an easier, meaningful and successful life. Build your personal leadership ability so people always need you.

Hiring a New Employee

If you needed to hire a new employee in your company, **would you hire someone who is skilled or unskilled**? You would hire someone who is skilled because unskilled people waste money, time, and often jeopardize companies.

Say you needed to hire a team leader for a new department in your company, and there are three people up for the position.

1. **Richard has a good attitude, but is unskilled and lacks leadership ability.**
2. **Mike has a good attitude and is very skilled, but lacks leadership ability.**
3. **John has a good attitude, is very skilled, and has strong personal leadership ability.**

Out of these three people, which one would you hire?

More than likely, you will hire John. If you hire Richard or Mike, your company would be thrown into chaos. Why? First off, Richard wouldn't even know what to do in this new job because he doesn't have the necessary skills. Mike has the necessary skills, but like Richard, he also lacks personal leadership. With their lack of personal leadership, both men would create lots of stress that would send the entire department spiraling in the wrong direction. When this happens, it only creates even more headaches and offers no hope for the future.

All of the previous examples illustrate that nobody likes being around an unnecessary person.

We need to be necessary people to survive and build strong relationships in the real world no matter where we are or what we do. If we

want to be needed by others, our lives to be easier and our future limitless, we have to be necessary.

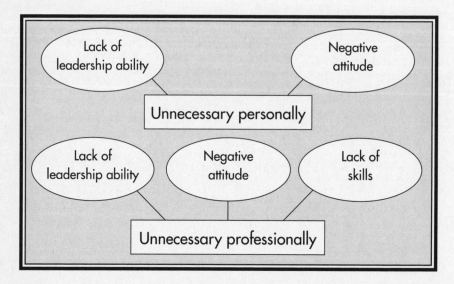

An unnecessary person is like an irreparable used car. While there
are some used cars that can be repaired, others require so much work
that repairs are impossible. If a used car is beyond repair, it's sent to a
junkyard.

The problems we face as people are the same as used cars. Just like
a used car that can be repaired, some individuals have problems, but
possess the desire to change, which helps them become a better person.
On the other hand, some people have deep-seated problems and no
desire to change, thus junking their lives.

What kind of people are unnecessary people? Unnecessary people
are typically lazy, unskilled, negative, unreliable, cowardly, ignorant,
and/or dishonest.

If we become unnecessary, we will fail to build good personal and
professional relationships. Professionally, if we lack the skills needed for
our industry or have a negative attitude, no one will like to work with or
hire us. Skill alone can't build relationships, but a lack of skill can help

destroy them. Personally, if we lack leadership ability or have a negative attitude, no one will want to be our friend. Being an unnecessary person will make your life miserable.

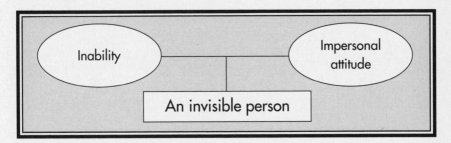

An invisible person is someone who has the capability to manage his or her own life, but chooses not to for one reason or another. This kind of person is incapable of managing his or her life without someone's help. It is because of these things that no one is interested in an invisible person.

An invisible person's inability to manage his or her life signifies a lack of leadership. Such a person does nothing but waste food, money, and time. Nobody is interested in a person who has the ability, but not the will, to help himself or herself.

How to Be a Necessary Person!

Being a necessary person is important in relationships on both a personal and professional level. On a personal level, from the time you are born and young, you need your parents. As you grow older, you want and need your friends. When you are an adult, if you want to get married, you need to date. When you are sick, you need a medical doctor for treatment. If you have your own business or manage a department, you need employees to operate it. Depending on whom you meet and how you build your relationships, your life can take many turns.

With the exception of your parents, you choose whom you want to associate with and whether to form good or bad relationships with

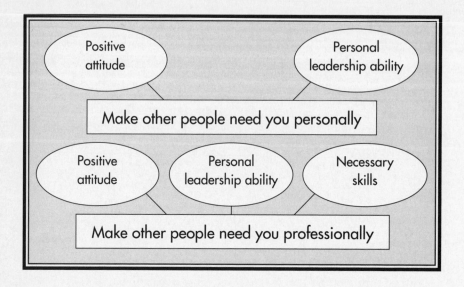

them. However even with your parents, if you are a likeable and necessary person, you can build better relationships with them.

Attitude is the foundation of relationships, in the sense that it can help determine whether or not others like you. Personal leadership acts as attitude's tool in the sense that it helps a person lead himself or herself and eventually lead others in any relationship setting. Simply put, attitude causes others to like or not like you. Personal leadership causes others to need or not need you. When you get others to like and need you, your life becomes much more enriched.

In addition, a necessary person should always learn new skills and improve necessary skills in the workplace. By combining them with their personal leadership ability and a positive attitude, these people will earn trust and respect from others, which also makes finding a job or starting a business that much easier.

People need people. It's learning how to hone that need that makes a person a leader.

In order for you to be necessary on a personal level, you must have more than a positive attitude; you need personal leadership ability as well. On a professional level, you need to have a positive attitude, personal leadership ability, and the necessary skills for your profession. Once you become a necessary person, you will be one of the luckiest people on Earth.

To be chosen or not is the people's choice! To be a necessary person is your choice!

STEP FOUR: DEVELOP PROPER COMMUNICATION SKILLS

Communication is the act of understanding another person through expression and listening, which counts for 99% of the kinds of relationships that are formed. Even entire nations can become best friends or bitter enemies through communication.

There are two primary ways in which we communicate:

1. **INTERNAL OR SILENT COMMUNICATION.** This form of communication is expressed through feelings and emotions. It cannot be heard, but can be felt.

2. **EXTERNAL COMMUNICATION** is verbal and body language. This form of communication also includes writing, sign language, and artistic expression, such as drawings, music, songs, or poetry.

The best way to communicate externally is to **listen sincerely** and **express yourself properly**.

Listen Sincerely

Have you ever really thought about why we have two ears, two eyes, and yet only one mouth? I believe we are blessed with two ears and two eyes for a reason: So we can be good listeners and observers. We are born to be better listeners and observers, so we can gain more knowledge and become better communicators. By sincerely listening to others, we will find out what their needs are to better understand them, thus helping to build win-win relationships.

How do you listen sincerely?

- ❖ Give your undivided attention to whoever is talking.
- ❖ Do not interrupt others unless absolutely necessary.
- ❖ Instead of interrupting while someone is talking, listen and write down important points.

Express Yourself Properly

We can express ourselves properly by following CCU:

- ❖ Choose the right word.
- ❖ Control the tone, volume, and speed of your voice.
- ❖ Use proper body language.

CHOOSE THE RIGHT WORD

One word!
One rude word can hurt someone's feelings the whole day.
One warm word can make someone feel good the whole day.

One careless word can ruin a relationship.
One caring word can build a good relationship.

One critical word can create an enemy.
One motivational word can change a person's life.

One inappropriate word can destroy a person's life.
One appropriate word can save a person's life.
Choose the right word by thinking right!

Turn an average word into a better word

Good to *excellent*
Valuable to *invaluable*
Reliable character to honorable *character*

Strong spirit to indomitable *spirit*
Beautiful to *gorgeous*
Different to *extraordinary*

The first step to expressing yourself properly is choosing the right or appropriate words based on the situation. What's the difference between right and wrong words? Consider the following examples to further understand the difference:

1. It's the Christmas holidays, and you're eager to show how much you appreciate and respect your loved ones. You decide to take the money you've saved and spend the day gift shopping for family members. On Christmas Eve, you head to your family's house to exchange gifts, and your Uncle Joe and Aunt Susan just opened their presents from you. Let's see how they react.

   UNCLE JOE: "This looks like crap. Where the heck did you get this sweater?"
   AUNT SUSAN: "Wow, this is such a thoughtful gift. How did you know I needed a new waffle maker? Thank you so much!"

How would you react to Uncle Joe? How would you react to Aunt Susan? The wrong word can ruin your holiday while the right word can make it the best holiday ever.

2. Mike is attending his father's funeral, and he is very sad and tired. His two best friends, Milton and Mark, come up to him after the ceremony and offer their condolences.

   MILTON: "Sorry about your dad. So...how much money do you think he left for you in the will? Think you're gonna be rich?"

MARK: "I'm sorry for your loss. Your dad was a great man. If there's anything I can do, please let me know."

Milton's comments would only make Mike's grief worse or even anger him, while Mark's words would be soothing and helpful. You can really feel the difference between the right word and the wrong word in this case.

3. Two couples, Elaine and Ed and Jack and Diane, go on a double date, but the conversations are entirely different:

> **ED:** "Baby, you look like a total pig, and you make me sick."
> **ELAINE:** "You pig!" (Slaps Ed across the face)

> **JACK:** "Diane, I am the luckiest man alive to be with you. You know why?"
> **DIANE:** "Why?"
> **JACK:** "Because you aren't just beautiful outside, but inside, too."
> **DIANE:** "That's the sweetest thing anyone has ever said to me (Kisses Jack)."

Ed just ruined his evening with Elaine because of his careless choice of words while Jack just made his evening a whole lot better because he chose the right thing to say.

4. Bobby's mom and dad just saw his report card, and it was full of bad grades.

> **MOM:** "How did I raise such a stupid little boy? What do you wanna be when you grow up, a loser?"

> **DAD:** "Bobby, don't feel bad. Everyone has trouble in school some

times. Whatever subjects you are struggling with, I will be more than happy to help you. I am always proud of you because I know you are smart, strong, and are my son."

Think for a moment. Mom's way of raising Bobby would send that child into the wrong direction. His father's way of raising him will help Bobby become a very successful individual, and make his parents very proud.

Choosing the right words is the first step to becoming a good communicator.

CONTROL THE TONE, VOLUME AND SPEED OF YOUR VOICE

In communication, using the proper tone and volume, as well as controlling the speed of your voice is just as important as choosing the right words. You may choose the right or appropriate words in a conversation with someone, but if you don't control the tone, volume, and speed of your voice, the meaning behind your words will be misinterpreted.

For example, John and Mary are on a date in a public park and John wants to show Mary how much he loves her. He thinks very carefully before saying what he wants to say. *"I love you. You complete me!"* John was so excited before this lovely statement that he couldn't control the volume, tone, and speed of his voice, sounding like he was crazy. Do you think Mary will feel good after hearing this statement? If John yells this statement, Mary will probably be stunned, and might even run away and never talk to John again.

If John controlled his voice and made the same statement in a very soft, sincere tone, in the right speed, do you think Mary would have felt good or bad hearing this statement? Mary would feel wonderful and therefore shower him with affection because John used the right voice along with the right choice of words.

Now despite John being very tender towards her after telling her he loved her, Mary replied with "I don't like you. You're too rough," in a soft, light-hearted tone. Do you think John would hate her? Not at all. Even though she chose the wrong word, Mary controlled her tone, volume, and the speed of her voice in making what she said sound very humorous.

Remember: Controlling the speed of your voice is just as important as controlling your tone and volume. If you talk too fast, what you say won't be understood at all, no matter how correct your tone of voice is. If you talk too slowly, you will bore whomever you talk to, regardless of your voice's tone or volume. So control the speed of your voice as well, depending on what you are saying and what kind of message you are trying to convey.

Controlling your voice is as important as choosing the right word. You can try acting the above scenarios out if you would like a better grasp on the importance of controlling the tone, volume, and speed of your voice.

Controlling the tone, volume, and speed of your voice can work wonders in all relationships, even between parents and children. Do you remember how you felt when you did something wrong and your father sometimes scolded you nicely in a calm tone, and other times by yelling? If you control your tone, volume, and speed of your voice when you speak, you will become a great communicator.

Use Proper Body Language

When communicating with others, it is absolutely important to use proper body language because action is always louder than words. When you meet people, you can immediately tell if they are comfortable or uncomfortable in talking to you through their body language. They can convey a range of feelings and emotions, including arrogance or modesty, without saying a word.

If you choose the right word and control the tone of your voice, but not your body language, the wrong message will be sent. For example, you could say, "I love you," to someone with a frowning face or with a warm smile and convey two completely different meanings. You could even say, "I hate you," with a big smile or with a scowl and you would know the difference. Take a moment and try it so you understand what I'm saying.

Yes, body language can even be perceived from a non-visual standpoint. If you were to say, "I love you," to your girlfriend or boyfriend with an ugly face over the phone, he or she will be able to hear that face and may never want to see you again.

The best facial expression in our body language is a smile. Try smiling with me now. It's so easy. Smile when you are face-to-face with someone you love or even over the telephone.

Always choose the right words, control the tone, volume, and speed of your voice, and use proper body language to properly express yourself. However, the best way to communicate is to understand others, then get others to understand you.

STEP FIVE: EMBRACE THE TOOLS OF WIN-WIN RELATIONSHIPS

- ❖ **UNDERSTAND OTHERS:** Understanding others is one of the best ways to build win-win relationships.
- ❖ **RECOGNIZE OTHERS:** By recognizing others, you recognize yourself.
- ❖ **ADMIRE OTHERS:** Admiring others shows that you have strong self-confidence.
- ❖ **SHOW APPRECIATION:** Showing appreciation reflects an outstanding character.
- ❖ **CARE ABOUT OTHERS:** Caring about others builds strong bonds in win-win relationships.
- ❖ **TREAT PEOPLE FAIRLY, NOT EQUALLY:** We have to treat everyone fairly because everyone is different.
- ❖ **SHARE WITH OTHERS:** We must share with others in order to have successful relationships.

Understand Others

In the martial arts, students endure promotional testing to advance to the next belt of their respective style. Following the completion of a test at the school, some students' families came to me complaining about the fairness of the testing. One parent in particular named Mr. Hunter wanted to pull his child out of my school because of my testing methods. I couldn't understand why they were complaining because I knew these methods were valid. All the students did great and were very happy about the rewards of their hard work. I asked Mr. Hunter to please elaborate on his concerns. He said that he noticed one of the students made 10 attempts to break the board and barely broke it. Mr. Hunter went on to say that the student had lousy technique and couldn't understand how he earned the new belt. He finished his diatribe by accusing me of only being interested in making money from my students, not fairly advancing their belt rank saying, "Looks to me like you just sold the (new) belt."

I was crushed after I finished listening to Mr. Hunter because the student he referred to, Matthew, may have looked like a normal 12-year old boy, but he wasn't. Matthew had the mental capacity of a 3-year old, was physically challenged, and had a severe learning disability. When Matthew joined the school, he couldn't stand properly. After training diligently, his learning ability and physical coordination improved incredibly. I was worried about the uproar that was being caused because I knew it would hurt his parents' feelings. Matthew's parents were very proud of him for taking martial arts. They saw the remarkable improvement in him since he began taking lessons. In fact, both parents and Matthew's brother knew the benefits of martial arts personally because they were black belts.

Facing Mr. Hunter and the other angry parents, I took a deep breath and explained the purpose of testing. I told them that, as an instructor and evaluator, I knew that technique was important in testing but not as much as attitude. When I look at a student, I first notice their attitude, desire, and improvement because testing is not a competition in which a championship is at stake, it's a measure of individual progress. I also accounted for the fact that everybody has different levels of coordination and intelligence. I then told them about the child's disabilities and went on to say how proud I was to be teaching this brave kid. After I finished, Mr. Hunter and those around him were at a loss for words.

I think everyone learned a lesson that day: it is important to accept people for who they are.

By understanding others, people will want to be with you and you can successfully build win-win relationships. Put yourself in other people's shoes. When you can see their point of view, you can easily understand others.

Recognize Others

When the Former Director of KCIA (Korean Central Intelligence Agency) Sea Dong Chang finished his term, he was jailed three times during the terms of Presidents Tae Woo Ro and Young Sam Kim for political reasons. Although previous political victims blamed their bosses or others for their predicaments, Mr. Chang never blamed his boss, former President Doo Hwan Chun. Even when the new administration demanded that Mr. Chang be questioned about any improprieties that former President Chun might have committed, he refused to cooperate and chose to go to prison instead. Chang's sentence could have been reduced or eliminated all together if he blamed former President Chun for his problems, but Chang chose not to.

Once Chang was released from prison, a reporter questioned him about his refusal to blame former President Chun for his problems and Chang replied that he would die in prison for a man who recognizes others. He also said that former President Chun was a great leader and that he had always recognized and acknowledged him.

President Chun always recognized Chang, from when Chang was an Army officer, to his post as Chief of Staff of the Blue House and then his position as the Director of the KCIA. Chun recognized Chang as a great soldier, someone he liked and could trust, and that he (Chun) was the luckiest person to have Chang. Mr. Chang's personal sacrifice is something we can all learn from.

If you always recognize others as unique and important, you will win them over. By recognizing others, you can motivate, encourage, and energize them. Recognition is the real power behind building win-win relationships. Find other people's strong points, positive qualities, and good characteristics, and recognize them for these things.

If you see or hear that someone you know has improved in some way (for example, a new haircut, a new job, even a new outfit), make sure you take a moment to recognize him or her for this improvement personally. Just a short phrase of recognition can make anyone feel great all day.

Remembering names is a powerful way to recognize others. Always remember someone's name after you meet him or her the first time. When you meet them again and you are able to call them by name, they will recognize you and be your friend. The best way you can remember someone's name is to ask questions about his or her family, job, or hobbies.

Admire Others

When I was younger, I remembered a day when my neighbors watched me practice my kicks. Some of them said my legs were as flexible as an octopus's tentacles. I was so motivated and energized by this compliment that I felt like I could kick all day long and never get tired. I began having more confidence in myself, which motivated me to do more stretching exercises to increase my flexibility. I have this same attitude when I teach the martial arts. I tell all of my students, young and old, that they have improved their techniques to build their self-confidence. Admiration is incredibly powerful.

By admiring others you not only demonstrate your self-confidence, intelligence, and personal leadership ability, you admire yourself. Also, by admiring others, you motivate and encourage people to enhance their performances.

When you admire others, they will admire you back, building win-win relationships in the process. Show admiration towards someone when you've seen them do good things or if they have improved in something. Compliment people on their positive qualities. Say at least one nice thing to everyone you meet.

Show Appreciation

Imagine if two of your friends bought new houses, and both needed your help to paint them within the span of a week. The first weekend you woke up at 5 a.m. and prepared to help your friend paint his new house. You worked with him until 7 p.m. that night. Upon finishing the job, your friend took you out to a nice restaurant for dinner. He showed real appreciation for your help and offered to help you if you ever needed assistance with something. This made you very happy, as you were able to go home and sleep peacefully.

The next weekend, you did the same thing for your other friend. You used your own paints, time, and sweat all day and night to help him paint his house. After finishing, your friend's attitude was very nonchalant, like he expected this kind of favor, telling you he would see you tomorrow. You went home feeling empty and used.

Both of your friends have the same talents and skills, but if you had to choose a new partner for your business or home project, whom would you choose? And if they each asked for help again, whom would you be more likely to help?

Showing appreciation demonstrates that you have great character, which helps build win-win relationships. Always show appreciation when others treat you well. Say thank you. Give a gift to the person you want to appreciate. The gift doesn't have to be big or expensive, but it must come from the heart. And show the attitude of gratitude when someone does something nice for you, even if it was something small.

Care About Others

What goes around, comes around. If you don't care about others, no one will care about you; but, if you care about others, they will do the same to you. The bottom line is that we should care for others.

There may be no greater example of a person that cared deeply about others than Mother Teresa, who was known all over the world for her concern, love, and compassion for the human race. She spent her entire life caring about others, helping millions of unfortunate people worldwide and touching their hearts. The whole world cared about Mother Teresa because she cared about them. In fact, the world actually gave her the Nobel Peace Prize as a symbol of their gratitude.

What we can learn from her example is that if you care about others, they will care about you. Doing so is one of the best ways to build win-win relationships. Start caring about your family, friends, co-workers, and even your neighbors. Care about them, and they will care about you.   Invest your time, energy, heart, experience, and if you have it, wealth, to help and care about others.

Treat People Fairly, Not Equally

Even though we all have equal opportunity and civil rights, being treated fairly is more important than being treated equally. For example, Bobby and his classmates are in a 100-meter race. Bobby has one leg while everyone else has two. Therefore, it's important that we treat Bobby fairly in his race against his classmates. Perhaps Bobby can have a 90-meter head start in the race, accounting for his handicap.

Despite our differences (beliefs, level of education, cultures, religions, strengths, level of speech, etc.) we should always strive to treat people fairly, not equally. Not everyone is at your level in whatever you do, and you may not be at someone else's level. If you don't care about treating others fairly, then you will have nothing but trouble in your relationships. By treating people fairly, you will build win-win relationships. It's important always to be flexible to make sure everyone is treated fairly, but at the same time, be strict to prevent unfairness.

Share with Others

People love those who are generous towards them because such generosity makes people feel respected, recognized, and cared for; win-win relationships are built because of sharing. You show that you are a successful, confident, caring, a respectful individual, and a leader when you share with others. Sharing isn't just about giving money, clothes, and/or food. You should share your knowledge, experience, time, strength, and heart. Make a habit out of being selfless by always taking the time out to share your knowledge, experience, time, energy, heart, and wealth (if you have that) with others.

STEP SIX: AVOID THE ENEMIES OF WIN-WIN RELATIONSHIPS

- ❖ **CRITICIZING OTHERS:** Criticism can create enemies.
- ❖ **ARGUING WITH OTHERS:** Winning arguments means losing friends.
- ❖ **DISCOURAGING OTHERS:** Discouragement destroys relationships.
- ❖ **BEING ARROGANT TOWARDS OTHERS:** Nobody likes arrogant people.
- ❖ **BEING NEGATIVE TOWARDS OTHERS:** No one likes dealing with negative people.
- ❖ **BEING SELFISH TOWARDS OTHERS:** Nobody is interested in selfish people.
- ❖ **LYING TO OTHERS:** Everybody avoids a liar.

Criticizing Others

How do you feel when other people criticize you? Horrible. Criticism is the worst thing that anyone receives in a relationship. For instance, if you told an overweight person he looked like a pig, how would he react? He probably would give you an earful of abuse or a punch in the face. Why? Nobody likes criticism because of its potential to humiliate and hurt others. If you want to build good relationships, don't criticize people.

However, there are times when we all must offer constructive criticism in order to help someone correct a weak point. In fact, there are times that we recognize a weak point in a person, and we offer constructive criticism because we care about him. When you are criticizing someone to prevent him or her from doing something bad or wrong, that is also considered constructive criticism. Because of criticism's power to embarrass and humiliate people, the person you criticize will think twice about doing something that might be harmful or wrong.

Calling an overweight person a pig is an example of destructive criticism. This type of criticism only serves to hurt others and annihilate relationships. Many times, destructive criticism comes from a person who is only looking to excuse him or herself as a defensive measure, or from someone that seeks revenge.

Let's take a look at the contrasts between constructive and destructive criticism: Mike is a terrible shot on his school's basketball team. Here are two ways his coach can remedy the situation:

CONSTRUCTIVE CRITICISM: *"Mike, you have a great arm but your aim needs a little work. If you flick your wrist as you throw the ball, your shots should be more accurate."*
DESTRUCTIVE CRITICISM: *"Mike, you are a terrible shot. You are so bad you shouldn't even be on the court."*

There are several ways that we normally react to criticism. We get angry, embarrassed, or argumentative, and even become vengeful towards these critics for their harsh words. Sometimes we feel defeated, allowing these criticisms to fill our hearts and minds with self-doubt.

All of these reactions hurt us.

When you hear criticism or discouragement, take a couple of deep breaths. As you listen to these words, determine if the criticism is constructive or destructive. If constructive, take the criticism to heart and use it as advice for self-improvement. In fact, we all need to discipline the way we handle and accept constructive criticism from a self-improvement standpoint. If destructive, ignore it or just laugh it away. By doing these things, you can become a leader.

When criticizing constructively, you must do so by first admiring someone and then informing him or her of the mistake. Most of us can handle criticism easier when we are admired by our critics. Another useful method in constructive criticism is informing the guilty party that you've made the same kind of mistake. This approach helps the guilty party handle criticism more easily.

Arguing with Others

All of us think winning an argument is important and often necessary. I speak from experience when I say that arguing with others is a bad thing.

As a kid, I used to be pretty proud of myself whenever I won an argument with a friend. In those days, I was confident in my arguing abilities. My need to be always right came back to haunt me one day when my teacher caught one of my classmates, Park, and I fighting.

> "What happened?" my teacher asked me.
> "I did nothing wrong at all," I replied.
> "I didn't do anything, either," Park answered.
> "You're a liar!"
> "Just tell me what happened," my teacher replied calmly.
> "Park took my pen and threw it away. When I asked him for my pen back, he claimed he never touched it. I have witnesses who will say the same thing." I pointed to Lee, my classmate and friend.

"He saw everything."

"Lee, please come over here," the teacher said. Lee walked over to the three of us. "Did you see what happened between these two boys?"

"No. I didn't see or hear anything."

"You're a liar too, Lee!" I shouted. "You saw everything! I know you did."

I was shocked when I heard Lee lie to the teacher. I knew I did nothing wrong to Park, but Lee lied to the teacher to get me in big trouble and hurt my feelings. I later found out he lied because I would always win in our arguments. By lying on purpose, he avenged my behavior.

I realized that though I've won arguments over the years, I've lost friends and actually hurt myself. I learned a hard lesson that day in school: Never deliberately argue with people again. If I ever did have to argue, I would stop the discussion without hurting anybody's feelings.

In reality, most of us argue because we want to show how right we are, and how wrong someone else is. This kind of self-righteous behavior reflects an "I'm smart, you're dumb," attitude on behalf of both parties. It's hard to deny that whenever any of us starts an argument, we don't want to give up or concede because we feel that we will lose our honor or pride. The harsh reality of arguing is that everybody walks away a loser.

Do not tell facts, truths, or lies to avoid arguing with others, unless it is totally necessary. Why?

- **IF YOU PROVIDE FACTS,** you make yourself out to be smart while the other person feels stupid.
- **IF YOU TELL THE TRUTH,** you make yourself out to be righteous while the other person is made to look like a bad guy.
- **DON'T LIE** or agree with a wrong or untruth because then you will be a liar.

However, if the other person is going to do something that can potentially harm himself and others, then argue with him so you can help him. Otherwise, as long as you don't tell facts, truths, or lies in an argument with others, you will keep your relationships intact.

The best solution for avoiding arguments is trying to understand others by putting yourself in their shoes. If you do this, you will see why arguing is pointless. When you act selflessly, you can avoid confrontation. For example, if you make a mistake, acknowledge it and don't argue about it. Admitting that the other person is right prevents the potential destruction of a good relationship and helps to build a better one.

There is an exception to this, though! Keep in mind that we have a reasonable right to argue in situations that require us to defend ourselves such as political debates, court arguments, or even during a law-enforcement investigation. In cases like these only, we should argue to win.

Discouraging Others

When you hear the following, how do these words make you feel?

"That's a stupid idea. It'll never work."

"You'll never amount to anything."

"Don't even try it. You'll just fail again."

"You are useless. Who would want to hire you?"

"You can't do anything right. You're an idiot."

"You are such a loser."

Much like criticism, discouraging words destroy good relationships, inflict depression, can entirely crush desire, and cause others to be equally discouraging. There may come a time when you need encouragement, but if you have discouraged others, discouragement is what you will receive in return; everyone hates discouragement. In fact, the acid of discouraging words can melt away the strongest bonds. Unfortunately some people have a habit of discouraging others, no matter what. Therefore, avoid being discouraging and ignore people who discourage you. If you have a great idea or goal, don't tell your idea to someone you know that will discourage you. (Often family members discourage you more than anyone else because your family worries about risks or knows your strengths and weaknesses.)

However, discouragement can be good for us at times. If you are contemplating a bad idea or personal move, or struggling with some sort of self-destructive behavior, discouraging words can help stop you from making a bad choice. In fact, this sort of discouragement can reflect a genuine caring attitude. Don't bring other people's weak points to their attention unless it will help them. If someone close to you is doing something wrong, tell that person.

Don't discourage others. If you wish to help them without making them feel discouraged, use proper communication. To go from being discouraging to encouraging, build self-confidence so you encourage yourself and always encourage others.

Being Arrogant towards Others

What are the differences between respectful and arrogant people?

Respectful people have high self-esteem, confidence, intelligence, and they respect and recognize others. **Arrogant people** lack self-confidence, have low self-esteem, and are ignorant and disrespectful of others.

Arrogant people reflect an "I'm smart, you're dumb;" "I'm rich, you're poor;" "I'm strong, you're weak;" "I'm beautiful, you're ugly;" or "I'm better than you are" attitude, which shows how rude and ignorant they are towards other people. When they aren't ignoring others, arrogant people intimidate and order others around, making them feel like servants. What goes around, comes around. Remember: If you ignore others, you will be ignored too.

There may come a day when you really need that person you ignored previously, and he or she will turn his or her back on you. Consider that the person you once ignored may surpass you in power, wealth or fame, and because of your arrogance, you no longer remain in that person's favor. Your arrogance will become your loss. Therefore, don't dig your own grave by ignoring others.

Don't let arrogant people get to you. Avoid them if you can, but if you can't, just take what they give you at the moment and laugh away the way they made you feel. Just think of arrogant people as dog poop. Don't be afraid of it, but avoid it.

To change from being arrogant to being respectful, build self-confidence by loving yourself unconditionally.

Being Negative towards Others

Negative people are full of excuses, and are envious and hateful toward others. They resent everyone, always blaming others when something has gone wrong. Negative people drag everyone down by not only criticizing others, *but by being bad mouths, and complaining for the sake of complaining,* all of which make others feel insignificant and make it impossible for anyone to accomplish anything. The reason for their behavior and attitude is that negative people are insecure and are full of self-doubt. Remember that negativity poisons your body, your mind, and your relationships so avoid being negative.

When situations arise in which you can't avoid a bad mouth, listen to their words but don't mind them. Instead, thank them for the information so that he or she will think highly of you.

If people complain to you, be polite and listen until they are finished. Once they have finished, most likely they will feel better because they have nothing left to complain about. It is possible that their complaints could have some sort of merit, making it sometimes necessary to complain to improve something or fix a problem. When listening to a bad mouth or a complainer, it's important to determine if what they are saying is negative in the sense that it's a personal attack, or in the sense that it is information that is protective for personal and business reasons, or for decisions involving some form of improvement. A good or bad decision should not be made without having all the correct information.

To turn the negative into the positive, love yourself unconditionally and focus on positive things. You will become a very positive person, and you can build win-win relationships.

Being Selfish towards Others

Some people only think of themselves, reflecting an attitude and exhibiting behavior that always screams 'me, me, me!' Their thought processes is always the same:

"I win, you lose."
"Mine is mine, and yours is mine."

Relationships are constructed through dualism, not individualism. Therefore, selfishness goes against one of the basic principles of relationships and is just another way to make people feel bad.

It's important to know the difference between loving yourself and being selfish. We love ourselves by taking care of ourselves. In other words, taking care of yourself isn't selfish because loving yourself is not only good for you, but for others too. On the other hand, selfish behavior is bad and unfair. Nobody likes associating with selfish people because of their "I win, you lose" mentality. Never be selfish. Change your thinking, which is the seed of selfishness, by being generous. I know that it is not easy to change old habits, but if you realize that selfishness is bad for you in the long run and bad for others, it will be easier to take the next step that generosity is good for you and good for others. When you think and act with generosity, you will become generous instead of selfish.

The first thing you should do is try to ignore selfish people or avoid them all together. However, if you are put into a situation where you have to deal with a selfish person, then be generous to them regardless of their behavior. If you continually show a selfish person generosity, then most of the time he will eventually become generous.

Lying to Others

Can you trust liars? Absolutely not. However, if you don't know the difference between bad lying (against the truth) and good lying (following what is right), you won't know how to properly build win-win relationships.

For example, Joe is at a jewelry store, looking for diamonds. The owner, Bill, takes one look at Joe and thinks, "I can easily sucker this guy." Bill marks up $600 worth of diamonds to $5,000 but tells Joe, "These diamonds are worth $5,000, but I'm gonna do something special for you. For today, and today only, I will sell them to you for only $3,000." Joe, thinking that this was a great deal, purchased them right away. Bill smiled, thinking that he had successfully swindled another customer.

Joe gets home and tells his friend, Mitch, about the sweet deal he got at Bill's jewelry store, getting $5,000 in diamonds for just $3,000. Mitch replies, "How is that possible? It sounds too good to be true. Maybe, you should have those diamonds independently appraised." Taking Mitch's advice, Joe goes to another jeweler to have the diamonds appraised and discovers the truth; that the diamonds were worth only $600.

Bill made two mistakes. First, he mistook Joe's niceness for gullibility. Second, Bill had no idea that Joe was actually incredibly influential in their town.

Once he found out that the diamonds were worth only $600, Joe told all of his equally influential friends about the fraud, and those friends told their friends and so on.

Bill's lie was an example of "bad lying." Why? First, Bill's dishonest act hurts the customer. Second, it hurt the reputation of the jewelry store. The store becomes known for its unethical sales practices, receives bad press, eventually gets shut down, and the jeweler could go to jail for fraud. If Bill were honest with his customer and not interested in making a quick buck, he could have had hundreds of thousands of dollars in new business but instead he destroyed potential relationships.

Honesty is the best policy in building win-win relationships. However, true honesty isn't about telling the facts; it's actually about following what is right.

For example, one day your two good friends, Johnny and Mike, became angry at each other, venting their frustrations at you in separate conversations. Johnny said some negative things about Mike and vice versa. Both are disappointed with each other. Their relationship—either its continuation or demise—comes down to how you react to the situation.

If you tell each of them what the other said (the facts), they likely would get into a fight, ending their friendship. If you tell them the facts, you will be a loser. Why? You made your friends fight and destroy their relationship.

On the other hand, if you tell Mike and Johnny that you are surprised about how well they get along, and how each speaks highly of the other. This is a good lie, because it follows what is right. More than likely, when the men hear these complimentary remarks, they will build a good relationship. When they find out the facts later, Mike and Johnny should handle them well because they won't be angry at each other.

If you use wisdom, you are a leader. Why? Because you united your two friends. Leaders follow the truth to save friendships and unite people; they don't tell the facts blindly. Only a loser would allow a friendship to be destroyed and let others get hurt in the process.

If you have made the mistake of telling the facts when you weren't supposed to, that's ok. We can't change the past, but we definitely can improve the future. Follow the truth; don't always follow the facts.

Fact VS Truth (Being honest versus following what is right)

You have a choice between buying a shirt for the same price at two different stores: ABC Buy and XYZ Buy.

At ABC Buy, George, one of their salespersons says, "Hello," to you when you walk in and asks how you are feeling. You say you're feeling well and ask the same question of George. He responds with, "I feel terrible," in a weary voice, treating you rudely, and not caring if you make a purchase.

George reveals information that will discourage other people, proving he can't control himself. Physically, George is an adult but mentally, is as mature as a 6-year old.

At XYZ Buy, Mike, one of their salespersons, greets you with, "Hello, how may I help you?" but when you ask the salesperson how he feels, the salesperson says, "I feel wonderful," and is very kind to you, assisting with all of your shopping needs. Mike is a leader and encourages other people.

Both salespeople started the day by having a big fight with their spouse, and they each came to work feeling angry and disappointed. But the differences in their attitudes were like night and day. George, the ABC Buy salesperson, told you how he was actually feeling, while Mike, the XYZ Buy salesperson, didn't tell you all of the facts ("white lie" or "good lying") and controlled his emotions. Mike followed what was right.

Which store would you shop regularly at? The ABC Buy salesperson would potentially destroy many good relationships with customers and might cause the store to close. The XYZ Buy's salesperson didn't tell the facts, using wisdom instead, which would help build win-win relationships with customers. Eventually, they will have to expand the store.

We should rid our minds of any negative impressions that may result from misunderstanding these scenarios. Also, we should not confuse following what is right with fact. Always remember: Honesty and integrity are the best and only policies to follow when building win-win relationships.

BE A LEADER, NOT A LIAR, WITH MULTIPLE FACES

When you control your emotions, you can build win-win relationships, but if you can't, you will destroy them. Controlling your emotions fol-

lows the truth. How do you control them? You have to put on multiple faces to maintain a positive self-image in order to build win-win relationships. To this end, you should try to have at least the following five different faces that you can control under any circumstance—all based on honesty and integrity, of course.

The following are five faces you can put on to maintain a positive self-image and build win-win relationships:

SMILING FACE. You are in the Miss America contest, and you discover that a fellow contestant hates you, which angers you. If you lose control of your feelings and show an angry face during the competition, you will lose, disappointing the state that you represent. If you control your emotions and compete with a smiling face, you will have a chance to win. You lied about your true feelings, but because you controlled your emotions, you are not a liar. You are truly a good leader. (Babies or little children cannot control their emotions because they don't have the strength to do so.) If you want to build win-win relationships, control your emotions and start a smile campaign right now.

SYMPATHETIC FACE. You just won a million dollars in the lottery, and your wife just delivered a healthy baby; you feel wonderful. However, your happiness is soon tempered when you discover that your best friend's wife died on the same day in a tragic car accident. If you don't control your happiness at the hospital, you will inappropriately show a smiling, excited face as you talk about your good fortune at the hospital, which could destroy years of friendship. However, if you control your feelings and show a sympathetic face while sharing your friend's sadness, you will preserve your long relationship.

SINCERE FACE. Just before you are about to go in for an interview for a million-dollar job, your girlfriend calls you and breaks up with you. If you don't control your feelings, you will show a hateful, ugly face at the upcoming interview and not get the job. If you control your feelings and show a sincere face, you will present yourself professionally and have a solid chance of winning the position and even a new love later on.

BRAVE FACE. You are the Commander-in-Chief of NATO forces during a war against terrorist groups when you receive some terrible news in an e-mail: A car killed your beloved puppy dog last week. The news leaves you terribly depressed. If you can't control your feelings and proceed to show a face of depression, your demeanor could lower troop morale and you could lose a battle, even lose the war. If you control your emotions and show a brave face, you will have a strong chance at winning the war.

POSITIVE FACE. It's a normal day for you and anything is possible. If you want to cry, please go ahead. If you want to be angry, get angry and yell. If you want to laugh, please laugh as loud as you can. If you desire to be quiet, do so. Whatever you feel like doing, please do. There is one condition: Please show your emotions in isolation, whether it's in your car, house, the park, or office.

After you release your frustration, you will feel positive and energetic. You will also feel good that you didn't bother anybody. Most people will be comfortable around you if you are positive and energetic. If you can manage to be this way, you can open anyone's heart and build win-win relationships.

STEP SEVEN: STRENGTHEN YOUR SPECIAL RELATIONSHIPS

We all have two different special relationships in our lives: familial and non-familial.

Familial relationships are those relationships we have with our parents, siblings, spouse, children and other members of our family.

Non-familial relationships are those relationships we have with our girlfriend or boyfriend, friends, co-workers, teachers, etc.

Our lives begin in a familial relationship. As babies, we need protection and nurturing from our parents. As we get older, we attend school and begin our non-familial relationships by making friends. Later on, some of us develop a need for a lifetime companion and then, perhaps, children—all of whom bring us back full-circle to familial relationships.

Among all relationships we form, the most important one is that of husband and wife. No other relationship is as legally or morally binding as the association between a husband and wife, making this the most important relationship, especially because marriage is the foundation of familial relationships. So, without question, your lifetime partner is the closest and most-needed person on Earth.

Because our relationships aren't set in stone, we must learn how to form relationships the right way so they become special and unique over time.

Build the Four Special Relationships

1. Special Relationship with Your Parents: Big trees have big roots.
2. Special Relationship with Your Spouse: The closest and most important person to you is your spouse.
3. Special Relationship with Your Children: Your children are a reflection of you and your hope for the future.
4. Special Relationship with Your Best Friends: You are the luckiest person in the world if you have best friends.

SPECIAL RELATIONSHIP WITH PARENTS: BIG TREES HAVE BIG ROOTS.
Can a tree survive without its roots? No tree can survive without roots because they provide nourishment, stability, and support. For example, a big tree needs big roots to stand firm in storms and other types of severe weather. Without big roots, it could fall down when subjected to hurricane-force winds. Much like a tree needs roots to live, we need good role models to survive. Good role models provide us guidance and support, among other things.

I learned a lot about role models one evening while watching the Late Show with David Letterman on NBC. Letterman was interviewing a young African-American boxer, and he asked the boxer if he thought his coach was good. The young man told Letterman that his coach was great, and that he was like a brother to him. Letterman then jokingly asked the young man if his manager took his money. The boxer replied that the manager was like a father to him, and that Letterman shouldn't make jokes about their relationship. It was at that point of the interview that this young man got all of my attention. I finished watching the interview and went to bed, impressed by this young man's attitude. Because I believed this boxer was a good role model for young children, I instantly became a fan of his and never missed one of his matches. Then, one day on November 22nd, 1986, he beat the world heavyweight champion and became the world's youngest heavyweight boxing champion in history at the age of 20. That boxer was Mike Tyson.

Just like that, Mr. Tyson became rich and famous. This made me so proud because I felt the right guy had become a hero to millions. His rags-to-riches story played out like a Hollywood movie. Here was a guy who went from being a street thug to being the world heavyweight boxing champion. Wow!

Enamored with the young man, I told my students that Mike Tyson wasn't just a champion in the ring, but also a champion in life. I implored my students to learn from his attitude. I was, in my own little world, a public relations man for Tyson. However, that would soon change.

One day while watching TV, I was shocked to discover something was not quite right about my young role model. A reporter asked Tyson what happened to his coach, and he replied that he had fired him. Tyson went on to say that he could win without his coach and that he didn't need him. I was stunned.

Not long afterwards, Tyson was questioned at a news conference if he were going to fight Lennox Lewis and dedicate the fight to his manager. Tyson said he would not fight Lennox Lewis for his manager. He and his manager parted ways after that. This latest revelation perplexed me. I didn't know what happened to Tyson's previous attitude toward his coaches and managers. Needless to say, I was disappointed. With this latest turn of events, how could I continue to tell my students to learn from Mike Tyson's example?

After turning his back on his manager and coach, Tyson went to Japan in 1990 to defend his titles against then unknown boxer Buster Douglas and lost by knockout. Laid out on the ring mat, he lost his title and his honor, disgracing himself by losing to an unheard-of fighter.

His life unraveled from there. In 1992, Tyson was imprisoned for raping a former beauty contestant, Desiree Washington, spending nearly three years behind bars. Tyson's loss to Douglas and subsequent imprisonment left me in disbelief. Mike Tyson totally forgot where he came from and had cut his roots, leading to his downfall. If there is one thing we can learn from Mike Tyson, it's that we can't cut our roots.

> Your roots define who you are. Always care for them.

NOTE HOW DIFFERENT Tyson is from Michael Jordan. Remember, how Jordan stood up to the Bulls management and informed them he would not return for another season unless they re-signed Phil Jackson. Jordan did not cut his roots with his coach, who was a good role model to Jordan and his teammates. Jordan's decision prompted Chicago management to re-sign Jackson as head coach, and the Bulls went on to win their sixth NBA title. On the other hand, look at what happened to Tyson when he cut his roots. Without his manager, he was directionless and suffered the consequences, losing his world heavyweight title.

Both Jordan and Tyson were rich and powerful, but their lives went in totally different directions because of the way each chose to handle his roots.

All of our first roots in life lead to our parents. They're also our best role models. I've never seen rich and famous people who have turned against their parents, continue being happy. I certainly don't consider them to be successful for doing so. Your parents are your parents, good or bad, rich or poor. Even if they abandon you or turn to crime, your parents are still your parents. You may hate what they did, but never hate *them*. If you hate your parents, you only hurt yourself in the long run. Hating your parents is akin to having a time bomb or poison in your body. You can never be truly happy when you hate your parents.

Please understand, I'm not asking you to condone or copy a parent's bad actions. What I'm asking is for you to utilize the gift of forgiveness to forgive them for their wrongs, and love them for who they are. By forgiving your parents, you might be able to help them stop their improper behavior and set them on the right path.

To reiterate what I said before, I have never seen anybody who turned against his or her parents live a good life. Like it or not, our roots are our parents. If we cut our roots, we commit suicide. Take care of them. You always need to remember your parents' good qualities so you appreciate and love your parents even more.

These are the 3 things I like about my parents:

1. They are loyal. My father gave his life to protect his family and his country during the Korean war.
2. They are caring. When we had nothing, my mother sometimes went hungry to give food to my brother and me.
3. They have an indomitable spirit. My mother lost her husband and her daughter, then became homeless, but never gave up as a provider for my brother and me.

Please list the 3 things you like about your parents:

1. _____
_____

2. _____
_____

3. _____
_____

SPECIAL RELATIONSHIP WITH YOUR SPOUSE: THE CLOSEST AND MOST
IMPORTANT PERSON TO YOU IS YOUR SPOUSE.

❖ Find the Right Person to Marry: A healthy and wise person is the
best choice.
❖ Maintain Marital Happiness: The principles of win-win relationships are the keys to marital happiness.
❖ Practice the Seven Ways of Having a Great Marriage: These seven
ways will help to forge long lasting marriages.

To find the right person to marry:

1. Never marry someone only for money, fame, or power. If you do,
you will become either a prisoner or a gold digger. Remember
money, fame, or power can't buy happiness.
2. Avoid marrying someone who is lazy or has a negative attitude.
These kinds of attributes indicate a negative personality or bad
character, which will stress you out and lead you to a life of sickness and unhappiness.
3. Refuse to marry a person who is unable to manage his or her life.
(Not referring to a physically or mentally challenged person.) If you
do, you will become a babysitter for life.
4. Don't just use external beauty as a guide in marrying someone. If
you date someone because of his or her external beauty, a short-

term relationship is okay. If you marry someone for only his or her external beauty, you are asking for trouble.

5. Think deeply before marrying someone just out of love. Although love is essential for marriage, a couple must have more than that to maintain a long-term commitment. Some people are blinded by love, overlooking what the other person is like on the inside. Obviously, don't marry a person that you don't truly love.

6. Marry a person who can offer you personal power, a positive attitude, and love. You will have a happy relationship for life.

7. Marry someone who shares the same interests, hobbies, values, goals, and beliefs. Definitely date or marry someone who shares the same beliefs and hobbies along with leadership ability, especially if you consider them healthy, beautiful and loving. If you can find such a person, then you will have the kind of marriage that will motivate, energize and strengthen your life, making you the luckiest person in the world.

To this day, I still feel like I am the luckiest person on Earth to have met my wife, Sonja Kim. She is full of vitality, compassion, leadership, and is beautiful in every way. We have so much in common, especially our culture, beliefs, and values. Getting married to her was one of the best things to ever happen to me; I love her more than anything in the world.

However, many couples can attest that emotions and beliefs before and after marriage can vary greatly. In fact, my initial thoughts of my wife weren't enough to sustain a happy marriage.

We were both stubborn, had strong personalities, and our leadership abilities didn't mesh. I wanted to do things my way and change her to be like me. She wanted to do things her way and change me to be like her. Our selfish behavior was tearing this marriage apart. We became so frustrated with each other that we couldn't figure out how to solve this crisis, making our differences all the more exasperating.

One day, our conflict finally came to a head when I saw a note on my desk from my wife, listing all of my negative points. As I read it, I got very upset . . . so upset that I had to take a deep breath and wait a couple of minutes before I could continue reading. After finishing it, I wrote the same kind of note back to her. I felt much better after getting all of my anger out on paper, but I decided not to give her the note right away. Instead, I slept on it and waited until the next day to do it.

Tomorrow came and I re-read her letter. Unlike the day before, some of her criticisms made sense, and I understood why she needed me to change. I decided not to give her my letter and chose to wait until the next day to request a meeting with her.

The next day, we sat down to talk and agreed to write down 10 things that we felt the other should change so we could discuss them together. We promised that we wouldn't get angry, interrupt each other or walk away during our discussion; that promise didn't last long. Within minutes of critiquing each other, we got into a shouting match. Eventually, we calmed down, tried again, and finally realized we needed to try understanding one another. We agreed to work on improving ourselves and not each other.

Our letters of criticism and heart-to-heart talks helped us the most in maintaining a happy marriage. These talks worked so well that we agreed to have more of them as often as necessary throughout the years. These experiences helped me to understand that marriage is like a flower garden. Both are beautiful, emotionally moving, and wonderful. Yet, both need constant care to remain beautiful. If you don't take care of your garden, weeds will overrun it, and a beautiful garden can transform into a haven of weeds. In every marriage, a couple needs to take care of each other, much like you need to tend to your garden. By taking care of each other, you and your spouse will build a long-term win-win relationship.

I would like to share with you my seven ways of having a great marriage.

1. Love your spouse unconditionally.
2. Don't try to win arguments. Instead, make win-win situations, not "I win, you lose" or "you win, I lose," by communicating with your spouse.
3. Change yourself instead of trying to change your spouse.
4. Admire, appreciate, encourage, and motivate your spouse, in everything your spouse does.
5. Avoid discouraging your spouse, blaming your spouse for something, or criticizing your spouse.
6. Try to maintain a positive self-image around your spouse.
7. Build on the same beliefs, interests and hobbies with your spouse and set family goals.

In addition to following the seven ways to building a good marriage, make a commitment always to take care of your marriage so it will remain beautiful.

You always need to remember your spouse's good qualities so you appreciate your spouse even more.

These are the 3 things I love about my wife:

---

1. She is very beautiful, both inside and outside.
2. She is caring. When I could not move, she took care of me like a baby, while continuing to work full time and take care of our children.
3. She has personal leadership ability. She is the President and CEO of a strong, successful company.

Please list the 3 things you love about your spouse:

```
┌─────────────────────────────────────────────────────────┐
│ 1. _____      │
│    _____      │
│ 2. _____      │
│    _____      │
│ 3. _____      │
│    _____      │
└─────────────────────────────────────────────────────────┘
```

SPECIAL RELATIONSHIP WITH YOUR CHILDREN: YOUR CHILDREN ARE A REFLECTION OF YOU AND YOUR HOPE FOR THE FUTURE.

I have a lovely daughter and son that my wife and I love more than anyone else. Even with my undying love for my children, I've had to learn to build good relationships with them, understanding not to associate raising children with instructing them at my martial arts school. Although I've been a successful martial arts teacher for many years, I realized that I couldn't raise my children in the same manner. The principle of discipline might be the same, but its application is quite different in the home than it is in the school. I learned this lesson the hard way through a particularly painful experience when my children were very young.

It started following a dinner at a restaurant with my family. I was upset and embarrassed about my pre-school aged children's behavior during dinner, and I yelled at them on the way home. However, my words fell on deaf ears, which just ticked me off even more. When we got home, I spanked them, sending them to bed crying.

A few hours later, I went upstairs to their rooms to check on them; staying in each of their rooms and watching them sleep for an hour. When I saw how peacefully and innocently they slept, I realized how small they were, and how I might have been too harsh punishing both my children. I questioned why I yelled and spanked them. Feelings of guilt washed over me. I was embarrassed and upset when I realized my discipline as a master instructor wasn't very effective with my own children. I even wondered what other people would think of me, and whether they thought I was capable of disciplining my own children.

I finally understood that my expectations of my children were way too high. I expected my children to think and act like adults, completely forgetting they were just children. After that incident, I decided to change the way I disciplined my children. The restaurant incident helped me learn a lot as a parent, but it didn't teach me everything.

One day, my wife told me that I was very immature. I laughed and asked her to explain. She told me that our son said that I was immature. My 11-year-old son thought I was immature! Imagine that . . . but I told myself that was exactly what I wanted to hear from him.

My son was 11 then, but I was still talking to him as if he were five or six years younger. I had simply forgotten he was getting older and wiser. From that experience, I've learned to grow with my children and understand their problems, helping me become a better parent.

MOST CHILDREN LOSE confidence and stray into the wrong direction when you stop loving them. At the same time, if you stop disciplining your children, they start losing confidence and their positive habits. **Always love your children unconditionally, no matter what.**

> Love and discipline are the diet of a healthy parent-child relationship.

The following are some invaluable tips on raising children to build win-win relationships with them:

❖ Love your children unconditionally, no matter what.
❖ Find what talents your children have, support them, and help them achieve their goals. Also, help your children in other things that they are not as talented in, to help improve their lives.
❖ Talk at your child's level, not yours, when disciplining them.
❖ Help them know right from wrong and instill discipline.

❖ Spanking is not the right way to raise a child with love. Try reasoning with them instead. After my restaurant episode, I promised never to spank them again.

❖ Be honest and understanding when communicating with your children.

❖ Don't make promises you can't keep.

❖ Admit your mistakes.

❖ Help your children set positive goals and achieve goals to help them create winning habits.

❖ Make sure you spend some private one on one quality time with your children regularly.

❖ Make your children responsible for their own chores to help develop their character and personal leadership ability. One way you can work toward this goal is to post a list of their daily and weekly chores so they can see what they need to do.

1. Cleaning up their own room.
2. Making their own bed.
3. Doing their own laundry.
4. Doing their own dishes.
5. Doing yard work.
6. Doing homework.

❖ After they have done their chores, reward them. But you need to set up a fair reward system beforehand.

You always need to remember your children's good qualities to appreciate and love your children even more.

These are the 3 things I love about my children:

> **1.** They are healthy. I am proud that they eat wisely and practice martial arts with me.
> **2.** They are intelligent. They are both honor roll students.
> **3.** They are creative. They constantly surprise me with beautiful artwork, writing, and projects around the house.

Please list the 3 things you love about your children:

> **1.**
>
> **2.**
>
> **3.**

SPECIAL RELATIONSHIP WITH YOUR BEST FRIENDS: YOU ARE THE LUCK-IEST PERSON IN THE WORLD IF YOU HAVE BEST FRIENDS.
True friends are valuable in the sense that they are extensions of your body and mind. The more true friends you have, the greater your life will be.

How many true friends do you have? If you can say that you have at least one, then let me say that you are very lucky. If you can say that you have two true friends, then I say your life has been worthwhile, and that you have a bright future. If you can say that you have three, then you can do just about anything, and have or will have a successful life. If you can say that you have four true friends, then I say you are a leader, and that you have broken the mold. You are a true winner. If you can say that you have five true friends, you can change the world.

What defines a true friend?

1. They are very comfortable whenever or wherever you meet.
2. A true friend sticks by you in good or bad times and shares with you big or small things.
3. A true friend is available 24 hours a day, without hesitation. Don't misunderstand this, though. A true friend should always be available in times of need and will support you, but won't bother you unnecessarily.
4. You both share the same interests and beliefs.
5. You both understand, trust, support, care for, encourage, motivate, and respect each other as true friends.

True friendships are built on unselfish behavior. If you and your friend each have a "We win" attitude, then you are true friends. However, if either of you have an "I win and you lose" attitude, then you don't have a true friendship.

To build true friendships:

❖ **INVEST TIME AND ENERGY** by caring, understanding, sharing, sacrificing for/with each other in order to build trust. When you and your friend(s) are honest, responsible, and show integrity, you will respect and be loyal to each other.

❖ **EXERCISE FAIRNESS** to create win-win situations.

❖ **DEVELOP THE SAME INTERESTS AND BELIEFS** by setting common goals and achieving them together.

The measure of true friendships is the amount of unwavering loyalty between two people. Many relationships are superficial. In other words, people are conditionally your friend for one reason or another. Superficial relationships are short-term associations that can be hurtful and wasteful.

If you are successful, a lot of people will want to be around you as you achieve greater things. If things go bad, these people won't stick around. Likewise, some people only stick together through difficult times. When things become easier, these people go away. Whether you succeed or fail, or go through good or bad times, a true friend stays with you, no matter the circumstances.

If you have the type of person you can share things with, trust and depend on—anytime, anywhere, all your life—then you have a true friend. If you have a true friend, then you are the luckiest person in the world. True friends make life valuable and worthwhile.

These are my true friends, and the reasons they are my true friends.

---

1. Sonja Kim: I love and respect her more than anything on Earth. She keeps me on balance, providing some of the good qualities I lack to make our family happy.
2. Master Tim McCarthy: I trust, respect, and love him. His honesty, loyalty, teamwork, and educational background help us build a stronger organization.
3. Master Keith Winkle: I trust, respect, and love him. His loyalty, enthusiasm, outstanding leadership and indomitable spirit have helped our organization grow to its current level of success.
4. Master Kirk Pelt: I trust, respect, and love him. His exceptional leadership ability and organizational skills represent the future of our organization.
5. Master Mike Bugg: I trust, respect, and love him. His hard work, dedication, and courageous leadership have made our organization strong.

Please write down who your true friends are, and explain why they are your true friends.

```
1. _____

2. _____

3. _____

4. _____

5. _____
```

STEP EIGHT: MAKE INTERNATIONAL FRIENDS

The world is a grand, beautiful place, rich with history, full of potential and opportunities that await you. Businesses, education, entertainment, communication, even politics have all become global. The world is literally now at your fingertips. If you know how to build international relationships, your future will be limitless and your life will be incredibly triumphant.

The best international relationships follow the same principle of win-win relationships: "You win, I win, therefore we win." In order to make international friends:

FIRST, understand and accept people for who they are and what culture they come from. Doing so will get those people to understand your culture and accept you for who you are, becoming their friend and building a great relationship in the process.

SECOND, use the universal languages of smiling and showing appreciation. The power of smiling opens minds while showing appreciation opens hearts. By smiling and showing appreciation, you can make good international friends anywhere and everywhere on Earth.

We need to educate ourselves on our vast differences to better accept and understand others. By knowing how others are different, we can accept them for who they are.

To understand the value of international friendships, it might help if I shared with you my knowledge and experience of living in two different cultures: Eastern and Western.

Culture's Effect on Personality & Character

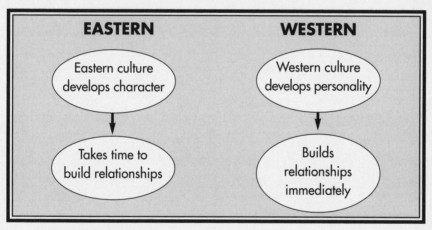

EASTERN	WESTERN
Eastern culture develops character	Western culture develops personality
Takes time to build relationships	Builds relationships immediately

I have always been amazed at the discrepancies in Eastern and Western relationships. Two people from the West can form quick and lasting relationships after just one meeting. The same can't be said about Easterners.

I've also noticed differences in cross-cultural relations: Some Westerners liked only Easterners and vice versa. A Korean friend of mine said that Koreans who formed friendships with Westerners so quickly were "Americanized." On the other hand, when I noticed that an American student of mine struggled to form close friendships with Easterners the first time around, I told him he was like a Korean.

Utilizing my own experiences along with extensive research, I observed some basic differences in social behavior between the two cultures. Please understand that the following observations will be simplified generalizations. No one can accurately describe any individual, much less an entire culture, in a few pages, but I will offer these comments as an elementary understanding of the differences between the two cultures.

Eastern culture is intangible and invisible, with much concern for the spiritual and the causes that affect life. **The Eastern person says: "If I do this, that will happen."** Easterners believe in what they can feel or perceive, not see. This development of character, coupled with their introverted social behavior, makes relationship-building a slow process.

Western culture is tangible or visible, emphasizing material possessions and the effects of causes. **The Western person says: "This happened because I did that."** Westerners believe in what they can touch or see. This development of personality, coupled with their extroverted social behavior, makes for fast-starting relationships.

Interestingly, the immediate contrasts between the cultures produced striking similarities in the end. From these studies of the East, I found that their introverted social behavior and intangible relationships created a society that had good character, but introverted personality. My research of the West showed their extroverted social behavior and tangible relationships created a society that had positive personality, but a lower expectation of character. The end result for both was that lasting relationships were difficult to develop.

Consider how the East formerly lagged behind the West in economic development. China, Japan, Korea, Malaysia, Singapore, and Thailand were considerably less wealthy than their Western counterparts. That all changed when these Asian countries began adopting Western culture, thus developing a booming economy. In the 1980s, Japan's economy nearly dwarfed America's.

Although there were many factors that contributed to this economic turnaround, the Asians' decision to become more extroverted in their social behavior and develop more efficient communication skills was one of the more important ones. They even learned how to build better relationships between family members, schoolmates, co-workers, and friends.

Cultural crossovers were even felt in the West, when many people began adopting the Eastern culture through the martial arts. This decision helped many Westerners, especially children, get in shape physically, and strengthen their character. The benefits of martial arts were especially good for children because through its discipline, children improved their school grades and built better relationships with their parents, teachers, and classmates. Personally, I have found that children who hold a black belt earn mostly "A's" in school. The martial arts enabled Westerners to develop character to go along with their outgoing personalities, bridging the gap between the East and the West.

To better understand how to make the best international friendships, we must look at our cultural differences and see how we can combine the best of the East and the West to create global win-win relationships. The following examples illustrate ways that both cultures deal with similar situations:

HOUSEHOLD LEADERSHIP

- ❖ **EAST.** The home is considered a place of respect, growth, and harmony. The family has high regard for its elders, parents, and grandparents. There is typically one leader of the family, usually a grandparent, who makes family decisions until such time as he or she hands the responsibilities over to the parents. Opinions of family members are regarded in order of seniority: grandparents, parents and eldest of grandchildren. The younger the family member, the less likely he or she will be able to express him or herself.

Although every group needs a strong leader, it is important to consider individual opinions equally. The Eastern outward expression of respect and care for elderly grandparents and parents is motivating, dynamic, and great! However, suppressing the opinions of younger members of the family is unfair. Independent expressive ability is so delayed that it takes younger people longer before they can adjust socially. Children need to improve communication skills to have a better quality of life.

❖ **WEST.** Individual growth, liberty, and happiness are top priorities. The family has highest regard for the parents, with the father and mother usually holding equal power. Grandparents are rarely a factor, since they don't usually live with the family. Family members are usually free to express themselves, allowing for more democratic decision-making. However, younger members often end up with a lack of respect for their elders, including grandparents and parents.

Freedom of expression for all age groups, including children, allows for the development of individual independence and is motivating, dynamic, and great! However, younger members' lack of respect for their elders and parents is not right. All groups need to have some kind of unity and a strong leader. Children need discipline to build personal power so they can survive and succeed.

❖ **UNIVERSAL.** Utilize the best of the East and West. The home needs a team leader, but at the same time the family needs to have respect for individual rights.

DISCIPLINE OF CHILDREN

❖ **EAST.** Children are strictly disciplined to the point of inhibition and their desire to express themselves is often suppressed, which carries over into adolescence and contributes to a very modest demeanor.

Extreme disciplinary pressure on youngsters is not good. Without enough love and attention, children gain nothing from discipline and can become depressed.

❖ **WEST.** Parents often shower their newborn children with attention, setting the stage for children to grow up spoiled and allow them to do almost whatever they please. Their discipline of children lacks consistency.

Parents should listen sincerely to children's opinions, becoming a good coach or advisor in the process. Love and attention without reasonable discipline creates selfishness and spoils a child.

❖ **UNIVERSAL.** Children are the future leaders of the world. They need the opportunity to express their own ideas and build self-confidence. They also need discipline. When they have done well, they deserve praise; when they have done wrong, they need to be reprimanded. Both freedom and proper discipline during growth will yield stable leaders for the future.

"I" THE INDIVIDUAL OR "US" THE FAMILY?

❖ **EAST.** Emphasis is on the family as a unit, each member being part of a whole. Cooperation is important and many families work together at family-owned businesses.

❖ **WEST.** The individual is the unit, several of which make up the family. Independence from the household is often sought in adolescence. Some family members opt not to cooperate in family-owned businesses.

❖ **UNIVERSAL.** Individual independence is important, but family cooperation is more so.

The above topics are examples of the opposing customs, lifestyles and habits of the people of Eastern and Western cultures. However, Eastern and Western cultures also have many similarities. Both cultures value education. Human virtues like integrity and responsibility are universal; as are emotional needs like love and caring for others. All cultures have positive and negative aspects, yet the peoples of these cultures should find ways to preserve their finer, positive points. Build great relationships by combining the best of the East and West.

SUMMARY
Build Win-Win Relationships
Relationships are constantly changing, but with a win-win relationship dynamic, relationships can remain constant. Michael Jordan and Phil Jackson are living examples of the power of win-win relationship.

Eight Steps to Building Win-Win Relationships
Be a necessary person to build win-win relationships.

1. **DEVELOP THE PRINCIPLES OF WIN-WIN RELATIONSHIPS.** Relationships are fairness, negotiation, and investment.
2. **HELP OTHER PEOPLE LIKE YOU.** People like positive attitudes; attract others with a positive attitude by building a high-class character and a positive personality.
3. **BECOME A NECESSARY PERSON.** People need people so become a necessary person by building a positive attitude, personal leadership ability, and the necessary skills.
4. **DEVELOP PROPER COMMUNICATION SKILLS.** Relationships begin and end with communication. Choose the right word, control your voice, and use positive body language.
5. **EMBRACE THE FRIENDS OF WIN-WIN RELATIONSHIPS.** The seven ways to make others feel important while securing a win-win relationship are understanding others, recognize others, admire others, show appreciation, care about others, treat people fairly, not equally, and share with others.
6. **AVOID THE ENEMIES OF WIN-WIN RELATIONSHIPS.** Avoid making others feel bad. The seven enemies of win-win relationships are criticizing others, arguing with others, discouraging others, being arrogant to others, being negative to others, being selfish to others, and lying to others.
7. **STRENGTHEN YOUR SPECIAL RELATIONSHIPS.** Cherish the ones closest to you by tightening the bonds. These special relationships

are with your parents, your spouse, your children and your best
friends.

8. **MAKE INTERNATIONAL FRIENDS.** Open your heart and mind to
the world. Eastern culture is intangible, Western culture is tangible. East and West need to combine together to build win-win
relationships.

REVIEW OF "BUILD WIN-WIN RELATIONSHIPS"

What are the three principles of win-win relationships?

_____

_____

Can you apply the principles of win-win relationships in a competition? If yes, please explain how.

_____

_____

How do you help other people like you?

_____

_____

What two ingredients make up your attitude?

_____

_____

How would you react to the following personalities?

Positive:_____

Negative:_____

Impersonal:_____

_____

Describe how people think when they have the following kinds of character.

Low class:_____

Middle class:_____

High class:_____

What does it take to build a positive attitude?

_____

_____

What is the difference between a necessary, an unnecessary, and an invisible person?

_____

_____

How is personal leadership crucial to being a necessary person?

_____

_____

What is the best way to understand, recognize, and admire other people?

_____

_____

How do you show that you care about others?

_____

_____

Why should you treat people fairly, not equally?

_____

_____

How can you criticize others without hurting their feelings?

_____

_____

Why is telling the truth, facts, or lies dangerous in an argument?

_____

_____

How should you handle discouragement?

_____

_____

Who are the most important "roots" in your life and why?

_____

_____

What does it take to maintain happiness in a marriage?

_____

_____

Why are love and discipline so important in properly raising your children?

_____

_____

How do you build true friendship?

_____

_____

What is the main difference between Eastern and Western culture?

_____

_____

How does Eastern or Western culture influence the way you develop your personality and character?

_____

_____

Create
DYNAMIC
Organizations
Be triumphant in your life

THE SUNSET OF AMERICA

I came to America in 1977 with many of the same hopes and dreams millions of immigrants before me had envisioned. America was a land where the streets were paved with gold, with freedom for everyone and opportunity everywhere. I dreamt of great success and a new, wonderful place to call home. However, my vision was quickly clouded.

Under Jimmy Carter's Presidency, America was in turmoil. Rising oil prices were causing a critical shortage of gasoline, forcing millions of Americans to wait in line for hours just to put 10 to 15 gallons of gas in their cars. The nation's inflation rate climbed to a staggering 18%, the interest rate climbed even higher to 20% and the federal deficit doubled from $27.7 billion to $57 billion from 1979 to 1980. Prices on goods continued to climb as well, while the average person's salary remained the same.

Then there was the American hostage situation in Iran. On November 4, 1979, Iranian students stormed the U.S. embassy and held 52 hostages for 444 days, making it one of the most intense international incidents in world history. America could do little to solve the situation for more than a year; every rescue attempt failed.

The U.S. had even more trouble on the home front. In 1980, President Carter announced to the world that the Americans were boycotting the Summer Olympic Games in Moscow because of the Soviet Union's invasion of Afghanistan. Just like that, hundreds of American athletes had their dreams of Olympic gold crushed for political reasons. Carter's decision to pull the U.S. out of the Summer Games was a public and political disaster, plunging his administration into further disfavor with the American people.

If that wasn't enough, the crime rate was going up nationwide. Homicides, robberies, assaults, and rapes increased by the year, especially in New York City, Chicago, and Detroit, along with other major U.S. cities. During this period of time, many Americans lost confidence in their nation. Elsewhere, Japan, West Germany, Korea, and China gained more confidence as they strengthened their economies and increased productivity.

Meanwhile, America's federal and trade deficits continued snowballing out of control and these economic problems trickled down into mainstream society. Companies laid people off by the millions, hiking the unemployment rate even higher. With millions out of work and the U.S. struggling to right itself at home and abroad, its economic forecast was bleak.

As America searched for answers to its troubles, Americans became obsessed with products made abroad, especially ones made in Japan. Americans were so enamored with all things foreign, from electrical household appliances to automobiles that consumer surveys at the time showed most Americans favored Japanese products, believing they were far superior to their American counterparts. In fact, Japanese-made cars eventually comprised 25% of the U.S. automobile market. Americans were further enraged when the Japanese bought some of the symbols of Americana, the aftermath of the economical damage done during Carter's presidency. In 1985, a group of Japanese investors purchased

the Rockefeller Center (the Rockefeller Center was a symbol of capitalism in a free, democratic society and is located in the heart of America's business center, New York City). In 1989, Sony purchased Columbia Pictures (the Columbia picture logo features the Statue of Liberty).

Americans' decision to purchase imported goods and services further enlarged the nation's federal trade deficit. Japan's superior products and Korea and China's low-cost goods forced U.S. imports to exceed exports. The nation's ever-increasing purchases of foreign products also decreased the value of the American dollar at such a rapid rate. Many American manufacturers suffered, including such icons as General Motors, Ford, and Chrysler. With the U.S. economy steadily sinking, fears began to rise that Japan would eventually take over America's corporate world.

> Good things take time to build, while bad things fall apart within the blink of an eye.

MANY INTERNATIONAL WRITERS at the time began writing about the "Sunset of America," noting that world leaders were openly saying that America had become a nation full of lazy citizens, a "Paper Tiger."

Even more unbelievable to me, the people of my native country were treating Korean-Americans as second-class citizens. Korea was slowly becoming a rich and powerful nation, and America looked like a "sunset" country to Koreans. To them, America was no longer a leading nation but a directionless one.

All of these setbacks were disappointing. I came to America to pursue the American dream, not be dragged into a nightmare. I was so shocked that Americans were being so reactive instead of proactive. They were trying to cure the country's ills instead of finding, then eliminating the causes behind them to prevent future problems. At this point, America hated immigrants like me, and my homeland hated Korean-Americans like me. It felt like I belonged nowhere.

THE SUNRISE OF AMERICA

On June 20, 1998, the G7 and 10 Asian nations had an emergency currency meeting in Tokyo. (The G7 is a group of the wealthiest nations, including the United States, Canada, United Kingdom, France, Italy, Germany, and Japan.) Just 20 years after Americans feared a Japanese takeover of the U.S., Japan was now in the middle of an economic crisis of their own. Although the U.S. harbored bitter feelings toward the Japanese two decades ago, America had matured and grown wiser from its experiences and was deeply concerned over Japan's economic crisis.

Meanwhile, the U.S. government announced a federal budget surplus of more than $70 billion by the year's end. The U.S. was a world power again and its economic forecast was brighter than ever. I even noticed that most Americans were busier and more energetic than ever. They were filled with confidence.

After 20 years of native Koreans regarding Korean-Americans as second-class citizens, they were now treating Korean-Americans as first-class citizens once again. In the interim, Korea's economic system became so corrupted that the International Monetary Fund barely bailed the country out and saved Korea's economy.

I was ecstatic that America was doing well again, but I didn't understand.

Why was the Japanese economy so strong in the 1980s?

Why did it appear that the Japanese would take over America?

What made Americans burn Japanese cars and smash Japanese radios? What was it that changed the American way of thinking? How did America revive its economy in the mid-1990s to once again become a leader on the world stage?

Why did the Japanese economy suddenly begin to decline then?

Some said that the change in fortunes between the U.S. and Japan stemmed from land, or rather the size of it. I didn't believe that argument because there are plenty of countries that are bigger or more populated than the U.S. (China & India, for instance), but don't economically compare to the U.S. So what if Japan is the size of California? In the 1980s, Japan was a huge economic power that threatened to overtake the U.S.

Others said the economic turnaround in America could be traced to our abundance of natural resources. Sure, natural resources help, but I didn't think that alone made the difference. In fact, Korea has no natural resources and it was able to build itself into a huge economic power.

Some said that the U.S. was lucky because it had all the right citizens at the right time to turn the nation around—smart, handsome, and beautiful people. That may be true, but looks and smarts certainly didn't help America in the 1970s and 1980s. Also, countries everywhere are blessed with intelligent and beautiful people.

None of these theories answered my questions so I looked to my own native country of Korea for the answers.

When President Chung Hee Park came into power in the 1960s, Korea was extremely impoverished. Under Park's leadership, Korea became the 11th richest country in the world. However, things went south when President Young Sam Kim came into office in the mid 1990s. Under President Kim's leadership, Korea went from having a great economy to going into near economic collapse. It took a helping hand from the International Monetary Fund in 1997 to save it.

President Park, however, wasn't the only leader to turn around a nation in the modern era. Great Britain was filled with problems not too long ago, but former Prime Minister Margaret Thatcher rebuilt it into a strong and prosperous nation. The U.S. was no different under former President Bill Clinton. Under his leadership, the U.S. erased a deep federal deficit and created a $256 billion surplus.

It wasn't just the nation that turned its fortunes around. Take a look at Chrysler for instance. In the late 1970s, the automobile giant was on the verge of collapse, but Chairman Lee Iacocca turned the company around to where it was strong and profitable again. Walt Disney Company shared Chrysler's struggles until Michael Eisner was named CEO and chairman, a move that turned the company into a major media powerhouse–strong enough to buy ABC Networks.

American cities also turned their fortunes around. In New York City, former mayor Rudolph Giuliani took the reins of the nation's most powerful city in 1994, when the city's crime rate was at its highest. Under his leadership, New York's crime rate declined every year until it reached some of the lowest numbers in the city's history. As part of his war on crime, Giuliani cleaned up the formerly seedy Times Square, transforming it into a booming, bustling nerve center of business and entertainment. Gone were the pornographic shops and prostitutes, replaced by the likes of Disney Store, Virgin Records, other mega chain stores and businesses.

It became obvious to me why nations, companies and even cities have so many ups and downs; leaders make or break everything. A strong leader can make a great difference while a weak leader can make a disastrous one.

To BETTER UNDERSTAND the impact leaders have on the world, let's examine two different companies, and what made them what they are today.

> Strong leaders create the strong future they envision.

THE BEST CORPORATION ON EARTH

People are proud to work for General Electric. As of 2001, 32,000 GE employees held $12 billion of stock—the largest amount of employee-held stock in corporate history. In 1980, GE owned 10 businesses and had $11 billion in assets, all of which were in North America. By 2000, GE owned 24 businesses and had $370 billion in assets in 48 countries.

In 20 years, Chairman and CEO Jack Welch helped the company grow 3,400%. Under his leadership, he built the most productive, competitive, and modern corporation on Earth. His efforts helped General Electric's market value cap with more than $450 billion in 20 years.

When Jack Welch was named CEO of GE in 1981, he knew the conventional wisdom of corporateship could be distilled in three inevitable trends: oil, inflation, and America's manufacturing battle with the Japanese. Oil was at $35 a barrel and heading toward $100, if anyone could even afford it. Inflation rocketed to 20%, making some believe that it would be in double-digits forever. Japanese-made products, from simple household appliances to cars, invaded the U.S. It appeared that the Japanese manufacturing juggernaut was going to take over America. Despite all of these things, the business world saw General Electric as a strong and healthy corporation, secure in its position as an industrial world leader.

Still, Welch had visions that no one else had. He knew GE couldn't fight back against foreign businesses, especially Japan's, with the company's bureaucracy of the time. It desperately needed to be fundamentally reshaped in order for his company to be more productive and competitive among the world's corporations. Welch knew that he had a huge fight on his hands.

Welch began improving the company by examining its productivity. In his 20 years as a GE employee, he recognized that some of the workforce was unproductive, and that many positions in GE's 29-level hierarchy were totally redundant and harmful to the company's success.

Welch strongly believed that his company needed to rid itself of conventional bureaucracy and unnecessary management. He saw that some managers wasted time and created teamwork problems by solely monitoring other people, which only discouraged, stifled or hurt their staff in the process. At the same time, Welch knew he needed to develop more people into strong leaders so they could motivate, encourage, and energize others to form a winning team at General Electric. He did the following things to reach his goals:

1. GE went from having 411,000 employees at the end of 1980 to 299,000 by 1985, an approximate 25% cut in the workforce. Of the 112,000 people who left the GE payroll, about 37,000 were in businesses that he sold. The remaining 75,000 people lost their jobs for productivity reasons. Downsizing helped to form a strong, winning team that saved billions of dollars, which helped GE lay the foundation for better and more productive services.

2. Upon making the cuts, Welch sought to increase production by rewarding employees based on their personal performance. On an individual level, Welch's idea worked well, with some workers increasing their productivity by 165%. However there were others that made no progress. Welch then switched to the team reward system for more consistent productivity, and he found that the system worked. Comparatively speaking, the team reward system yielded much better results than the personal performance reward system.

3. Welch's biggest task in rebuilding GE was re-examining the company's profitability. Whether it was fixing, closing, selling or purchasing, Welch religiously believed that all of GE's businesses needed to be first or second in their respective market, and be profitable. Purchasing and reviving NBC television, Welch and NBC chairman Bob Wright, who came from GE, used the company's hard-driving culture to turn around NBC, GE's marquee property. From there, NBC, CNBC, and MSNBC turned huge profits. The turnaround led NBC news anchor Tom Brokaw to say, "I honestly believe that (Welch and Wright) saved the company."

4. Welch succeeded because he never stopped learning, and was adept at personal and professional improvement. He created and achieved excellent quality control through the MAIC. (Measuring, Analyzing, Improving, and Controlling system.)

5. Welch adopted new internet e-business for GE, and e-business became a part of the company's DNA. E-business transformed

GE, saving the company tens of billions of dollars per year, while modernizing it for efficiency, but this transformation didn't happen overnight. E-business wasn't something Welch was comfortable with. He feared the Internet because he didn't know how to type well, but Welch had the guts to overcome this personal obstacle and made e-mail useful and an ally to him.

6. Welch emphasized and lived the values of honesty and integrity both personally and professionally, which helped GE become a success. Honesty and integrity became GE values. In 1994, Welch fought with the federal government for three years over an issue of integrity. They battled over pre price-fixing. Welch and company counsel Ben Heinemann traveled to Washington, D.C., to meet with an assistant attorney general over GE's case. She couldn't have cared less about arguments. She was out to get an indictment, and nothing was going to get in her way.

To avoid an indictment for price-fixing, GE was asked by the assistant attorney general in February 1994 to plead guilty to a felony and pay a fine. Welch balked. He said: "There was no way I was going to do that. We hadn't done anything wrong. The government's case was built on a bunch of lies. We had to fight this all the way."

In an effort to gain some evidence, the government got the FBI to wire a dismissed GE employee. The FBI got nothing but a bunch of wasted time. The government then hired an expensive independent lawyer to try the case. Eight months later, on October 25th, 1994, the trial began in federal court in Columbus, Ohio. After listening to arguments on both sides, on December 5th, 1994, Judge George Smith threw out the entire case. Welch won a huge victory for the real foundation of GE, integrity.

Through vision, integrity, wisdom, courage, and passion, Welch developed the kind of leadership that helped rebuild one of the most competitive and modern corporations on Earth, revolutionizing the culture of the corporate world. Jack Welch is a role model to business-men everywhere. He helped rebuild America into a strong nation.

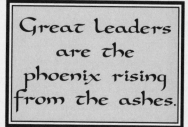

Great leaders are the phoenix rising from the ashes.

WELCH HAD STARTED at General Electric in 1960 as an engineer, earning $10,500 a year, the same as other entry-level employees. By the time he finished his career, he had climbed 29 levels in the company's hierarchy. I highly recommend his book, *Jack, Straight From the Gut*, as a business dictionary, a guidance tool, and even a business "Bible."

THE WORST COMPANY IN AMERICA

Just how did Enron, the 7th biggest corporation in America, go bankrupt in 2002? The answer is very simple: Bad leadership. Enron's leaders demonstrated bad leadership through their dishonest and un-ethical business practices. According to Sherron Watkins, former Vice President of Enron, the company was hiding hundreds of millions of dollars of debt through their numerous partnerships and accounting loopholes. Once these findings were brought to light, Enron was forced to reveal their true financial status and were forced into declaring bankruptcy.

Weak leaders are the termites that weaken the foundation of the world.

ENRON'S COLLAPSE hurt millions of people within their company and na-tionwide. Enron employees and their family members, investors, business partners, and hundreds of thousands of innocent people lost their life savings for retirement when Enron's stock was decommissioned by the Stock Ex-

change. The anguish from the fallout left many mentally and financially ruined. Equally as damaging was the fact that Enron had disgraced American corporate credibility to the rest of the world.

GE AND ENRON illustrate the importance of organizational leadership regarding dynamic organizations and why all of us need to develop organizational leadership in order to protect ourselves and make life successful.

FROM A "PAPER TIGER" TO A "PROUD EAGLE"

What fundamentally made America's transformation from a paper tiger into a proud eagle possible? Who had the unique ideas and vision to make that turning point a reality? Whose organizational leadership was the most influential in contributing to turning the American economy back into a superpower? Let's re-examine how America's economy emerged from the doldrums and became a world power once again in the 1990s.

Political Leaders

Former President Ronald Reagan's leadership started America's economic rebuilding process. It was Reagan who built the foundation of a strong U.S. economy during his presidential term (1981-1989). Under his courageous leadership, America was able to help boost its economy through reduced taxes and regulations.

Former President George Bush's leadership continued America's restoration, especially in the country's victory against Iraq during the Gulf War. That war woke up the American spirit and help breathe life into the economy.

From there, former President Bill Clinton's leadership strengthened the economy and the nation's confidence during his terms (1993-

2001). Clinton's tireless efforts and leadership skills helped not only to eliminate the federal deficit but also built a surplus.

Economic and Business Leaders

Also helping America's recovery was Federal Reserve Chairman Alan Greenspan, whose intelligent leadership and sharp judgment in adjusting Federal interest rates made the economy the strongest it had been in 40 years.

Jack Welch's leadership helped transform America's corporate culture, which also contributed to America's revival as an economic superpower. Subsequently, many business leaders followed Welch's ideas and vision to great success, thus reshaping American industry and making it more competitive in the world.

Also, Microsoft founder Bill Gates boosted the American economy by using his leadership and computer genius to create technology that not only enhanced the American corporate landscape, but changed technology all over the world.

Now that we understand the impact that leaders have, we can learn how to develop The Nine Qualities of Organizational Leadership.

THE NINE QUALITIES OF ORGANIZATIONAL LEADERSHIP

1. **PERSONAL POWER.** Personal leadership is the first step to leading organizations.
2. **TEAM BUILDING ABILITY.** Team building is the cornerstone of organizations.
3. **FINANCIAL MANAGEMENT ABILITY.** Cash flow is critical to dynamic organizations.
4. **VISION.** Vision gives organizations clear direction.

5. **INTELLIGENCE.** The smarter the leader, the better the organization.

6. **COURAGE.** Courage fuels dynamic organizations.

7. **TRUST.** Trust is the foundation of all organizations.

8. **FAIRNESS.** Fairness breeds strength in organizations.

9. **GENEROSITY.** Generosity creates loyalty in organizations.

These nine qualities will help you build the dynamic organizations that make life triumphant. Let's examine how these nine qualities of organization leadership impact our lives.

QUALITY ONE: PERSONAL POWER

Does anyone want to follow someone who is weaker than they are? Unless they have to, absolutely not. People naturally follow those who are stronger; they know that if they follow weakness, they themselves will become weak. When they follow those who are stronger, they have the chance to become strong and secure, too, leading themselves into a bright future.

In order to lead organizations, you must be strong so that you can lead and inspire others to follow you even if they don't have to, by developing personal power.

What is personal power in organizational leadership? Personal power, which is personal leadership, consists of physical, mental, and moral fitness. As we saw in Chapter 2, if you are physically sick, you can't physically act. If you are mentally ill, your brain won't be clear enough to think. If you are morally corrupt, your actions will only damage others. Having personal power is the first step to leading organizations.

Without personal power, you can't take the action necessary to lead others and yourself because nothing happens without action.

A powerful position means nothing without personal leadership. You must build personal power before you can earn a position of leadership. With personal power, you can use your powerful position well. The following is the best illustration of why we need personal power and how dangerous a position of power is without it.

Consider King Louis XVI. At the turn of the 19th century, this man inherited the throne of one of the most privileged countries of the Western World: France. As king, Louis commanded a massive army and controlled the purse strings of an equally impressive national treasury. So, how did he eventually face a national revolution in which he lost both his crown and his head?

Simple. Although he enjoyed many of the trappings of a grand leader, he lacked the qualities of true leadership. The title of "King of France" was given to Louis because it was his birthright, not because he won great battles or garnered any great amount of popularity from his subjects. In fact, while Louis XVI held the title of King, he bled the French treasury dry in the pursuit of pretentious personal fashion and luxury, all the while taxing his subjects into abject poverty. The citizens of France responded by rebelling against his leadership, and Louis's vision died with him. By disgracing himself and his family and hurting many innocent people in the process, Louis XVI destroyed his country—all because of his lack of leadership.

WHAT ARE THE MOST fundamental differences between personal and positional power?

Positional power is used by a person who lacks personal leadership. Nobody wants to follow people who use positional power, unless they have to, because these kinds of leaders only stifle or oppress those who follow them. People know that to follow them is to throw away their future.

Personal power is used by a person who has personal leadership. Most people want to follow leaders who use personal power, even if they don't have to, because this kind of leader motivates, energizes, and empowers those who follow them to succeed.

To develop personal power, you need to go back to Chapter 3 "Develop Personal Power," so you can discover who you really are, build physical, mental, and moral fitness, learn how to manage your time and money, build a positive self-image, and build self-esteem by loving yourself unconditionally.

QUALITY TWO: TEAM BUILDING ABILITY

Team building is key to having a dynamic organization. Why? A winning team will work together to achieve all of the organization's goals.

To build winning teams in any organization:

❖ Recruit the right people for the right place.
❖ If you want to win the dogfight, you have to choose a strong dog.
❖ Create a team reward system: Teams will maximize their potential when they work towards the same goal.
❖ Develop an assessment system: Keep the right people and let go of the wrong people based on their performance, and leadership ability.

Recruit the Right People for the Right Place

For your organization to stay dynamic in the real world you must recruit the right people for the right place; this is extremely important because you don't want to put the right person in the wrong place or the wrong person in the right place. If you don't recruit the right people for the right place, you will fail to build a winning team and have a strong dynamic organization. For example, Jack is an excellent basketball player but has an awful attitude. If a NBA team drafts Jack, that means the **wrong person came to the right place**. In another case, Bob has a great attitude but lacks any basketball skill. If a NBA team drafts Bob, that means the **right person came to the wrong place**. Now in a third case, George has an excellent attitude and the skills to play basketball. If a NBA team drafts George, that means the **right person has come to the right place**.

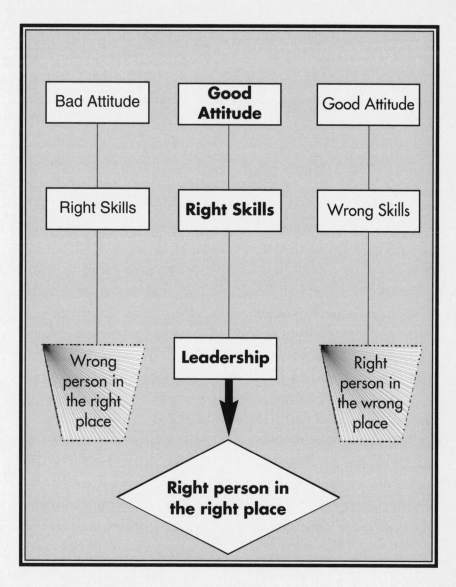

THE BEST WAY to start the process of building your team is to look at the following traits in finding the right person for the right place:

CREATE DYNAMIC ORGANIZATIONS

1. **ATTITUDE.** Attitude is essential because the right person must have the right attitude. Without the right attitude, creating and maintaining a teamwork dynamic is impossible.
2. **SKILLS.** A person must have the right skills to be put into the right place. A person who has the wrong skills or no skills at all would be in the wrong place because they would never get any work done.
3. **LEADERSHIP ABILITY.** People who have the passion, the ability to prioritize, and the ability to lead themselves and others will strengthen the team if put in the right place. Finding people with leadership ability will make your organization's future bright.

Before hiring people, check your own attitude, skills, and leadership ability to see if you meet the same standards you expect from others.

The right person isn't necessarily someone who has a great education or a high IQ. The right person is someone who has passion, a strong burning desire to succeed, and leadership ability, regardless of his or her IQ level or educational background. Without these things, even a genius or a college graduate from an Ivy League school can only use a limited amount of his or her potential, doing just a decent job by only having the right attitude and the right skills. Those who have passion, a strong burning desire to succeed, and leadership ability will maximize their potential in your organization while having the right attitude and the right skills, thus maximizing the organization itself. These are the kind of people you should be looking for to be a part of your organization.

Create a Team Reward System

In order to motivate the individual members of your team, create a team reward system that gives them a personal reward for achieving team goals. If you have a sales team, establish rewards based on sales. If you have a production team, establish rewards based on production.

The following is just an example of a team reward system. You can set up your own team reward system with monthly or yearly goals based on the needs of your organization. Encouragement and support are keys to achieving team goals.

MARKETING TEAM
Goals for November 2003

	Yellow belt level	Black belt level	Instructor level
New clients	20	35	50
Sales	$1,000,000	$2,000,000	$3,000,000
Retention	30%	60%	90%
Reduce expenses	3%	5%	10%

(The above figures are based on a team of 5 people.)
Reward for achieving the Yellow belt goal—$10,000/5=$2,000 per person
Reward for achieving the Black belt goal—$20,000/5=$4,000 per person
Reward for achieving the Instructor goal—$40,000/5=$8,000 per person

Additional requirements

❖ A team member must achieve 1/5th of at least two categories in any of the above categories in order to receive his or her portion of the team reward for the month.

❖ If the team has not achieved at least three goals, then the team reward will be voided for that month.

❖ Each team member is rewarded personally for his or her teamwork if the team has met all of the above requirements. The amount of the reward given is based on the goal level that the team has achieved.

❖ In order to receive the Black belt or higher reward, all categories of Yellow belt must be achieved.

Once you have created the team reward chart, set up a team and study each team member's strong characteristics. Then, arrange a meeting to discuss the system. Inform all team members of where, when, and what the meeting is about and encourage them to bring all of their difficulties and ideas regarding the subject.

To start the meeting, the team leader explains that the purpose of the team reward system is to create a win-win situation for everyone on the team and in the organization by striving for a common goal through teamwork.

Next, the team leader should use a friendly ice breaking exercise, such as having each team member introduce another team member, saying something that they admire about him or her, to make the team feel more comfortable and open to talk freely once the meeting begins. Then, the team leader should introduce each team member to the team and mention what that specific member's strong points or positive qualities are, even if some or all of the team knows each other. It's the team leader's responsibility to do the research necessary beforehand to make this exercise successful.

Finally, the team leader distributes the reward chart and identifies the team goals.

Then, the meeting turns to brainstorming and problem-solving. First, ask "why" questions to dig out the negative points, obstacles, and problems stopping the team from achieving a common goal. These obstacles can be anything from the product, customer service, productivity, management, marketing, etc.

FOR EXAMPLE, why can't we sell our product?
- ❖ No money to advertise our product.
- ❖ No one knows how to sell it properly.
- ❖ The product is bad.

- We need a projector for a sales presentation.
- We have responsibilities but no rights as salespeople.

The purpose of brainstorming for problems is to bring them to light so everyone can work together to solve them during the solution phase of the meeting. With the team working together, problems can be brought to light so the team can easily solve them later on.

During this "why" part of the meeting, no one should bring up solutions. Normally, when people hear problems, they want to offer solutions right away, but not everyone will agree to the problems being brought up during this portion of the meeting. Some may even wonder why such and easily solved problem was brought to everyone's attention, which will hurt individual pride and damage the teamwork dynamic. Solve problems only when it's time to do so.

Next, ask the question "how" to find the answers to the problems that have been identified. When asking "how," everyone works together to brainstorm solutions for the obstacles, negative points, and problems that were brought up earlier. By doing so, the team will discover how to achieve their goals.

Why is this session a discussion about solutions and not problems? If you discuss problems again, the meeting will never be finished and all the problems will go unsolved.

FOR EXAMPLE, how can we sell our product?

No money to advertise our product.
Solution: We can advertise for free through a direct phone promotion.

No one knows how to sell it properly.
Solution: Spend 2 hours a day training and role-playing the sales presentation.

The product is bad.
Solution: Find out why the product is bad and improve it.

We need a projector for a sales presentation.
Solution: Purchase or rent a new projector.

We have responsibilities but no rights as salespeople.
Solution: Salespeople have 100% freedom but 100% responsibility.

The team should not try solving all of their problems at once. Fix them one at a time, even when things appear dismal. To make things easier, break down your problem-solving tasks anywhere from two to four phases. For example, work on sales the first week; dig out all the problems and find the solutions in the second week; learn how to make a proper phone presentation in the third week; practice how to handle a live customer in the fourth week; create a proper sales presentation during week five. If the team leader feels this schedule might be too long, then they should do it in daily increments.

After the team gathers their solutions, the team leader must execute them right away. If the team needs money, the team leader needs to provide the resources quickly. If the product is bad, the team leader should set up another meeting to find out the problems with the product, the solutions, and execute the solutions with the team's help.

Finally, when the team achieves their goals, the team leader checks individual goal achievements and rewards team members accordingly. After they have achieved a goal, maintain and improve the quality of the product or service, and set higher goals.

THERE ARE THREE reasons that the team reward system is the best tool for team building:

1. When the team digs out the problems in their organization, they rid themselves of stress.
2. When the team brainstorms for solutions, everyone on the team feels that they are an important part of the organization and equally responsible in achieving their goals.
3. One person can make a boulder move up a mountain a little but five people can make a boulder move up a mountain a lot; a team effort is much stronger than individual efforts in achieving goals.

Overall, this system boosts performance 100% and builds a winning team because the team supports each other, improving productivity and morale to achieve common goals.

Develop an Assessment System

After finding the right people for your winning team, you have to retain them to keep your organization dynamic and ferociously competitive in the real world. You do so by setting up a system that will assess people on three levels,

❖ **"A" CLASS (ELITE):** People on this level have a great attitude, are highly skilled, and show great leadership ability. They have vision and passion, demonstrate prioritization, are committed to the organization they belong to and its values, and achieve personal and team goals. Even after they have achieved their goals, these people immediately move up to the next level and also help others to become leaders.

❖ **"B" CLASS (GOOD):** People on this level have a good attitude, are adequately skilled, and try developing their leadership ability. They have passion, are committed, and demonstrate the values of the organization they belong to, and they achieve personal and team goals.

❖ **"C" CLASS (POOR):** People on this level have the wrong attitude, lack the right skills, and/or lack leadership ability. They also have no desire or passion. These people show that they are against the values of their organization, and cannot achieve personal or team goals.

Retain "A" class and "B" class people. They are the right people for the right place. Let go of "C" class people. They are either the right person in the wrong place, the wrong person in the right place, or the wrong person in the wrong place.

In order to refine your team building ability, you must develop your organizational skills. To develop your organizational skills, you must:

❖ Get information about what you need for your organization and organize it in written form.

❖ Analyze the information you have received.

❖ Divide each piece of information into small chunks and write an outline with details under each piece of information.

❖ Write down what you will need to execute your plans.

If you are running a small organization, you're the leader. However, in a big organization, you'll need to find leaders for each department and train them in team-building methods, which includes how to conduct team meetings and how to find and retain the right people in the right place in your organization.

QUALITY THREE: BUILD FINANCIAL MANAGEMENT ABILITY

Who puts their financial future in the hands of someone who has no financial management ability? No one at all. Everyone knows that if they put their money into the hands of someone with no financial management ability, they commit financial suicide. People like to follow someone with strong financial management ability because they know that their financial future won't be just secure, but bright. Even if they don't like a person, people will follow him or her if they have strong financial management ability so that they can survive and succeed. In order to lead an organization, you must have strong financial management ability.

Financial management is crucial to the survival and success of any dynamic organization. If your financial management abilities are weak, you will suck the lifeblood, cash flow, out of your organization, and cause it to go bankrupt. Therefore, it is absolutely necessary that you build your financial management abilities to make you and your organization stronger.

Financial management ability is simply the ability to manage the financial aspects of your organization so it is generating more income (assets) and paying fewer expenses (liabilities).

As we've seen, two of the best examples of the power of good financial management abilities and the price of poor financial management are Jack Welch, former Chairman and CEO of General Electric and the people who ran Enron.

In the almost twenty years that Jack Welch was CEO and chairman of GE, he turned what was an $11 billion North American business into a $370 billion international powerhouse. No company has ever achieved such amazing growth in such a short amount of time.

Jack Welch had excellent financial management abilities. He wasn't afraid to cut the unnecessary fat out of his company, which sometimes included unproductive workers. He wasn't afraid to sell off liabilities and invest in assets. Welch was also open-minded and always found ways to cut expenses and make more money

On the other hand, Enron did none of the things Jack Welch did. On paper, Enron was making money hand over fist, but in reality Enron was hiding hundreds of millions of dollars in debt through their numer-

ous partnerships and other accounting loopholes. It was because of such poor financial management that the company went bankrupt, hurting their employees, their stockholders, and American corporate credibility.

To build financial management abilities:

- ❖ Think big but spend wisely. Cut liabilities (unnecessary expenses) and generate more assets (income).
- ❖ Always pay attention to your finances. Analyze your expenses and see which ones can be cut in order to save money and make sure that you are paying the least amount of expenses to generate the most amount of income. At the same time, research new ways to generate income for your organization. For example, whatever operational money you have in the bank, put it into a safe money market account so you can generate even more income, instead of paying checking account expenses to the bank. Keep seeking out new, more efficient ways to manage your organization's finances and make the right investments to generate future assets.
- ❖ Keep the cash flowing.
- ❖ Don't spend more than what you earn unless it is an emergency or an investment for future profit.
- ❖ Generate only flexible, not high fixed expenses for your organization. For example, your organization had a profitable year so you doubled your staff's salaries. In the next year your organization struggled, but you can't cut salaries without losing staff. In that case, the organization spent more than it earned. The solution would be to set up a team reward system based on performance so not only will the organization make more money, those who perform well will also make money, keeping the organization stable.
- ❖ Build a professional financial team.

If you are the head of a big organization, you'll need to use your financial abilities to create and train a team that will help you with your organization's financial management.

By doing these things, you are utilizing proper money management, which will help you lead organizations. Become a rich leader!

QUALITY FOUR: VISION

Vision is an organization's path to the future. How you use vision can make that path filled with pitfalls that send your organization into a dark, dismally insecure future, or a path so clear in direction and purpose that the future of your organization will be so bright that it will inspire hope in all who belong to it. Those who are near-sighted with their vision will always smash into a wall without even knowing it. Then there are those who see the wall coming but choose to deal with it at the last minute; some of these people survive and some don't. Those who are visionaries will see the wall well before anyone else and have already figured out a strategy around or through it. It is because of this that everyone loves following visionaries because they provide a clear direction that leads to a bright and secure future . In order to build a dynamic organization, you must create vision.

Vision is the ability to mentally picture the future. Vision can be many things; it's envisioning a huge shopping center on an empty lot, a recreational center to keep teenagers off the streets, a special hospital for burn victims, a new park for children, or even the vision of a political goal to promote better understanding. Having vision means that your dreams are alive! All leaders have to have vision.

Dr. Martin Luther King, Jr., campaigned for African-American civil rights in the U.S. during the 1960's. He had a vision of freedom and equality for every person regardless of their skin color or religious beliefs. King's vision is outlined in his famous "I Have a Dream," speech, which still influences people over 30 years later; his vision ultimately gave him great power.

Vision comes from imagination, and imagination comes through mental concentration. You develop vision by focusing 100% on whatever you do or on whatever you want to do. By having vision, you create the possibility of a new future and will generate hope for you and for others; anyone can have vision. When you have vision, you generate power. Vision is the driving power behind leadership.

QUALITY FIVE: INTELLIGENCE

Who willingly follows stupid people? Unless we have to follow them, no one does. We don't follow stupidity because we can't learn from it. And if we follow stupid people, we become unproductive. Most of us like following intelligent people because they not only help us to learn new things, but lead us to a great future. Intelligence builds organizations while stupidity destroys them. With intelligence, people not only need to follow you but like to follow you as well. You must have intelligence to lead any organization.

Dynamic organizations need intelligent people. The more intelligence there is in a dynamic organization, the more dynamic that organization becomes. Intelligence in organizational leadership consists of wisdom, vision, and good communication skills, all of which come from acquiring knowledge. These traits assist in understanding, analyzing, forming sharp judgments, making decisions, planning, organizing, which puts the organization on a clear and right direction.

Intelligence is a gift that should never be abused. When used selfishly or immorally, intelligence is very dangerous to everyone, including to the person abusing it. In fact, most good, intelligent people will avoid those who abuse intelligence because they realize following them would lead their lives into ruin. Good, intelligent people use their intelligence for the benefit of others, which causes people to flock to them.

For example, Adolf Hitler was incredibly intelligent and had strong leadership abilities, but he immorally and diabolically exercised his intelligence to engineer the slaughter of millions of innocent people in order to create a master race, becoming one of the most evil leaders in human history. In the end, Hitler committed suicide.

Now consider George Washington. Besides his role as the first President of the United States and a Founding Father, Washington still earns the respect of people today. Why? He exercised his intelligence for the right reasons. Although he held the title of General of the Continental Army and then President, he didn't lead the nation through position alone. He led America with great leadership, believing in a system of government that favored the election of strong leaders over the mere succession of inherited titles. Because of the strength of his convictions and conscience, his intelligence helped establish the democratic system of government we enjoy today.

To be a good, intelligent leader in an organization:

❖ Bear in mind what Thomas Edison once said, "Success is 1% inspiration and 99% perspiration." Therefore, you must "perspire" in constantly developing wisdom, vision, and good communication skills by acquiring more knowledge. By developing these traits, you will become more understanding, be better at forming sharp judgements, and have strong decision-making skills, giving your organization a clear and right direction.

❖ Without having all of the correct and necessary information, you can't make the right decisions for your organization. Therefore, you must stay informed always, learning and listening to everything you can. Information is power.

QUALITY SIX: COURAGE

Is anyone willing to follow a coward? No one is, because nobody wants to follow someone weaker than they are unless they have to. Cowards weaken or destroy organizations. If you decide to follow a coward, your future will be uncertain. Naturally, people follow courageous leaders because they offer security and the promise of a prosperous future.

Courage creates a fighting spirit, generating passion, determination, energy, enthusiasm, flexibility, and adaptability. Courageous leaders have all of these qualities. Also, they have the ability to take action, which is necessary for anything to happen in an organization or in life. If you have courage, you are seen as a strong leader. If you don't have courage, you are seen as a weak leader. Therefore to lead a dynamic organization, you have to build courageous leadership.

Courageous leadership is the type of leadership that embraces and utilizes courage in the decision-making and leadership processes in organizations. Courageous leaders always encourage, energize, and motivate others, never giving up until they achieve their goals. Courageous leaders fight to win and always stand for justice. Courage helps make things happen in an organization.

In the same fashion that an intelligent person can use his or her intellect the wrong way, a courageous person can use his or her courage for personal gain or for hurtful, illegal, or immoral purposes. However, people have a choice not to associate with someone who is selfish, immoral, and dangerous. A person who uses courageous leadership for the right reasons is beneficial to others; people gravitate towards courageous leaders. Let's compare the Presidencies of Jimmy Carter and Ronald Reagan to further illustrate the impact weak and strong leaders have on society.

Consider the U.S. hostage crisis in Iran from November 1979 to January 1981.

Jimmy Carter was President at the time when Iranian extremists took Americans hostages at the U.S. Embassy in Iran. Apparently afraid the conflict would get out of control, rather than threatening military aggression, he reacted by severing diplomatic ties with Iran and set up a trade embargo. More than a year later, the embargo had little effect on resolving the hostage crisis. Carter then tried a rescue operation, but that practically failed before it began. Failure is not the opposite of courage, but the timing and scale of the operation showed weakness, in my opinion. The crisis continued until the last day of his presidency. Once the new, stronger leadership of Ronald Reagan came into the White House, the extremists became afraid and released the hostages immediately.

The American people lost confidence in Carter. During his Presidency, countries around the world joked about America's new image, comparing it to that of "a paper tiger." Carter's weak leadership created economic havoc: Soaring inflation, outrageous interest rates, and sky-high gasoline prices, which depleted the federal budget and created trade deficits.

The former Soviet Union also took advantage of Carter's weak leadership by invading Afghanistan. In 1980, the U.S. responded by boycotting the Summer Olympics in Moscow. That boycott crushed the dreams of many young U.S. Olympic hopefuls, ruining years of training and left many disappointed and depressed.

Carter's weak leadership not only disgraced the nation, but it hurt countless Americans. His leadership was so damaging that he did not get reelected. The Carter presidency illustrates the danger of weak leadership.

In contrast, President Ronald Reagan believed in the principles of the American democratic system: Personal freedom and capitalism. He reinforced these principles in his fight against aggressive Communism. Reagan took a strong stance against negotiating with terrorists and built up our national defenses.

In addition to wearing down Communism during the Cold War, Reagan built a strong foundation for the American economic system by cutting taxes and reducing government regulations for business, despite the risk of making the inflation rate soar even higher. He remained positive and full of courage, believing his economic strategy would turn America around. Reagan told his advisers over and over an anecdote about two boys, one a pessimist and the other an optimist. The pessimist was given a pile of new toys and responded by crying because he was afraid someone would come and take them away. The optimist was given the job of going down to the barn and shoveling out the stalls. He tackled the chore with great enthusiasm, heartily digging into the manure, because he was convinced that "there's got to be a pony in here somewhere." Reagan had the courage to take a hit in popularity over a short-term recession in order to have a stronger economy in the long run.

Ronald Reagan's strong leadership was key in demolishing the Berlin Wall, a symbol of the Cold War that stood between East and West Germany. During a speech outside the Berlin Wall in 1987 he had the courage to speak to challenge Russian leaders publicly by saying "General Secretary Gorbachev, if you seek peace, if you seek prosperity for the Soviet Union and Eastern Europe, if you seek liberalization: Come here to this gate! Mr. Gorbachev, open this gate! Mr. Gorbachev, tear down this wall!"

When it crumbled, it changed the course of human history by helping end the reign of communism is the Soviet Union. In this chapter, I assessed as poor former President Jimmy Carter's leadership during, not after, his Presidency. After his Presidency, however, Jimmy Carter showed more great personal leadership than any other retired President in U.S. history. He traveled tirelessly to countries all over the world to insure that citizens received fair elections. He won the Nobel Peace Prize in 2002. If he hadn't show great leadership after his time in office, I don't think Carter would have won such an honor. It's a great example for all of us that we cannot change the past, but we can change the future.

Courage comes from confidence so in order to be a courageous leader, love yourself and believe in yourself to build self-confidence and become a courageous leader.

QUALITY SEVEN: TRUST

Is anyone willing to follow liars? No, everyone knows that liars can't be depended on. Without trust, you cannot gain the influence you need to get others to cooperate with you in an organization. People prefer working with those who are trustworthy—people who are dependable, reliable, responsible, and act with honesty and integrity. Trustworthy people give everyone peace of mind. In fact, people will not only have a need to follow trustworthy people, they will enjoy following them as well. Leading organizations also takes trust not only to guarantee that people will follow you, but also build winning teams. Without trust, organizations have no foundation.

Trust in organizational leadership consists of honesty, integrity, responsibility, and proven ability, all of which follow the truth.

Leaders who wrongfully exercise their trustworthiness can hurt others and even ruin their own lives. A truly trustworthy leader exercises his or her leadership to touch countless hearts and change countless lives. Here are two examples of the importance and impact of trustworthiness in our lives.

Charles Manson was a self-proclaimed 1960s "messiah" whose cult followed his beliefs, committing murder and suicide in his name. Manson used his trust to build the wrong kind of leadership, hurting many innocent people in the process. His actions landed him in prison, where Manson remains to this day.

On the other hand, evangelist Billy Graham tirelessly travels around the world, using his trustworthiness to touch and change hundreds of millions of people's lives. Trust creates power. If people did not trust Billy Graham, they would not take the leap of faith he asks them to take in his crusades. Graham is so trustworthy that he led the U.S. Presidential inaugurations for Dwight Eisenhower, John F. Kennedy, Richard Nixon, Jimmy Carter, Ronald Reagan, George Bush, and Bill Clinton, crossing all political party lines. A good leader believes in the principles he preaches, lives by those principles and promotes them. A bad leader believes that a separate set of rules only apply to him or her, directing others to work for his or her benefit, rather than for the good of all. Honesty, integrity, and reliability all are part of trust, which is the foundation of an organization.

If you aspire to be a trustworthy leader, follow the truth, always exercise your principles, do the right thing, take responsibility for your actions, educate, and discipline yourself.

QUALITY EIGHT: FAIRNESS

Is anyone willing to follow unfair people? Not unless they have to. People hate being treated unfairly. Fair people try to understand others, making them that much easier to work with. In fact, those that treat others fairly will get others not only to need to follow them, but to like following them as well. In order to build dynamic organizations, you must exercise fairness by using flexibility and strictness.

It is very important to maintain rules and regulations to prevent chaos in an organization. Yet no rule or regulation is perfect. With flexibility, it becomes incredibly easy to handle any obstacle and problem while maintaining and improving a competitive organization. Flexibility also improves adaptability, making the chances of you achieving your goals that much greater.

Flexibility is the ability to bend, not break, in handling life's situations. Flexibility leads to equality, fairness, open-mindedness, and cooperation, allowing a leader to work with people equally, despite their strengths and weaknesses. Flexibility does not mean that leaders can follow their feelings whenever they feel like it, or ignore rules and regulations; flexibility is used to benefit the organization, not the leader. Organizations need flexibility in order to adapt and improve in our rapidly changing environment to not only survive, but also succeed.

However, there are times where you cannot be flexible; you must be strict when a situation calls for it, always keeping fairness in mind. Strictness in an organization is order. When applied properly, strictness ensures that punishments and rewards are given to those who deserve them. For example, those who do well in an organization get rewarded, while those who break the rules get punished. Strictness strengthens organizations and prevents them from falling into chaos. When this balance is achieved, no one is treated like they are above or below the law; everyone is treated fairly.

Early on as a martial arts instructor, I was very strict. In fact, I was so strict that I allowed no water or bathroom breaks to be taken during practice. In one particular class, an elementary school student named Joey raised his hand and asked to go to the bathroom. "No!" I angrily replied. A minute later, I heard liquid splashing on the practice mats. I looked over and saw that Joey just relieved himself. I was mortified. I couldn't believe it! My inflexibility had caused this child to wet the floor and his pants. I wanted to just run right out the door; we both felt humiliated. When Joey's parents arrived to pick him up, I apologized profusely. Now, I am much more flexible, especially when it comes to bathroom breaks.

It's always painful to work with someone who is inconsistently or irrationally strict. These kinds of people don't know right from wrong, are unfair, and are only strict when it's convenient to them. They confuse, discourage, or enrage others with their unfair treatment of people.

Inconsistently strict people also make bad and biased decisions. For example, an inconsistently strict person would give a raise to an unproductive worker over a productive one.

True strictness is achieved through consistency.

Most positive people love working with someone who believes in fairness because he or she loves maintaining a positive environment. However, most negative people hate working with fair and consistent people.

HERE IS ONE of the best examples of the impact that fairness has on organizations.

Jack Welch was the strictest, yet most flexible CEO on Earth. How did he use fairness to help build the best company in the world?

CREATE DYNAMIC ORGANIZATIONS

In the 1980s, no one could understand why Welch continued to downsize GE. His strictness eliminated tens of thousands of useless positions based on performance, saving the company billions of dollars. His flexibility also helped 35,000 GE employees share in $12 billion worth of stock. General Electric didn't just save money, it helped build and maintain quality people in the company that made GE the strongest corporation in the world.

How to develop fairness in organizational leadership:

❖ Follow your principles, keeping in mind what is right for your organization, when exercising strictness and flexibility.

❖ Keep in mind that flexibility and strictness are for the benefit of your organization only, not for your own.

QUALITY NINE: GENEROSITY

One of the best ways to generate the loyalty that builds successful organizations is generosity. People will work harder for a generous leader instead of a selfish one because generous leaders have an "I win, you win, so we win" attitude.

Generosity in organizational leadership consists of selflessness, compassion, and care for everyone within the organization.

Companies that make a lot of profit while they overwork and underpay their employees are selfish. Sooner or later these companies would lose quality people unless they became more generous. Employees can be equally as selfish, i.e. demanding more money without equal work, causing a good company to go bankrupt and actually hurting themselves. Selfishness hurts everyone.

In order to be a generous leader, you must have a big heart, be willing to make personal sacrifices, and take the time to always share your experiences, time, and knowledge with others so that you always care for, support, and help those in your organization. Build an attitude of gratitude. Share with others and become a generous organizational leader.

ORGANIZATIONAL LEADERSHIP IS HARMONY

The foundation of a dynamic organization lies in the nine qualities of organizational leadership: Personal power, team building ability, financial management ability, vision, intelligence, courage, trustworthiness, fairness, and generosity. In order to make other people love to follow you even if they don't have to, you have to develop all nine organizational leadership qualities to build a competitive and productive organization.

Each of us has different ratios of these qualities. If one of your qualities is stronger than the others, don't despair. As long as you continue to improve the remaining eight, you will become a good organizational leader.

For example, Mother Teresa was remembered for being generous; Dr. Martin Luther King, Jr. for his vision, Ronald Reagan for his courage; Teddy Roosevelt for his personal power, Alan Greenspan for his financial management ability, Thomas Edison for his intelligence, Phil Jackson for his team building ability, Billy Graham for his trustworthiness, and Jack Welch for his fairness. They used their strongest qualities of organizational leadership to help build the remaining eight.

However, if you are completely missing one of the nine qualities of organizational leadership, it will be difficult for you to become a great leader. No one wants to follow a sickly, unorganized, financially irresponsible, clouded, dumb, cowardly, untrustworthy, unfair, or selfish leader. You need all nine qualities to lead an organization.

Do you have all nine of these organizational leadership qualities? If not, which ones do you think you need improvement in? Try to improve those qualities so that you will have all that you need to lead an organization.

THE IMPORTANCE OF ORGANIZATIONAL LEADERSHIP

We all participate in organizations directly and indirectly for many reasons. For example, some people join an academic organization in high school or college to help them professionally. When we go to work, we are participating in a company. People join a religious group for worship or join the military to protect their country. There are also a variety of organizations that we join based on our personal beliefs, like political parties, different business or sports associations.

Then there are organizations that we are indirectly involved in such as companies and governments in which we are stockholders and voters. Stockholders can vote in company matters while voters can vote for a candidate to fill a local, state, or a federal government office. To be indirectly involved in an organization is to have a say in said organization but not be a part of its day-to-day operations. The state of our society is the direct result of the organizational leadership exhibited by its leaders and its people, so how you choose to participate in an organization will impact your future.

Though experience is important, organizational leadership needs more than experience. I believe experience only accounts for a fifth of leadership ability, contradicting the common belief that experience largely makes leaders what they are. If experience were the most vital part of being a leader, then all of the elderly would be great leaders based on the accumulation of their life experiences. Despite having less than 5 years of political experience, for instance, George W. Bush ran for President and won, beating more experienced opponents. Why does experience account for only a fifth of actual leadership? The answer lies in the interpretation of experience itself.

Even though experience is very important, organizational leadership requires much more than experience. Physical, mental, and moral fitness along with all the other necessary characteristics of organizational leadership must also be developed. Organizational leadership creates harmony. If you are missing one of the nine qualities, you will weaken your organization when you are in a leadership position. If you develop the nine qualities of organizational leadership, on the other hand, you can lead any organization, a nation, and even the world.

Assessment of Organizational Leadership:
The U.S. Presidencies 1977-2004

Here, I present my personal assessment of the organizational leadership of the US's last five Presidents (1977–2003), based on their performance and results.

KEY
GREAT 5 points GOOD 4 points AVERAGE 3 points
POOR 2 points AWFUL 1 point

	JIMMY CARTER	RONALD REAGAN	GEORGE H.W.BUSH	BILL CLINTON	GEORGE W. BUSH
Personal power	5	5	5	4	5
Team building ability	4	4	5	5	5
Financial mgmt ability	3	5	3	5	5
Vision	4	5	5	5	5
Intelligence	5	5	5	5	5
Courage	3	5	5	5	5
Trust	5	5	5	3	5
Fairness	4	5	5	5	5
Generosity	5	4	3	5	3
Total	38	43	41	42	43

40 + pts = great leader
36-39 pts = good leader
30-35 pts = average leader
21-29 pts = poor leader
20 pts & under = awful leader

1977–1981 Jimmy Carter (38 pts: Good leader)

After his presidency, he became one of the best ex-Presidents in history because of his strong personal leadership ability. Unfortunately, he didn't demonstrate strong organizational leadership while he was president because of the struggling economy and the American hostage crisis in Iran.

1981–1989 Ronald Reagan (43 pts: Great leader)

He proved his strong leadership ability through two historical events, building the foundation of a strong U.S. economy and defeating Communism.

1989–1993 George H.W. Bush (41 pts: Great leader)

He proved his strong leadership ability as a president by winning the Gulf War, and proved it again after his presidency, by helping one of his sons win the 2000 presidential election and the other win the Florida governor's office. However, his organizational leadership was unbalanced because he broke promises about not raising taxes, weakening the economy under his presidency.

1993–2001 Bill Clinton (42 pts: Great leader)

By balancing the budget, creating 23 million jobs, and creating a surplus of money by strengthening the economy, he proved his strong leadership ability. However, Clinton showed he wasn't trustworthy through several scandals, including one that got him impeached by the U.S. House of Representatives.

2001–2004 George W. Bush (43 pts: Great leader)

He showed strong leadership in handling the tragedy of September 11th, and then led the U.S. in liberating Iraq and capturing Saddam Hussein, finally bringing him to justice. Also, Bush demonstrated his economic leadership ability when he cut taxes despite an increase in the U.S. Federal deficit and the national unemployment rate, which sparked an economic recovery.

Assessment of Organizational Leadership:
American CEO's from 1980–2004

This is my personal assessment of organizational leadership between the five most prominent American CEO's based on their performance and results from 1980-2004.

KEY
GREAT 5 points   GOOD 4 points   AVERAGE 3 points
POOR 2 points   AWFUL 1 point

	JACK WELCH	BILL GATE	MICHAEL EISNER	TED TURNER	WARREN BUFFET
Personal power	4	5	5	4	5
Team building ability	5	5	4	5	5
Financial mgmt ability	5	5	5	3	5
Vision	5	5	5	5	5
Intelligence	5	5	5	5	5
Courage	5	5	5	5	5
Trust	5	4	4	5	5
Fairness	5	4	4	4	5
Generosity	4	5	3	5	3
Total	43	43	40	41	43

40 + pts = great leader
36-39 pts = good leader
30-35 pts = average leader
21-29 pts = poor leader
20 pts & under = awful leader

Of course, presidents and CEOs have very different responsibilities, so you cannot directly compare their leadership qualities or the assessments of their leadership qualities. I have been careful to assess each leader based upon their responsibilities in the positions I've noted. For instance, I assessed George W. Bush as a president and not as a businessman; he might score very differently as a businessman. Similarly, I have assessed Ted Turner as the founder of CNN, not as a political advocate.

JACK WELCH, FORMER CEO OF GENERAL ELECTRIC
(43 PTS: GREAT LEADER)

Through his strong leadership, Welch built General Electric into one of the best companies on Earth. GE is so good to its employees that they own over $12 billion in GE stock. It was because of Welch's leadership that American corporate culture was forever changed, making him partially responsible for America's resurgence as an economic superpower.

BILL GATES, FOUNDER OF MICROSOFT AND THE RICHEST PERSON
IN THE WORLD (43 PTS: GREAT LEADER)

Gates used his strong leadership abilities to invent user-friendly PC software that totally changed the world, making lots of other people millionaires and billionaires. He also founded a charity foundation that donates billions of dollars worldwide.

MICHAEL EISNER, CEO OF WALT DISNEY (40 PTS: GREAT LEADER)

Eisner's strong leadership made Disney so strong at one point that they were able to buy the ABC Network, creating a potential media giant. However, even great leaders can fall if they do not continue to fight within themselves to maintain great leadership. Now among the four networks, ABC has the weakest ratings. In addition, Roy Disney, Walt Disney's nephew, quit the company because he believed that Eisner's leadership caused Disney to lose "its focus, its creative energy, and its heritage" and called for Eisner to step down. Eisner subsequently lost his position as chairman.

TED TURNER, FOUNDER OF CNN (41 PTS: GREAT LEADER)

Ted Turner used his strong leadership to do something that no one ever dreamed of, create a 24-hour news network. He stunned the world with his creation of CNN, which made him very rich. Turner also became the first person to donate $1 billion to the United Nations for charitable purposes, which was almost one-third of his wealth at the time.

WARREN BUFFETT, THE WORLD'S GREATEST INVESTOR (SECOND RICHEST PERSON IN THE WORLD) (43 PTS: GREAT LEADER)

Buffett's strong leadership not only made him the 2nd richest person in the world; he made lots of other people millionaires, too.

Your Assessments of Leadership

Now take some time and assess how good of an organizational leader you, your boss, your mayor, your governor, and your president are based on performance and results.

40 + pts = great leader
36-39 pts = good leader
30-35 pts = average leader
21-29 pts = poor leader
20 pts & under = awful leader

Discover the qualities that need improvement, maintain your strengths, and improve your weaknesses to become a great organizational leader.

ASSESSMENT OF
ORGANIZATIONAL LEADERSHIP
KEY
GREAT 5 points   GOOD 4 points   AVERAGE 3 points
POOR 2 points   AWFUL 1 point

	YOU	YOUR BOSS	MAYOR	GOVER-NOR	PRESI-DENT
Personal power					
Team building ability					
Financial mgmt ability					
Vision					
Intelligence					
Courage					
Trust					
Fairness					
Generosity					
Total					

SUMMARY

The Sunset of America
Leading an organization requires strong leadership. Weak leadership creates disaster.

The Sunrise of America
Strong leadership brings significant changes, and the difference is like night and day.

The Best Company on Earth
Jack Welch, former CEO of GE, showed us how strong leadership impacts organizations and society.

The Worst Company in America
Enron showed us we have to build strong organizational leadership.

The Nine Qualities of Organizational Leadership
These nine qualities are necessary to successfully build dynamic organizations.
1. **PERSONAL POWER.** Personal leadership is the first step to leading organizations.
2. **TEAM BUILDING ABILITY.** Team building is the cornerstone of organizations.
3. **FINANCIAL MANAGEMENT ABILITY.** Cash flow is critical to dynamic organizations.
4. **VISION.** Vision gives organizations clear direction.
5. **INTELLIGENCE.** The smarter the organization, the better.
6. **COURAGE.** Courage fuels dynamic organizations.
7. **TRUST.** Trust is the foundation of all organizations.
8. **FAIRNESS.** Fairness breeds strength in organizations.
9. **GENEROSITY.** Generosity creates loyalty in organizations.

REVIEW OF "CREATE DYNAMIC ORGANIZATIONS"

What are the Nine Qualities of Organizational Leadership?

_____

_____

Why are the three dimensions of personal power necessary for organizational leadership?

_____

_____

Why is team building ability vital for developing dynamic organizations, and how do you build a winning team?

_____

_____

Why is financial management ability critical in the development of dynamic organizations, and how do you develop the ability?

_____

_____

What is vision, why is it so important for the future of any organization, and how do you develop vision for your organization?

_____

_____

Why do organizations need an intelligent leader, and what does it take to become an intelligent leader in an organization?

_____

_____

Why is it important for an organization to have a courageous leader, and what is the best way to develop courageous leadership in an organization?

_____

_____

Why must organizations have a trustworthy leader, and how do you become a trustworthy leader in your organization?

_____

_____

Why must an organization have a fair leader, and how do you develop fair organizational leadership?

_____

_____

What is the main reason an organization must have a generous leader, and how do you become a generous organizational leader?

_____

_____

Among the Nine Qualities of Organizational Leadership, which is your strongest, and which needs the most improvement?

_____

_____

Lead the Real World

CHAPTER six

Transform your dreeams into reality

On November 5, 1994, the whole world was stunned by what they heard, and no one could stop talking about it. They had to see it to believe it, people said. It was almost as if it were a miracle. The event was inspirational to the world, proving that a "Yes, I can," positive attitude had the power to do anything, touching the young and old alike; this one event helped change the way many people thought and lived.

That night in Las Vegas, George Foreman knocked out the world heavyweight boxing champion, Michael Moorer, and became the new heavyweight champion. Winning the championship itself wasn't what stunned people. Boxers win and lose titles all the time. But Foreman was 45 years old, the oldest heavyweight champion ever. When Foreman had come back into the ring seven years before, he was seen as a sideshow, an anomaly. Everyone wondered what would possess a grandfather to step into the ring and fight boxers almost half his age. Most people thought he was either insane for risking suicide or just as a foolish old man trying to recapture his youth and his glory days as a former world champion. After Foreman's amazing victory, though, everyone began to look up to and respect Foreman for his determination and indomitable spirit. These things, plus his "Yes, I can" positive attitude, began to inspire everyone.

George Foreman made the most of his regained respect and popularity, becoming the highest paid endorser in boxing history. A year after he won the heavyweight title, he partnered up with Salton and lent his name to their new grill product, the George Foreman Lean Grilling Machine. By 1999, Salton sold so many grills (10 million) that they decided to pay Foreman $137.5 million for the rights to his name. Thanks to Foreman, 50 million of these grills have been sold worldwide, not just making him a king in the ring, but a "King of the Grill." Foreman achieved great fame, wealth, and power, becoming the most successful ex-boxer ever.

George Foreman was one of seven children living in a struggling household in Marshall, Texas. Seeing no other way out of his life of poverty, Foreman dropped out of junior high school and lived on the streets, mugging and brawling with whoever got in his way. At the age of 15, Foreman finally realized that his life was going nowhere, and he needed to find a way out. One day while watching television, he saw an athletic idol on a commercial saying, "If you have dropped out of school and want a second chance in life, then the Job Corps is for you." Foreman immediately took the first train to Oregon where he joined up and did forestry and construction. Eventually he moved to California to finish his training in the Job Corps.

In 1967, Foreman went to Camp Parks, an industrial training center in California to earn his high school equivalency diploma. There he met Doc Broaddus, a Job Corps counselor and boxing coach, who told George to redirect his life from alley fighting and dedicate himself to a single task—boxing. Broaddus believed that George had the potential to be a world champion. Foreman fought his way up the amateur ranks and became the national heavyweight boxing champion in 1968, earning a spot on the U.S. Olympic boxing team that year. He made the most of his op-

portunity and earned a gold medal at the Summer Olympic Games.

Foreman started his professional career with a third-round knock-out victory over Don Waldhelm in New York City in 1969, and in the next three and a half years, he defeated 36 consecutive opponents. In 1973, Foreman finally became the world heavyweight champion, knocking Joe Frazier out in the second round. His domination in the ring continued as he defeated two world heavyweight contenders, bringing his total to 40 consecutive fights without a defeat. It seemed like no one could stop him at all.

However, in October 1974 he lost the heavyweight title to Muhammad Ali by a knockout in the famous "Rumble in the Jungle" match, the first heavyweight championship bout fought in Africa. Several years later, he experienced a religious vision that moved him to quit boxing and dedicate his life to God. He returned to Houston and became an evangelical minister.

Because Foreman was only 28 years old and at his physical peak—a leading contender still in a position to make large amounts of money—his retirement seemed bizarre. Everyone thought he was going through a phase and in a year or two, the old Foreman would return and make his millions beating men unconscious. Foreman was serious when he retired, so serious that he was not seen in the public eye again for ten years. During that time, he established a small church and a youth center, in which he could help kids stay out of trouble.

In 1987, needing money to support his family and his center, he decided to return to boxing. Everyone wondered what would possess a 38-year old man to climb back into the ring. Foreman began proving, though, that he was no sideshow. He fought Evander Holyfield in 1991, and though he lost the bout by decision, he gained even more respect. People began seriously seeing Foreman as a real boxer. And finally in 1994, two months shy of his 46th birthday, he knocked out Thomas Moorer. He was the oldest man to hold the title, completing one of the most improbable comebacks in sports history.

Advertisers saw Foreman as a great spokesperson because of his sideshow appeal, also noting his self-depreciating humor, his easygoing nature, and his tremendous positive attitude. His return to the ring brought companies such as Thompson's Water Sealant, McDonald's, Doritos, Nike, and Kentucky Fried Chicken banging down his door for endorsements. These personality traits also landed him in 1993 his own ABC sitcom George, which was short-lived. He co-wrote his autobiography *By George,* wrote George Foreman's *Knock-Out-the-Fat Barbecue and Grilling Cookbook* and the critically acclaimed *George Foreman's Guide to Life: How to Get Up Off the Canvas When Life Knocks You Down.*

No one thought George Foreman could accomplish any of these things. Yet he constantly overcame the odds, achieving things people could only dream about. Foreman made all of this possible by being incredibly tough, in and out of the ring, savvy with his street smarts, his superb communication skills and public speaking ability, which were key in his transformation from boxer to beloved spokesperson, and by always staying competitive. George Foreman is a true champion of life and a living, breathing example of someone who truly leads the real world.

Now it is your turn to lead the real world and make your dreams come true through the following five steps.

Five Steps to Lead the Real World

1. **BUILD LIFE TOUGHNESS.** To survive in the real world, you must have toughness.
2. **DEVELOP STREET SMARTS.** In reality, you need street smarts to survive.
3. **BUILD PRACTICAL COMMUNICATION SKILLS.** To succeed in the real world, you need practical communication skills.

4. **BE A GREAT PUBLIC SPEAKER.** You must be a great public speaker to make your dreams come true.
5. **BE COMPETITIVE.** Keep your mind and heart open to always improve yourself.

These five steps will help you triumph in life. The real world is waiting for you.

STEP ONE: BUILD LIFE TOUGHNESS

The real world is all about survival of the fittest. In the real world, if you are strong, you will survive; if you are weak, you will fail. The real world can be cold and merciless, chewing you up and spitting you back out onto the ground if you are weak; but if you are strong, the real world can be amazing, filled with tremendous opportunities that will lead you to incredible success.

The real world is like a war. There are many enemies that try to take you down in so many ways. Some people do it by criticizing you. Some try to con you and rip you off. Some people do it by being arrogant. If you let these enemies take you down and keep you there, they will swarm over you and destroy you. However, other people are not your worst enemy in the real world; you are your own worst enemy and yet your own best friend.

All of us get taken down at one point in the real world. Falling down is never the problem; staying down is. When you stay down, that means you have let your own worst enemy achieve ultimate victory. To survive in the real world, you have to not only stay standing but also keep moving. When you keep moving, you can take advantage of what is awesome about the real world.

In order to stay standing and keep moving, first, you need life toughness to be strong. Life toughness consists of three elements: physical toughness, mental toughness, and moral toughness. Physical toughness gives you the physical power to carry out your ideas and actualize your goals. Mental toughness is the ability to remain positive in the face of the fiercest of adversity. Moral toughness comes from the internal strength that you need to fight for what is right and fight against what is wrong.

To build life toughness, discipline yourself to train yourself physically, mentally, and morally. When you do these things, you will generate physical strength, a positive mental attitude, and self-confidence, which will make you that much tougher in the real world; the more physical strength, positive mental attitude, and self-confidence you have, the tougher you will be.

STEP TWO: DEVELOP STREET SMARTS

The key thing to remember about surviving is that the real world is not a classroom. It is reality. Though you must use book smarts to acquire knowledge and develop skills needed to become a necessary person, these things will not guarantee your survival in the real world. However, street smarts will.

Street smarts are the wisdom (common sense) that comes from the practical application of instinct and knowledge. Instincts, such as eating when we are hungry, going to the bathroom when necessary, knowing when to rest, just to name a few, are the foundation of our common sense, giving us the desire to survive and succeed. Knowledge is what we know, which helps our judgment in determining what is appropriate and inappropriate, or what is right and what is wrong.

Without discipline, your instincts will control you, instead of you controlling them. Without knowledge, you cannot have the right judgment. To develop street smarts, discipline your instincts and continue educating yourself.

STEP THREE: BUILD PRACTICAL COMMUNICATION

Now that you know what it takes to survive, how do you succeed in the real world? In the real world, you have to deal with real people. If you can deal with real people, success will be yours. What is the best tool

for dealing with real people in the real world? Communication.

You need communication to maintain your relationships with family, friends, and other loved ones. You need communication to lead other people properly and stay competitive in the workplace, as an employee or as an employer. Without communication, there would be absolutely no progress on any level in the real world. Therefore, communication is vital in every aspect of the real world and is crucial to success.

The following are three true stories that illustrate the powerful impact of communication in the real world.

WHO STOPPED THE RISE of the KKK in 1991? The government? The police? The NAACP? Human rights groups? No.

In 1991, former Grand Wizard David Duke ran for governor in Louisiana. Legally, there was nothing wrong with his beliefs. Morally, Duke's beliefs were corrupt, which could have affected our entire country had he won. He had a lot of opponents, but their was one gentleman who cut the sprout of this revival before it could strangle the South without using weapons, organizing protests, or exerting any political power. He only used his excellent communication skills and personal toughness. That man is Tim Russert, the current host of *Meet the Press.*

On November 10, 1991, I watched NBC's *Meet the Press,* and Tim Russert was part of a panel interviewing David Duke regarding his qualifications to be Louisiana's next governor. The rest of the panel, moderator Garrick Utley and guest panelist David S. Broder, focused their questions on Duke's past and current affiliations with anti-black and anti-Semitic groups. It seemed Duke was able to counter all of their questions, making himself look like a smart and able candidate until Russert stepped away from asking about Duke's personal beliefs and refocused on one of the most important issues in the Louisiana race, the state's economy:

MR. RUSSERT: What manufacturers are the three biggest employers in the state of Louisiana?

MR. DUKE: Well, we have a number of employers in our state.

MR. RUSSERT: But who are the three biggest manufacturers who are the biggest employers in the state of Louisiana?

MR. DUKE: I couldn't give you their names, right off, sir.

MR. RUSSERT: You don't know who the biggest employers in the state of Louisiana are?

MR. DUKE: Well, I don't have the statistics in front of me, I know a lot of the—

MR. RUSSERT: Sir, you're talking about economic development and you don't know who—

MR. DUKE: I tell you what. The state of Louisiana is the biggest employer in our state. And because it is so big and there are so many employees and there's so much waste and inefficiency and there's so many selling of positions and there's so much corruption in the government, it's hurting every business in the state of Louisiana. That's the biggest employer.

Duke was unable to answer this question in detail, which didn't paint a good picture of his intelligence; it also showed how little he knew and cared about his own state's economy. Duke only discredited himself further when he failed to answer other crucial questions during the interview. By allowing Duke to discredit himself, Tim Russert helped squash his gubernatorial bid. Russert's street smarts, toughness, and great communication skills prevented potential violence, bloodshed, and economic collapse. He used the true power of communication.

TIM RUSSERT demonstrates that communication is the most powerful weapon we have in the real world.

> One appropriate word can save or take lives in the real world.

Who decides life and death in the real world?

Communication has the power of life and death in many situations. Consider the O.J. Simpson murder trial, which mesmerized the nation from 1994 to 1995. Simpson, a former NFL player, movie star, and commercial spokesman was accused of murdering his estranged wife and her boyfriend. Played out on television, this case featured a "Dream Team" defense created by Robert Shapiro, which consisted of Alan Dershowitz, F. Lee Bailey, Barry Scheck (a specialist in DNA and fingerprinting), Harland Braun, Sara Caplan, Shawn Chapman, and Anthony Glassman, all led by Johnnie Cochran. The prosecution team of Marcia Clark and Christopher Darden, which was supported by L.A. County District Attorney's office and Los Angeles Police Department, had their hands full. Though the prosecution had medical evidence and testimony that could have very well convicted Simpson of murder, his Dream Team used their excellent communication skills to exploit the weaknesses in the prosecution's case. The two critical events of the case that occurred involving two vital pieces of evidence, the glove and Mark Furhman's testimony, were just a small example of how effective Simpson's Dream Team was in getting him acquitted.

Critical pieces of the evidence during the Simpson trial were a pair of bloody gloves. During the June 15, 1995 court session, Simpson put on the gloves and they appeared to be too small. The prosecution contended that the gloves, once drenched in blood, had shrunk. The defense believed that if the glove doesn't fit, Simpson is not the killer. "If the glove does not fit, you must acquit," Cochran famously stated. Even after the prosecution brought in the president of Isotoner Gloves to agree that the gloves did indeed shrink, seeds of doubt were planted in the jury.

The most damaging blow to the prosecution's case was when Mark Furhman, the LAPD Detective leading the O.J. investigation, was called to the stand by the defense after several witnesses and audio tapes illustrated that Furhman was a racist. When F. Lee Bailey asked Furhman if he had made a racial slur in the past ten years, he denied doing so; Furhman was immediately charged with perjury, further destroying the credibility of the case against O.J. Simpson.

In the end, it was the defense team's convincing argument of racism and improper police procedure that led to Simpson's acquittal. The defense team's communication with toughness was far more influential than that of the prosecution's, and that helped make Simpson a free man. Had the prosecution proceeded more carefully with their evidence and communicated more clearly with the jury, they might have convicted Simpson.

THE O.J. SIMPSON trial illustrates that communication makes or breaks peoples' lives.

A final example of the power of communication is Senator John F. Kennedy's presidential campaign.

Kennedy trailed Nixon in the polls during the 1960 campaign for the Presidency, until the Presidential debates were televised for the first time. Why? Kennedy knew that television deviated greatly from radio because of its visual impact. He knew that television would allow millions of Americans to see their candidates in action, and to the American voter, appearance was everything. Kennedy understood that this new medium of communication would be the best way to get voters to vote for him. Meanwhile, Nixon, with all of his political experience, ignored television's impact on the American opinion.

With the power of TV in mind, Kennedy practiced his speech. Nixon didn't. Kennedy also made it a point to get in shape and dress well while Nixon looked sloppy and disheveled. Once the cameras went on, Kennedy conveyed an energetic, positive image while getting the most important points of the debate across. However, Nixon looked pale and pasty on camera, which caused the viewers at home to ignore his points. Kennedy also asserted himself with confidence well through his body language. Nixon looked awkward and unsure. Overall, Kennedy looked positive, energetic, sharp, strong, intelligent, and charismatic, while Nixon appeared weak and negative.

The debate proved to be a turning point for Kennedy as he made up ground in the polls and eventually defeated Nixon in one of the closest elections in American history. If John F. Kennedy didn't properly exercise his communication skills, he would never have been elected President and become one of the best Presidents in American history.

AS YOU CAN SEE, practical communication is incredibly powerful and can lead you to great success. What's even more amazing about practical communication is that anyone and everyone can have it, if they choose to build practical communication skills. Keep in mind that even if you have lots of life toughness and lots of street smarts, being a lousy communicator will only hurt you and can even cost you your life. Practical communication is that critical in the real world.

All the skills needed to be a practical communicator were discussed in detail in Chapter 4. Listen sincerely and express yourself properly by choosing the right word, controlling the tone, volume, and speed of your voice, and using proper body language.

STEP FOUR: BE A GREAT PUBLIC SPEAKER

To achieve the highest levels of success, you must master the most powerful form of communication: public speaking. By sharing your thoughts, ideas, and feelings publicly, you can reach, influence, and impact countless numbers of people.

However, many people have the wrong idea about public speaking.

Public speaking isn't just about making speeches in front of a crowd. It's speaking at seminars, giving interviews, debating opinions, hosting talk shows, speaking out at town hall meetings, or even just participating in conversation at dinner parties and other events. Anytime you are talking in front of a group of people, whether the audience is with you in person or your words are being broadcasted through radio, T.V., and the Internet, you are speaking in public. Even if you are not a celebrity, elected official, or senior executive, honing your public speaking abilities can help you lead the real world successfully.

SOME EXAMPLES of leaders that led and changed the real world through public speaking include Abraham Lincoln, Mohandis K. Gandhi, Dr. Martin Luther King, Jr. and Rev. Billy Graham. Their speeches inspired millions worldwide, changed entire societies, and left a lasting mark on countless generations.

> Public speaking is the steering wheel that can guide the real world.

Excellent public speakers have the opportunity to become respectable, rich, famous, and/or powerful. Some are fortunate enough to become all four and make their dreams a reality, giving them the power to change the world. Just look at our most prominent politicians, entertainers, media personalities, and business leaders as examples.

You are just as special and unique as any politician, entertainer, media personality, and business leader, and in fact, you can be even more special than they are. You have tremendous potential in becoming a great public speaker. Make your dreams a reality through public speaking.

Please allow me to show you how I used to drown on stage through my misadventures in public speaking. I hope these experiences make you laugh, make you think, show you the lessons I learned, and make your transformation into a great public speaker easier.

Be Yourself!

I love doing martial arts exhibitions but hated having to deliver a speech afterwards to explain what the martial arts was really all about. Just the thought of having to speak in front of all of those people terrified me.

A few days before putting on my annual martial arts exhibition for charity in Orlando, I sought out some help from an advisor about my speech. He suggested that I speak slowly and pronounce each word correctly because the way I pronounced some of my English made it difficult for people to understand me. My advisor said that by doing so, I would get my message across and people would respect me.

But when I began my speech, pronouncing my words very slowly in the hopes that I would sound just like any other American, I saw how bored everyone looked. Some were so bored that they just got up and left. I was stunned.

After the speech, I mentally pictured my past performances as a speaker, and I saw myself performing with lots of energy and passion, speaking and moving, hoping to move others. This time, I was neither energetic nor passionate. In fact, I put everybody to sleep. Like my audience, I left that speech feeling empty.

I learned two very important lessons from this experience. First, always prepare well and practice before a speech, especially pronunciation, so I wouldn't sound like I was practicing reading English in front of an audience. Second, never to be anyone else except myself during a speech.

Give Yourself Energy

At a Marriott Hotel in Dallas, I was so busy preparing and setting up a seminar that I didn't eat dinner the night before and had no time for breakfast in the morning. After the morning session, I ate a lot at lunchtime and the results were disastrous.

With a full stomach, I began getting sleepy during my afternoon speech and was so tired that my speech slurred, and I had to end it two hours ahead of schedule. I felt humiliated.

Afterwards, I realized that my eating habits during the seminar were bad. Falling asleep on stage was a result of my body expending a lot of energy in digestion, instead of generating creativity to my brain. I learned a hard lesson: don't eat heavily before speaking.

After that experience, I avoid eating any heavy food before speaking. I settle for soups, drinks, and other forms of liquid nourishment. When I eat energetic food, it helps me feel 100%. If I eat junk food, it slows me down. Energy is everything to a speaker and is so important in public speaking. Figure out what gives you energy—and, just as important, what saps your energy—so that you can prepare your body as well as your mind for your speeches.

Respect the Audience

For a keynote speech I had to make at another martial arts industry convention in Las Vegas, I deliberately chose to use complex vocabulary in my speech. Even though I knew that most people would have a hard time understanding it, I wanted to show everybody that I was better than anyone else in the industry. I envisioned that people would be so blown away by my brilliantly crafted speech that they would just all want to mob me, shake my hand, and sing praises up and down the halls.

However, these were not the reactions I got when I finished my speech. Instead of being praised, I was shunned. It was a very lonely weekend in Vegas after that. I reflected on my performance and realized my speech came across as haughty, pompous, and way too academic to the audience. Unknowingly, I had belittled the audience with my choice of words…a bad move.

After that experience, I always show respect and appreciation for the audience. Respecting the audience is extremely important whether through subject matter or delivery.

THE FIRST STEP in being a great public speaker is preparation. Preparation will relieve stress, eliminate mistakes, make you more fearless, and generate the energy and passion needed for a great performance. Preparation also makes your speech fun, exciting, and beneficial for your audience, showing that you have respect for them. Here are the four keys to prepare a great speech .

Obtain Details About Your Speaking Engagement

By obtaining details about a speaking engagement, who, what, where, when, why, and how, it helps you deliver a better speech. For example, Bob is a speaker and he has to prepare to write a speech. These are the details he needs:

- ❖ **WHO:** 500 CEOs of the top 500 corporations in America.
- ❖ **WHAT:** The topic is leadership development and building winning teams.
- ❖ **WHERE:** Marriott Hotel ballroom, New York City, NY.
- ❖ **WHEN:** 9 a.m. to noon, Saturday, April 25th, 2003.
- ❖ **WHY:** U.S. companies need to build more competitive companies throughout the world.
- ❖ **HOW:** As a Keynote speaker, I will use a well-paced speech with lots of motivation and energy (no other speaker).

Identify Your Audience's Wants and Needs

Before you deliver a speech, you must identify the audience's wants and needs. In general, what an audience or an organization wants is what they dream about or desire. What an audience or organization needs is answers to how they can achieve their dreams or desires. For example, a businessman wants to succeed. He needs to know how to succeed. A student wants to have straight "A"s. She needs to know how to get straight "A"s.

Once you've identified the audience's wants and needs, you can come up with the answers. Organize and write down your findings in detail. If you are delivering the speech without reading from text, prepare an outline. Then, if you need to, write out your speech, keeping your audience's perspective in mind.

Check on Last-Minute Particulars

❖ Check the weather of your destination to determine appropriate clothing for the area, if traveling out of town or country.

❖ Inquire how the venue—convention hall or room, banquet room or ballroom—will be set up so you know how your audience will be seated and you can prepare the movement and delivery of your speech accordingly, based on the seating arrangements.

❖ Ask event organizers to prepare a wireless microphone (choose a hand microphone, headset, or lavaliere). Speakers need a hands-free mike because they use a lot of body language while speaking.

❖ Request a pot of hot water, herbal tea, and plenty of honey to protect your voice.

❖ Check your hair. If necessary, get a trim or haircut to have a neat, proper appearance. You can change your clothes in an instant, but you can't cut your hair in the same amount of time.

❖ Ask event organizers and/or hotel staff to prepare special food for you in case you have heavy speaking duties or an all-day seminar, which will allow your energy to be used for speaking, not digesting.

❖ If speaking at a town hall meeting, prepare for a possible question-and-answer session and find out your host's and your opponent's strong points and weak points.

Practice, Practice, Practice

❖ Write, rewrite, record and listen to your speech.

❖ These things improve your organizational, memorization, and performance skills.

❖ Rehearse your speech, noticing voice control, body language and passion.

❖ By looking at your body language and gestures in a mirror, you notice all of your little nuances as a speaker.

❖ Mentally rehearse your speech, whether walking, driving or sleeping.

❖ Doing so gives you the self-confidence needed for a great delivery and will reinforce knowledge of the topic.

Other practice routines:

❖ If appearing on a talk show, find a partner to practice with. Express yourself with sincerity, smiles, and passion.

❖ If speaking at a town hall meeting, find an audience and have a practice question-and-answer session with them, expressing yourself with enthusiasm.

❖ If speaking at a debate, find a partner and have a practice question-and-answer session, expressing yourself with a smile, sincerity and desire.

❖ If being interviewed, find a partner and practice your answers with enthusiasm.

Now that you're prepared, here are a few more tips to keep in mind to deliver your best performance.

Perform Your Best with Passion and Respect

How does a speaker make a good or bad first impression? Attitude. How do we discover a speaker's attitude? We discover it through his or her physical and mental outlook. Physical outlook is determined by physical appearance while facial expressions, body language, and verbal expression illustrate the speaker's mental outlook.

The first thing we see when meeting a speaker is his or her physical appearance. A good speaker that takes his or her job seriously will be properly groomed (fresh haircut, clean appearance) and dress professionally, which demonstrates that the speaker respects his or her audience. An unprofessional speaker is usually nonchalant about dress (except in special cases) because he or she is careless or lacks self-respect.

We then notice if the speaker has the right mental outlook. Does he or she express him or herself appropriately for the occasion? Does he or she smile; show a sincere or sympathetic face, or a depressed, sad one? What about an angry face? We then assess the speaker's body language. Does the speaker show good or bad posture? Does the speaker stand or sit straight with confidence, hunch or bend his or her shoulders or back? Although it's important for a speaker to be conscious of his or her body language, it's just as necessary for him or her to be him or herself.

When on stage, always make yourself and the audience smile; smile with sincerity and passion. Smiling will open your mind, charge you up, and help you and the audience to relax. (Notable exception: When reading a eulogy at a funeral or memorial service, control your facial expressions appropriately.)

Communicate with passion, by doing the following:

- ❖ Always choose the right or appropriate words to say.
- ❖ Control your voice by varying its tone, volume, and speed.
- ❖ Use proper body language, such as natural facial expressions and gestures with your speech.
- ❖ Make sure that the speech is beneficial, and that you are delivering it clearly.
- ❖ Use examples or illustrations with your speech.
- ❖ When speaking, always do your best to maintain a positive attitude, show appreciation, and respect to your audience.

Always end your speeches strongly by finalizing and summarizing your speech with a flurry of energy and sincerity so that your audience will take your speech with them wherever they go.

Hold the Audience's Attention From Beginning to End

No matter how responsive audiences are, challenges always pop up during speeches. An audience can wander off mentally during my seminars (I would hope they wouldn't wander off physically). I've learned that my routine must be varied throughout the day because many people get sleepy after eating, especially after lunch. Although it's the body's natural way of handling digestion, sleepiness after meals can be avoided by eating smart.

In the beginning of a speech, I like doing something special and unique to seize my audience's attention immediately, regardless of the time, place, or situation. One of my best tricks is bringing out a couple of big stones to try breaking them with my hand, foot, or forehead. After failing to do so, I ask the audience if anyone thinks he or she can break one of my stones, and if so, please come to the stage. To make it even more interesting, I offer the first person that can break a stone $1,000 in cash. A confident audience member always tries breaking one, but no one ever does. No one can break a stone with his or her body alone. After everyone who tries to break the stones fails, I bring out a big hammer and pulverize one. This captures the audience's attention immediately, opening their minds and ears to what I have to say because this action gives the audience a special message that relates to the topic of the speech. In this case its "don't give up, for there is always a solution."

Another favorite attention-grabber I use is something I call "pushing the limit." I ask my audience to raise their hand if they think they are strong and can do one hundred push-ups, and then I pick five to ten people depending on the size of the stage. All of them come up on stage, and I ask them to get into push up position because they are about to have a push up contest, and I ask them do 120 push-ups. I also ask the audience to count together aloud. As the people on stage keep going towards that mark, I see some of them struggle. At this point, I tell everyone, "Without pain, you cannot win. If you can't overcome pain, you cannot win. Only when you overcome pain will you be a winner."

The "break the rock" and "pushing the limit" challenges are some of many things I use to keep an audience's attention. Each attention grabber is tailored to the audience and the topic of the speech. I don't want their minds to wander; I want their attention on me until I'm finished. Why is their attention so important? It is important because I respect the audience, and I especially don't want to waste their time, energy, or money. Instead, I want them to spend their time with me learning valuable and vital information, including the answers to the problems they may be facing in their business or within themselves. Here are some ways you can grab your audience's attention, too:

❖ **SMILE CAMPAIGN.** You should start a smile campaign when speaking because smiling prompts introductions, opens people's minds, and enables people to be friendly with each other right away. This campaign entices people to stay with you.

❖ **ASK A TOUGH OR INTERESTING QUESTION.** Another method you could use to keep an audience's attention is asking a very tough or interesting question that is relevant to the topic of your speech or to the audience. For example, sometimes I'll ask: "What is the most important thing in your life?" or, "in your business?" or "in your family?" "What is the most powerful thing on earth?" "What would you like to do if you had only one week to live?" "What is your definition of success?"

❖ **MAKE AN INTRIGUING STATEMENT.** Yet another way to grab the audience's attention is making an intriguing statement, such as:

"Ladies and gentlemen, I will show you three steps to make one million dollars within three months." Or,

"I will show you three ways to double your income in your business within one month without having to spend a penny."

❖ **APPLAUSE.** Applause is a great audience picker-upper. Start off by telling the audience to pay attention because you have something very important to say. Then say something like, "The sun rises in the east, and sets in the west," or something similar that the audience cannot disagree with. After making your statement, ask the audience that if they agree with your statement, to please give you a big hand. Then all of the audience should applaud, which keeps them from dozing off.

❖ **GET THEM MOVING WITH A SEMINAR EXERCISE.** To take the audience's mind off of wanting to sleep, interact with them. Say, "If you believe you can do it, stand up, raise both arms and say, 'I can do it' loudly." Other times say "If you think you are a leader, make the person next to you happy by talking, motivating, and encouraging them, and shake their hand." You can also ask the audience to do a simple exercise in their seat, like asking them to put their hands up, clench them into a fist, and then unclench them, repeating it 100 times. They will think it's easy but in actuality, their muscles will become sore. You can also come up with special seminar exercises of your own. By asking your audience to physically do something, they remain awake, have fun, and stay alert.

❖ **BRAINSTORMING.** Another great fatigue-buster is brainstorming. Ask the audience for their help in solving a problem. For example, "Why can't many people lose weight?" The audience then may dig 20 problems out of that one question and then find the answers to all of them. Going through this kind of question-and-answer session makes it difficult for the audience to sleep because the mind is occupied.

❖ **REPEAT AFTER ME.** Interacting with the audience is such a great way to make them forget about being sleepy. I especially love verbally interacting with them. Sometimes I'll say: "If you want to have lots of self-esteem and maintain successful habits, please repeat after me three times, 'I love myself, I love my family, I love my country.'" Other times I'll say, "Repeat after me loudly, 'No fear,' 'No fear,' 'No fear,' and 'I can do it,' 'I can do it,' 'I can do it.'" When the audience responds in kind, they begin having fun and don't think about sleep anymore.

STEP FIVE: BE COMPETITIVE

The real world is rapidly and constantly changing. In order to survive and succeed in the real world, you must stay competitive personally and professionally by adapting and changing with it. Even if you are successful, if you do not stay competitive, then you will lose it all in the blink of an eye.

I once heard about a little girl who made herself so competitive that she beat such insurmountable odds and not only grew up to be one of the most successful people ever but also has stayed at the top of her industry for a long time. Her story is an amazing inspiration.

In Mississippi, in 1954, there was a little girl born in a small rural town. Her grandmother tried the best she could to raise her, despite being extremely poor. When she was six, the little girl moved in with her mother in Milwaukee, WI.

The little girl grew up to be a troubled teen. She experimented with sex and drugs and eventually got pregnant. The baby was born prematurely and soon died after birth. The troubled teen knew she had to make a choice: Stay where she was and let her habits kill her, or go to Nashville, TN, to live with her father. She went to Nashville, little knowing that her choice to leave would forever change her life.

The troubled teen grew into a beauty queen. When she was 17, she was hired to Nashville radio station WVOL and two years later, was hired by WTVF-TV in Nashville as a reporter/anchor. At the same time, the beauty queen was attending Tennessee State University, but she saw a bigger opportunity on the horizon.

In 1976, she quit school to move to Baltimore, MD and joined WJZ-TV news as a co-anchor, and in 1978 discovered her talent for hosting talk shows when she became a co-host to WJZ-TV's People Are Talking, while continuing to serve as an anchor and news reporter. Even with all of this success, she still struggled with her weight and her image. The station managers constantly wanted the young broadcaster to change just about everything about her, which took a toll on her self-esteem. It was when she moved to Chicago in 1984 that she would find a permanent home.

In January 1984, she came to Chicago, IL, to host WLS-TV's AM Chicago, a faltering talk show, which was then put up against Phil Donahue's popular morning talk show. This television station was the first to let the broadcaster be herself, which allowed her to throw all of her energy into her new show. Within a month, she was beating Donahue in the ratings, and the show's format was soon expanded to one hour. In September 1985, the broadcaster's dream was coming true when AM Chicago was renamed after her: The Oprah Winfrey Show. Oprah Winfrey, after years of struggling, was beginning to reap the rewards of all of her hard work.

Since it went into national syndication in 1986, The Oprah Winfrey Show has won several Emmys, with Oprah eventually owning the talk show outright in 1988, becoming the first woman ever to own and produce a talk show.

Oprah has become so powerful that she has major influence in all forms of media. Any book that Oprah's Book Club listed became an instant bestseller. Her magazine, O!, has made $140 million in its two years of existence. Her production company, Harpo, has made films for television and movie screens that have not only been critically acclaimed, but have been moneymakers as well. All of these things made Oprah Winfrey the first ever black female billionaire.

She isn't just a billionaire. Oprah has a big heart that allows her to help everyone. Her show alone has changed countless lives worldwide. Oprah helped to establish a national database tracking child abusers all over the U.S. She has given her time and money to so many charitable organizations and in 2000, her own charity, Oprah's Angel Network began presenting a $100,000 "Use Your Life Award" to people who are using their lives to improve the lives of others. Through these actions, she established herself as rich, famous, powerful, and respectable.

How was Oprah's phenomenal success possible? How did Oprah

beat such insurmountable odds? She used her incredible toughness and stunning street smarts to discipline and improve herself so that she would have outstanding communication skills, great public speaking ability and always remain fiercely competitive. Her self-confidence (toughness) and wisdom (street smarts) helped her to survive all of her struggles, but when Oprah combined all that with her practical communication skills, public speaking ability, and her competitiveness, she achieved things that no one ever has.

Even after reaching the top, Oprah has not slowed down at all. She remains incredibly competitive to keep her crown as the Queen of Talk Shows. With all of her accomplishments, people are now wondering aloud more and more when Oprah will take the next big step and run for the U.S. Presidency. Oprah is a living example of survival and success in the real world. She has to stay competitive to keep her show at the top.

To stay competitive in the real world, you have to continue toughening yourself personally and professionally through discipline and training, keep an open mind and heart as you continue acquiring knowledge to sharpen your street smarts, and always practice and improve your communication skills and public speaking ability. As long as you never stop improving yourself personally and professionally, and you stay flexible enough to change with the times, you will always be competitive so you can continue surviving, succeeding, and enjoying your life in the real world.

SUMMARY
Lead the Real World

George Foreman overcame insurmountable odds with his toughness, street smarts, practical communication skills, public speaking ability, and competitive drive to live a successful life.

Five Steps to Lead the Real World

1. **BUILD LIFE TOUGHNESS.** To survive in the real world, you must have toughness.

2. **DEVELOP STREET SMARTS.** In reality, you desperately need street smarts to survive.

3. **BUILD PRACTICAL COMMUNICATION SKILLS.** To succeed in the real world, you need practical communication skills.

4. **BE A GREAT PUBLIC SPEAKER.** You must be a great public speaker to make your dreams come true.

5. **BE COMPETITIVE.** Keep your mind and heart open to always improve yourself.

REVIEW OF "LEAD THE REAL WORLD"

What are the five steps to lead the real world?

_____

_____

What are the three dimensions of life toughness?

_____

_____

How do you build life toughness?

_____

_____

What is the difference between book smarts and street smarts?

_____

_____

How do you become street smart?

_____

_____

Why are practical communication skills vital to success in leading the real world?

_____

_____

What benefits do you receive by becoming a great public speaker?

_____

_____

What is the most important ingredient for a successful speech?

_____

_____

Why is staying competitive critically important for success in the real world?

_____

_____

How can you stay competitive in the real world?

_____

_____

Success
IS YOUR
Choice

Think big and success will be easy

CHAPTER

seven

EVERY DREAM HAS A PRICE TAG

The journey to success can be long and hard. It's when we reach the end of the journey that we find the payoff to be worth all the work and struggle involved in getting there. Today, I am fortunate enough to be living out my dreams of building a successful multi-million dollar organization; please let me share with you how I got here. I hope that my journey to success makes you laugh, think, and helps you on your own journey to success.

New York City is known all over the world as being the most amazing city to live in, yet the toughest one, too. As the saying goes, if you can make it in New York, then you can truly make it anywhere. My own journey towards a piece of the American dream started right here, in New York in 1977.

I came to the Big Apple with only two things: A black belt and a strong burning desire to succeed. I thought that this great city would help me feed that burning desire, and the rest would take care of itself. All I cared about was having my piece of the American dream, even though I was homeless and had no green card. I wasn't going to let anything stand in my way, not my lack of money, not my lack of knowledge of American culture, and especially not my lack of English. My heart brimmed with hopes and dreams. However, I didn't realize right away that these hopes and dreams would have such a high price.

One of the first things I discovered was how much of a liability my lack of English really was. I went to a grocery store one day in Queens to pick up something quick to eat because I was hungry. I scanned the shelves and found a can of food with delicious looking meat chunks on the label. "Mmmmm, this looks really good," I thought to myself. I grabbed the can, paid for it, and rushed back to the place where I was staying. Once I got home, I opened the can and inside I found what was on the label; delicious looking meat chunks drowning in gravy. I took my spoon and dug in.

After my stomach stopped gnawing at itself, I was concerned because something wasn't quite right about the meat. It tasted kind of funny, but I couldn't figure out why. Maybe the meat had expired. I put the can down and grabbed my English to Korean dictionary to translate the words on the label. My eyes widened when I discovered what I ate… dog food. I ate…dog food? I actually ate dog food? This was an experience I would never forget.

My poor English and the fact that I had no green card also made it very hard to find a decent job. The only job skills I had were martial arts-related, and there were no full-time positions at any of the martial arts schools. I also had no money to open a martial arts school of my own at the time. The only jobs I qualified for were ones that were back-breaking and low paying, jobs that didn't utilize my full potential.

Even though my hectic schedule prevented me from training adequately, the martial arts still remained prominent in my life. Thankfully, I did manage to teach a class part-time, in a school in Manhattan. When I taught class, I was the happiest person alive, putting everything I had into it, my sweat, my energy, and my heart. If it weren't for this part-time martial arts class, my first year in America would have been totally wasted. Teaching part time kept not only me alive, but also kept the dream of opening my own martial arts school in America alive, too.

As I toiled in various odd jobs, I saved every penny I earned, hoping that one day I would have enough money to open my own school so I could do what I loved instead of doing what I had to just to survive. Every time payday came around, I knew I was just one step closer to realizing that goal, to begin living the American Dream. Penny by penny, I was getting there. After a year of doing these odd jobs, an opportunity came that would forever change my life.

That opportunity came in the form of an elder, Master Instructor Dong K. Park. He knew I was looking to open my own school and since he had to leave his school behind in Winter Park, Florida, to go back home to New Jersey, he gave me a call and asked me if I could take over his school. I hopped on the first plane down to Florida, my heart racing a thousand miles a second. This was it, this was the opportunity I came to America for, and I was about to finally get it.

When I arrived at Master Park's school, he gave me some advice: If I wanted to have a successful school, I should open my own school in nearby Orlando instead of using this location. I thought it over…I was diving into an even more dangerous unknown with no safety net to break my fall. I asked myself if it was worth taking such a risk. Owning my own school and teaching the martial arts full time was my dream, and I would do whatever it took to make that dream finally a reality. So I took all the money I saved and opened my first martial arts school in America. Once the school opened, Senior Master Park sent me his ten students, who now made up my first core class. My dreams were finally beginning to take shape.

Owning a martial arts school was financially draining. After paying deposits for rent, utilities, and office equipment, my savings were depleted. Although I had total confidence in my teaching abilities, I knew little about running a business.

However, my excitement exceeded all of my worries. I loved teaching so much that I didn't mind sleeping on the floor at the school, showering with a hose outside of the school at night, or drinking only water because I had no money for food.

I learned the hard way that enthusiasm could only carry a person so far. The due dates for my bills crept closer while my pockets stayed empty. Soon I would have to pay them, but with what? I couldn't tell bill collectors, "Hey, I'm a struggling martial arts master. Please don't charge me for your services." I knew if the bills didn't get paid that the phone would stop ringing, I would be teaching class in the dark with no water to drink or shower with, and my landlord would evict me. I was desperate and looked for solutions everywhere, even bookstores and libraries, for that one book that would teach me how to run a business. I found nothing. My dreams were being crashed by reality. I realized running a business would be a problem I'd have to solve on my own.

I searched everywhere for the answers to all of my financial problems, but none were to be found until I was walking outside of the school, and I suddenly realized that the solution to all of my problems might be right under my nose.

There were lots of restaurants all around my school. Some had lines forming around the block waiting to get in, while others had few to no customers at all. Why were some of these restaurants struggling? How could I get long lines of people to wait to get into my school? I figured the best way to get these answers was to visit as many restaurants as humanly possible, visiting 36 of them during my research.

There were huge differences in the restaurants I visited. The busy ones were very clean, had great food, and great service. The restaurants that were slow or empty had bad food, bad service, and/or they were just disgusting. I also noticed how the attitudes of the owners and managers reflected the kind of restaurants they ran. Busy restaurants had positive owners and managers, while the slow or bad restaurants had owners and managers with negative attitudes.

However, there was one new restaurant that puzzled me. It had great food and service, and it was clean to boot, yet, few people frequented it. I asked the manager why this great restaurant was so empty, and he told me the owner spent nothing on advertising. Because of this lack of advertising, hardly anybody knew about the place. That was it: advertising was the answer!

Like that good restaurant, my martial arts school offered the best instruction but had few students. As I learned from my research, offering the best of anything doesn't matter if no one knows about it. I realized that I needed to advertise the school in order to drum up much needed students, but I didn't have the money to put it all together. I thought I was doomed.

Fate smiled on me when a couple of students paid their monthly lesson fees early, and I used that money for advertising. I knew that if I spent money on food instead of advertising, it would be impossible to sign up new students. I told myself a thousand times that my martial arts school would never close down, no matter the cost. I quickly figured out that the cheapest way to advertise the school would be through a flyer.

Luckily, one of my students helped me write and design a flyer. At this point, the only way I could get my flyers out there was with my feet because I had no transportation. So at night, I walked all over town, sometimes more than 15 miles at a stretch, distributing my fliers, hanging them on lampposts, walls, electrical poles, anything that could hold a flyer had one on it. After I was finished, every muscle in my legs and feet throbbed. I would grab a couple of hours of sleep at the school before teaching my morning class. This routine was killing me, but I knew I needed to press on.

All my efforts seemed for nothing. No one was responding to the flyers, which just added to the crushing financial pressure I felt. I knew that if the bills weren't paid, I would lose the school. I couldn't figure out what was wrong. Maybe the flyers were misprinted. Maybe I put them in the wrong place. Maybe the flyers just didn't look all that interesting.

I pictured what was needed to make my flyers stand out. All of a sudden, I remembered another flyer I saw that promoted a grand-opening special free gift when people brought in the flyer. That's it! I needed to do the same thing. I decided to print new flyers that would offer a grand-opening free trial lesson from my school to lure prospective students in. So when a few more students paid their lesson fees, I took that money and printed my new grand-opening special flyer.

I was hanging one of these new flyers on a street pole in downtown Orlando one Sunday morning when a police patrol car stopped me. My heart began thumping. Beads of sweat trickled down my face. Terror and fear crept up in my chest as the police officer got out of his car and walked towards me. "Oh no, it's the police. Please don't let them take my flyers down. Please don't let them arrest me," I thought to myself. I was scared to death. These flyers were like my life's blood.

So the policeman walked over, looked at my flyer, took one, and left without saying a word. I was so relieved that I celebrated by hanging flyers on every corner of the downtown area. The next day, that policeman came to my school and signed up for a class. These new flyers were finally working.

Thanks to the new flyers, the phone was ringing at last. However, I had no idea what to say because of my lack of English. I asked one of my students for his help in writing a detailed phone script that guided me on the right way to receive calls. After it was done, I memorized it until I knew it by heart. Now, people were making appointments to come in or asking me where the school was instead of hanging up on me.

The rush of new students became just too much even with my new phone skills. I still had problems talking face to face with other people at the school. I had to learn quickly or all this new business would slip through my fingers. Luckily, another student came to my aid and helped me develop a presentation sheet for potential students.

Thanks to all of my students' help, I no longer worried about paying the bills. Tenacity helped me triumph. For the first time living in America, I could finally fully concentrate on teaching class and my mind was at ease.

Now that the bills were getting paid, I began to expand my dreams. Because the martial arts had changed my life in so many ways, I believed that they could change other people's lives and that if other people changed their lives, they could change the world. With this dream in mind, I set a new goal: Build a martial arts university in America that would mold future world leaders. However, my vision needed a foundation, which would be to change the way the public saw the martial arts.

At the time, Americans viewed martial arts as violent because of how they were seen in movies and on TV. I could speak from personal experience as people greeted me with kicking or punching gestures when they saw me outside of the school. To change that image, I would teach my students the true meaning of martial arts through action philosophy:

- ❖ To achieve physical, mental, moral, financial, and life fitness.
- ❖ To build the personal power that makes people leaders and great public speakers.
- ❖ To build the winning habits that make people healthier, stronger, smarter, richer, happier, and more successful, leading to inner peace.

Once I established this action philosophy of the martial arts, I realized the best way to change how the public perceived the martial arts was through community involvement. I looked for local organizations that needed help, and the one that broke my heart was the orphanage. How could I help all of those poor children? It didn't take long to find the answer: Put on a martial arts exhibition for charity.

However, putting on an exhibition for charity wasn't going to be easy. I knew I couldn't do it alone, so I turned to my students and fellow instructors to help produce this event. To my surprise, the other instructors didn't share my vision. They told me, "You're just an instructor, not a promoter. How are you gonna get a big enough crowd to fill a gym? Forget it. Quit dreaming!" in between their laughter. They pretended I knew it all, saying "Yes, Master Kim. You can do it, Master Kim." I could hear the edge of sarcasm in their voices, but I ignored them. I refused to let their comments and jokes get to me, and I moved forward with the exhibition.

The exhibition was getting closer. Though local newspapers, radio stations, and especially local CBS affiliate WCPX-TV 6 (now WKMG) supported this charitable event, ticket sales were still very very slow. Then Charley Reese, at the time one of the most respected columnists of *The Orlando Sentinel,* wrote a column about the event, putting his support behind it. Once that column got published, the phones wouldn't stop ringing and the tickets wouldn't stop selling. In the end, all of this hard work was satisfying when my exhibition team and I walked into the Rollins College gymnasium in Winter Park on Saturday, May 30th, 1981 and saw a standing room only crowd. This event was so successful that we did it annually.

As my martial arts school began attracting more and more students, my facilities couldn't keep up with the demand. The following year, I moved to a building that was four times bigger. Even with the increased amount of space, I still couldn't accommodate all of these new, incoming students. Every inch of the school was filled. I had to move to a new location. So I scouted the area for a bigger building and couldn't find one for rent close enough to the existing school. Instead, I searched for land and discovered a plot big enough to build a new school.

Once I decided that building a new school was the way to go, I told my students and instructors that I was building a new school. I didn't hear, "Wow, that's a great idea." I heard, "How are you going to buy the land? You have no capital, credit, or collateral. How are you going to get a loan?" Their lack of faith didn't slow me down. My students desperately needed a bigger school, and I was determined to get it.

I went to the bank for a loan, waded through a lot of paperwork, and accommodated all of the bank's requests. Shortly thereafter, I received a letter from the bank and I thought, "Finally, I can build my new school." When I opened it, I read that the bank had rejected my request. I reapplied 11 more times and was rejected each time.

After being rejected the 12th time, I invited one of the vice presidents of Sun Bank to my martial arts school. After he watched one of my classes, I told him someday, I would buy his bank and that my school wasn't going to fold unless America did. Sun Bank then approved my loan.

Construction on the new school began in 1981 and was finished a year later. The new school was 7,000 sq. ft, double the size of the previous school, and the students were very happy. However, this new building quickly reached maximum capacity because my students brought more students, who brought even more. I opened a second location—a 14,000-sq. ft school—and filled that one up right away as well. I thought to myself, "How can things get any better?"

With the school doing great and all of my financial worries laid to rest, I was finally ready to face head on an obstacle that had been daunting me since I arrived in America: my lack of English. I knew that by improving my English, I would become a better communicator, thus becoming a better instructor. I decided the best way to improve my English was to write a Tae Kwon Do textbook for my students. When other instructors heard of my project, they thought I was insane. "How can someone who barely knows English, write a textbook in English?" they asked.

With the help of my students and five Korean-English dictionaries, my Tae Kwon Do World textbook was published in 1982. Writing the textbook was the hardest thing that I had ever done.

Then I noticed all this hard work didn't just improve the way I wrote, but the way I spoke and interacted with other people. I was full of energy, passion, and enthusiasm when I talked. I was filled with so much confidence because I could finally say what I wanted to in English. This new confidence helped me as I eventually began speaking in front of large groups of people in promoting the martial arts to the public.

Being able to speak English better gave me so much confidence that I begged for challenges that would let me show off my skills. Then I thought how I could use my English skills to promote the martial arts and the answer hit me: on TV and in movies. I realized by using the power of TV and movies, I could promote the martial arts to a massive amount of people in a short amount of time. This belief led me to my first ever weekly TV show, called Y.K. Kim's Practical Self-Defense, which aired in 1983. Even though it lasted six months, I still wanted so much more.

Then, a Korean independent filmmaker named Richard Park contacted me. Park had seen me being interviewed and performing an exhibition of my skills on Korea's most famous talk show. Park wanted to make me a martial arts action movie star but needed my help in producing the low-budget feature film he wanted me to star in. I didn't know anything about making a film but visions of red carpet premieres, spotlights, and my name up in big letters on the marquee danced through my head: Y. K. KIM, Action Hero. I liked the sound of that. I announced to Central Florida that production of an action movie called Miami Connection would start in 1985.

As with all of my ideas, everyone in Orlando thought I was nuts. In fact, many of my friends begged me not to make this movie, saying it was incredibly risky, and it would destroy everything I've worked hard for. Whenever someone tells me I can't do something, I just want to do it more so I started the film anyway. This movie was not only going to let me show off my years of experience and technique to the world, I was going to be a big time action star and producer, while helping my students and the martial arts on a global scale, just like Bruce Lee and Chuck Norris did before me. I was going to be famous.

HOWEVER, ALL OF my visions of fame and fortune began fading away once we started pre-production. When Park saw that my students and the community were more than willing to support the making of Miami

Connection, he started having more grandiose thoughts. His budget requests became way more than anticipated. He no longer wanted a low-budget film. Park wanted a big blockbuster. I said that it was a great idea, but I was worried I wasn't going to be able to keep up with his needs. I started having this nagging feeling that I was being taken advantage of. I shook that feeling off

> Risk is the most courageous thing anyone can take.

and did my best to accommodate all of his requests and kept signing the checks. I had no idea how to make a film, and I was so scared that without him and a lot of money, it would not be completed. Our original budget of $35,000 was drying up quickly and with so much money put into pre-production itself, there was little to no money for casting.

Production of *Miami Connection* started and right away we ran into problems. Our location choices didn't fit the director's needs, which sometimes left us little time to find a new location. The change of location then created scheduling problems. We didn't have enough time to inform the actors and extra crew of the change in location, forcing us to proceed without one of the main actors, sufficient extras, or the necessary props. Park changed his mind on everything almost every day because of his grand vision of making a big-budget action blockbuster. All of this chaos drove me crazy. Our filming schedule was so unpredictable that I was forced to use hundreds of my students as extras and as most of the film crew. The only professionals from Hollywood that were around to film the movie were the director, cameramen, special effects man, and special assistant director.

> When you don't plan, you plan to fail.

WE HAD FILMED some motorcycle scenes with cooperation from motorcycle aficionados—professionals who are weekend riders—and real bikers. All the bikers did as I asked, creating fantastic scenes for the movie. The hundreds of motorcycles and motorcyclists gave the film a huge look, pleasing the director and film crew.

After wrapping up the shoot, the director decided he wanted some more footage of the bikers inside the bar having some drinks and mingling around. So, we all went into the bar and followed Park's directions. We filmed people drinking and mingling, and after a while, their attitudes were changing. Sensing trouble, I told Mr. Park that we needed to leave because this situation was getting dangerous. He was unfazed, saying he wanted more scenes.

My instincts were dead on. With all the drinking going on, I saw that the real bikers were becoming surly, with some even hurting our crew with knives, and others wielded guns. It looked like there was going to be a brawl. My thoughts screamed, "Do something now! Do something now! If people got hurt, the movie could be shut down and we could go to jail." So, I jumped onto the stage, grabbed the microphone, and I praised everybody's contribution to the movie with great passion and sincerity. Everyone calmed down and paid attention. Once everyone settled down, we got out of there and didn't look back. Very fortunately, my actions prevented what could have been a major battle. We left and took a collective sigh at our good fortune.

I did my best to keep the movie rolling along. I borrowed money, found actors, sought out new locations, brought in hundreds of extras, had food catered, and arranged for more props when necessary. In addition, I was acting and preparing for out-of-town filming, which proved to be the costliest of our tasks. Moving a huge film crew and equipment, gaining a permit for a location, finding extras and working with nighttime filming proved extremely challenging. Working with the director was equally difficult. Because Park spoke mostly Korean, I had to be his translator because his English was very weak. In all, I felt like I had to do the jobs of 10 to 20 people.

The film's numerous problems brought me to the brink of personal and corporate bankruptcy. I had to face too many unexpected obstacles almost every minute. My assets were literally dried up. By the middle of filming, I had no company funds to draw on and nowhere else to turn. I was totally broke.

Miami Connection became a physically exhausting nightmare, so nightmarish that I couldn't close my eyes for a whole week sometimes. However, the lack of sleep didn't stop me. I kept going. I had to prepare for the film, day and night. My careless sleeping habits caught up with me the morning after a night shoot. Having had little sleep, I drove around looking for a new location and was so tired that I ended up in a ditch. I didn't realize how lucky I was not to get seriously hurt.

To tell you the truth, there were so many obstacles during filming that I wanted to stop making the movie a million times. It was just too hard, but I couldn't stop even if it killed me, because I vowed to my students and the city's residents that this movie would be put in movie theatres, no matter what the cost. Finishing this film was entirely left to my mind, not my wallet. Even if I lost everything that I achieved, my mind would never be bankrupt. As long as I didn't give up mentally, the money would always come back. I promised myself that I would finish, even if I lost everything.

FORTUNATELY, my students, and especially my wife, helped me through this crisis. Without my wife's help, I wouldn't have been able to finish the movie. We had just gotten married when I started *Miami Connection.* Making the movie was hard on her because she felt like she lost her husband almost immediately, but when I was exhausted, my wife stood by my side and did her best to support me. Without her help, as well as the assistance I received from my students and the community, there was no way I could have finished the film. With their help, I pushed on until the film wrapped. The seven-month project felt like a 70-year ordeal. Then we were off to Hollywood for editing and mixing.

> Without obstacles, there are no goals.

Unfortunately, the editing and mixing were awful and made *Miami Connection* even lower than a B movie. There was one good thing about the movie, the action. The action was great.

With the movie in hand, I traveled to Hollywood and met with film companies in the hopes of selling it. I started with the Hollywood people who helped make Bruce Lee, Chuck Norris, and other martial artists famous. At the time, the president of 20th Century Fox tried helping us as much as possible because his son was a Tae Kwon Do student. Unfortunately, he was unable to help us sell the movie.

So I pressed on and showed the film to the other four major Hollywood distribution companies: Universal, Warner Brothers, MGM, Paramount, and to about 30 other distribution companies. Every single company that saw *Miami Connection* said it was garbage and I shouldn't waste my money or time in continuing to sell it. Hearing these things was a big disappointment.

Then, a student and I went to the Cannes Film Festival in France and rented a theater so we could show the movie to an industry audience. We got the same feedback that Hollywood offered up. The film wasn't worth buying, which was another crushing setback, making me feel like the movie was a bust. I wondered how could I face my students and wife with such bad news.

I decided to try again by calling a couple of distribution companies. Fortunately, one company informed me that if I fixed the movie, it might be possible to sell it. Eventually, I made a verbal contract with Menson International Distribution Company in order to borrow some money privately and finish the film. I guaranteed to pay them back once the film was finished and distributed. I also bought a "how-to" book on making movies, and with one of my student's help I rewrote the script, having realized that the original version had no script! Park had gone back to Korea, having re-edited the film in Korean, so I was on my own.

With my students' help, we re-filmed, re-edited, and mixed the movie again. I went back to Hollywood with the new product in hand,

and finally the distribution company agreed to distribute the movie to the world. Thanks to them, I barely managed to pay off the private loan.

With the movie now in international distribution, I had one last big hope to open *Miami Connection* in the U.S. I had to ask for one of my student's financial support so that we could book ten movie theaters throughout Central Florida because there was no interest in the film's domestic distribution. However, there wasn't enough money for advertising. So instead I woke at 5 a.m. everyday and promoted the movie through news interviews at local TV stations, radio station interviews, newspapers and magazines, morning, noon, and night. It was like the way I used to promote my school, except on a grander scale. I also did several live promotions, signed autographs and shook hands at martial arts exhibitions.

Miami Connection finally opened on August 26, 1988.

I had a huge movie premiere in a local theater in Orlando with my students, community leaders and the media in attendance. Though the movie was successfully opened in the ten theaters we booked, the expenses exceeded ticket sales, so we received no return on the investment. Finally, the long epic that was *Miami Connection* had come to an end.

In the end, my critics were right. I lost almost everything that I had accomplished and ended up in debt, but I never regretted making the film because it taught some very valuable, but expensive, lessons. My original budget for the film was $35,000, but the film ended up costing more than 30 times that amount. I am not proud of what I went through, but not ashamed, either. I wish I could have controlled the end result of the movie's release, but nobody can do that. I was lucky to have good students and a good community behind me the entire time. I appreciate and owe my students and the entire Central Florida community for helping me finish the film.

WITH *Miami Connection* finally over and done, I was ready to get back to doing what I did best, teaching and promoting the school full-time. However, I immediately noticed that a whopping two-thirds of my students were no longer with the school. Getting them back wasn't a problem. Even though I didn't know how to make an Academy Award winning movie, I knew I could bring back all of my old students and bring in even more new ones, as well.

The one good thing about the *Miami Connection* experience was that it gave me so many new ideas that could be incorporated in the school's promotions. With a lot of hard work and the help of a tremendous promotional campaign, the old students came back and even more new students came along with them. After rebuilding the school, I used more of my newfound experience to produce instructional and exercise videos for the students so they could practice and exercise at home, as well. The school was doing great again.

> Breaking out of the box is painful, but it's worth it.

IT WAS BECAUSE I had a reputation for having a successful school that instructors around the country always visited my school during their vacations, and we shared martial arts related ideas. Some instructors came to Orlando just to seek out my advice on business, which made me busier and busier. I wanted to help all of them, but I couldn't keep up with the rush. I couldn't handle all of these instructors looking for answers. I already had enough on my plate between teaching class, managing, and promoting the school.

So I thought deeply on how to handle all of their problems and these instructors reminded me of what happened after I came back from finishing my movie. I thought to myself, "The school had lots of good instructors while I was involved in making the movie. Why did I lose so many students? How did this happen?" I had to come up with a better business structure for the school so that even if something horrible happened to me, it would run as usual. Then I realized that the structure I created for my school would also be really good for the entire martial arts industry.

So I sought out the help of my business partner, Master Tim McCarthy. We organized a business manual and rewrote it as a book and a business package called *Success in Martial Arts Business,* which consisted of six full training audiocassettes, two full-length basic and advanced business-training videos. This package was based on my successes, failures, and additional research. I was proud to create something that I believed the martial arts industry has needed for a long time.

Once it was released, I figured the best way to promote *Success in Martial Arts Business* was to set up a national seminar tour. I expected everyone in the martial arts industry to welcome me with open arms, and accept these new management and marketing business ideas to promote their schools. However, my ideals were totally different from reality.

On the road, I saw that half of the schools were pro-business in the way they ran their martial arts schools while the other half were anti-business, believing the martial arts shouldn't be tainted by business and money. Some instructors were so enraged by my presence that I was slapped, spit on, even threatened with extreme violence and death. I was accused of disgracing the honor of the martial arts, many asking if I had a "death wish." They hoped by threatening me, I would stop my seminars. I totally understood their point of view, but how pure can the martial arts be if the bills can't be paid, and the schools get shut down? I had a very tough time until the industry realized that I was promoting a new martial arts business movement, which would help the industry, not destroy it. Eventually, they finally began embracing it and together, the martial arts industry turned itself around. I continued promoting and lecturing all over the country, eventually expanding this new movement into Canada, and my homeland of Korea.

My seminar tour was unforgettable. I met so many great leaders in the martial arts industry, all of whom were doing well for their respective communities, and I learned many valuable lessons. These experiences taught me that the future of this industry was very bright.

After ten years of putting on these seminars, I was perplexed because I told every participant that if they used this successful format, they would have a successful school, yet some did not achieve the results I described. I knew that all of the instructors I encountered had the potential to succeed. So why were many instructors living out their dreams as successful martial arts business leaders, while others still suffered as they worried about paying the bills every month, forcing some to close their schools? I wondered if I was doing anything wrong. No matter whom I spoke to, where I went, or what day I was speaking, I was delivering the same information at all of my seminars. Still, these facts didn't negate my concerns. To find the answers, I visited more schools in various cities.

The first few schools I visited were doing really well. Their instructors had very impressive titles—some of them were Olympic-medal winning coaches. Because of their success, I thought maybe martial arts schools needed impressive titles, degrees, and awards in order to succeed. As I continued visiting more schools, I was surprised to see schools were doing very well, while their instructors didn't have any impressive titles, degrees, or awards. Sometimes, these instructors had schools that weren't in good locations, which was even more baffling.

Then, I met instructors who disappointed me. Despite having impressive titles, advanced degrees, or schools in excellent locations, their schools were failing, which was so puzzling to me. After doing some thinking about why some schools failed where others succeeded, I found the answers. I believe these answers applied to success in all fields, not just martial arts schools.

All the failing schools had instructors who were:

- ❖ **LAZY.** They constantly sat around and procrastinated, hesitated to do anything, and hated to work hard and smart.
- ❖ **NEGATIVE.** They spent their time making up excuses, blaming others, or complaining, showing they were not focused on their school.
- ❖ **IGNORANT.** They were close minded, never tried improving themselves or their school and/or they thought small and spent big by accumulating too many liabilities and not enough assets, buying big houses, luxury cars, and other things they could not afford.
- ❖ **FEARFUL.** They were afraid to do anything and even when they tried something, if they met an obstacle, they just gave up.

On the other hand all of the instructors at successful schools had:

- ❖ **PASSION.** These instructors were positive, totally focused, and unwavering in their dedication to their schools and students, loving the martial arts unconditionally.
- ❖ **CONFIDENCE.** These instructors weren't afraid to work hard and smarter to achieve their goals. They also saw obstacles as temporary and always managed to find solutions, never giving up until they were overcome.
- ❖ **LEADERSHIP ABILITY.** These instructors thought big, spent wisely by acquiring assets (income), and avoided creating liabilities (unnecessary expenses). They also remained consistent, kept an open mind in learning new things, and constantly looked for ways to improve themselves and their schools.

I thought I could make anyone successful no matter who they were; I was totally wrong. All I could do was share my experience, coaching these instructors on how to use a successful business format while motivating, energizing, and supporting them. I realized that I could only show them how to proverbially fish the proper way. No matter how

good the bait is, it's the fisherman that still has to go out there and make the effort to catch the fish. In other words, I couldn't make a difference if an individual doesn't have the desire to succeed, or if he or she focused on the wrong things.

Even though we are all special and have the potential to succeed, we must make the choice to succeed in life.

What is success? What does it mean to succeed? Let's find out what the right answers are together.

What Defines Success?

There were people that I thought appeared to be very successful, but in actuality, they were miserable. Then there were people I thought to be unsuccessful, yet they were incredibly happy and satisfied with their lives. Then, I saw a third group of people who appeared to be successful by everyone else's standard but were still looking for more success. I asked myself, "What really defines success? How do we know when we are successful?"

If you ask other people what defines success, you will get varying answers, depending on their age, education, where they live, values or culture. I believe the principles of success are always the same.

Based on my experience and research, to be truly successful you must have a balance between internal success (peace and health) and external success (relationships, financial freedom, and sharing.) The following are what I believe to be the five areas that define success:

❖ **PEACE OF MIND.** Peace of mind brings happiness. Happiness comes from peace of mind, and our purpose in life is to be happy. If your heart and mind are constantly anguished, then you can't say you are successful, no matter how rich, famous, or powerful you are. When you have peace of mind, your mind is at ease, allowing you not only to go about your day worry free but also be able to sleep peacefully so you can wake up with even more hope and energy. By having peace of mind, you have achieved the ultimate form of internal success.

- ❖ **HEALTH.** Health is the foundation of success in life. Health is the most important thing in life. Even if you own the world, without good health it means nothing. If you don't have health, you can't say you are successful.

- ❖ **PERSONAL RELATIONSHIPS.** Personal relationships give life meaning. Relationships balance our lives on many different levels. First, if you love, believe in, and understand yourself, you will have a great relationship within you, allowing you to lead yourself and become successful. If you doubt yourself, hate yourself, or don't understand who you are, you won't be able to lead yourself, allowing someone else to take control of your life, thus becoming a failure. Second, if you get along with and care for your family, co-workers, and other people, then your life will be balanced and wonderful. If your family, co-workers, or other people hate you, or don't want to associate with you, your life will be unbalanced and miserable. Good relationships, with yourself and with others, are a bridge to success in life.

- ❖ **FINANCIAL FITNESS.** Money cannot buy happiness, but it is a practical tool in life. Money can't buy peace of mind, health, and good personal relationships, but a lack of it can destroy them; financial pressure creates a lot of stress. You have no reason to be poor and have financial pressure. If you don't have financial fitness, which is financial freedom, you can't say you are entirely successful. How important is financial fitness? It will give you every practical tool needed to lead a successful life.

- ❖ **HELP OTHERS TO SUCCEED.** Real success means sharing with others. If you don't like sharing with others to help them succeed, you can't say you are successful because people hate to associate with selfish people. Why?

We all want happiness and, in fact, more of our happiness comes from others than from ourselves. Therefore when we make others happy, we make ourselves just as happy. If you can help others to succeed by sharing your success, you are a truly successful person. However, sharing involves more than just giving money to others; it also involves sharing your experience, knowledge, heart, and time. Real success is the balance of internal and external success.

Now that we know what success is, it's time to learn how to attain it.

THINK BIG

Success begins and ends with how you think because how you think is what you will be. If you think small, you will be small, limiting yourself. However, if you think big, you will be big, giving yourself the opportunity to succeed in life.

Look at Bill Gates and George W. Bush. Bill Gates was just another college dropout until he made his company, Microsoft, work. Once he built Microsoft Windows, he not only became the richest person in the world but also redefined its technological landscape. Bill Gates changed the world because he thought big. George W. Bush looked just like the average Joe, nothing special, but Bush became the most powerful person in the world, the President of the United States of America, because he thought big.

> The size of your thoughts reflects the size of your life.

LET ME ASK YOU THIS: What's the difference between you and Bill Gates or George W. Bush? They each have eyes, so do you. They have brains, so do you. There is nothing different between you and them, except that they thought big.

You don't have to strive for money and power to think big. When I make this statement, I think of a woman named Joan. A friend of mine hired Joan years ago as a temp secretary, and she was very overweight. It was hard for Joan to find a job because of her size. When she got the temporary position, she felt incredibly lucky and did her best for her new company. With this positive energy infused in her, Joan began thinking big and it changed her life.

First, Joan thought about what was holding her back. It was so obvious—it was her weight. Joan decided right away to lose weight by setting weight loss goals, putting her plans into action, and fighting even after she achieved her weight loss goals to maintain them. At the same time, Joan also put in 100% of her energy into her work. She not only became the best secretary in the company, but Joan studied and researched ways to improve the company she worked for. She began to know more than the executives she worked under. With all of her new knowledge, Joan was able to make suggestions that proved valuable to her company, which helped her get promoted time and time again. After losing all of that weight and becoming an important executive in her company, Joan finally discovered who she really was. All of these things happened for one reason: Joan changed her way of thinking and she thought big.

When you change your thinking, you can change your body. When you change your body, you can change your mind and your heart. When you change your mind and your heart, you can change your life. However, only you can change the way you think. When you change your thinking to big, success will be easy.

SUCCESS IS EASY

Please ask yourself the following questions:

1. Am I a success, a failure, or in the middle?

    If you think you are a failure, or even in the middle, please ask yourself, "Why?"

2. Am I strong, weak, or in the middle?
3. Am I positive, negative, or in the middle?
4. Am I intelligent, stupid, or in the middle?
5. Do I have good relationships, bad relationships, or somewhere in the middle?
6. Am I rich, poor, or in the middle?
7. Am I happy, unhappy, or in the middle?

There are three types of people in our society: those who are failures, those who are mediocre, and those who are successful.

In this chapter, I will show you how to be successful, how to be a failure, and how to stay in the middle. Success is your choice.

> *True success means you will have peace in your heart and cash in your hand.*

SUCCESS BEGINS and ends with thinking. If you think small, you will be small. If you think big and maximize your potential, success will be yours. It's that easy.

If success is so easy, then why hasn't everyone achieved it? Allow me to explain.

- ❖ Anyone who uses only 5% of his or her potential will become a failure.
- ❖ Anyone who uses only 20% of his or her potential lives an ordinary life.
- ❖ Anyone who uses more than 35% of his or her potential lives a successful life.
- ❖ Anyone who uses more than 50% of his or her potential leads a triumphant life, and helps others lead the same lifestyle, thus changing the world.

A Failure

Through psychological research and personal experience, I've determined that *people who use only 5% of their potential will be failures.* Such people fail because they are ignorant, lazy, negative, or fearful. They have no desire to succeed because

1. They don't know the meaning of dreams and goals; they don't know the importance of goal setting; they don't know how to set goals, and they don't know how to achieve goals.
2. They think small, focus on the wrong things, and hate to work. Whatever they start, they give up on, looking for excuses and blaming others, never achieving anything.

Ordinary Lives

Examining the research further, I've determined that *those who use only 20% of their potential lead ordinary lives,* because

1. They're afraid to work harder and smarter because they don't have dreams or vision.
2. Because they think small, they don't know the importance or impact of dreams and goals in their lives.
3. They stay "in the box" and never work outside of their comfort zone, refusing to do anything that will require hard work or that would cause pain, shying away from obstacles instead of trying to overcome them.

Successful Lives

People who use more than 35% of their potential lead successful lives because

1. They have positive goals, and no matter what comes in front of them, they never give up until they achieve their goals and make things happen.
2. They are not afraid to work harder, smarter and passionately, doing their best with love, as they believe in and take pride in what they are doing.

3. They think big, have an open mind, and never stop improving themselves.

Triumphant Lives

Finally, *people who use more than 50% of their potential lead triumphant lives.* They don't just become successful themselves. These people always build winning teams and help others to be successful, often becoming great leaders and help change the world. Triumphant people meet the same three categories as successful people do and:

1. They totally focus on their goals 24 hours a day, 7 days a week, eating, sleeping, breathing, and living with them. They are crazy about what they are doing.

2. They face any obstacle, no matter how insurmountable it is or how much pain it will involve to overcome it, always pushing themselves to the limit and going that extra mile to make things happen because they believe in their dreams and are far ahead of their time with their vision.

3. They share with others, motivating, energizing, and helping them to succeed.

Push the Limit

Now that you know what it means to use 5%, 20%, 35%, or more than 50% of your potential, allow me to show you why it is entirely your choice on how much of your potential you use.

Please go ahead, put the book aside, and try to do as many pushups as possible. If you can do 10, do 10. If you can do 20, do 20. If you can do 50 or more, do 50 or more (if you are in an airplane or a car, clench and unclench your fist 30, 50, 100, or 300 times based on your strength). Test yourself to see how far you can go and push yourself to do even more. I want you to do so many that you can't do any more pushups. Go ahead. The book won't go anywhere. I promise.

Done? Great.

- If you gave up when you started feeling uncomfortable, you didn't build any muscle at all. You can't get stronger if you don't build muscles. By giving up so soon, you show that you only use 5% of your potential and that you will be a failure in life.
- If you gave up when you started feeling a little pain, you built a little muscle, but it's still difficult for you to do anything. By giving in so quickly, you only used 20% of your potential, showing that you live an ordinary life.
- If you kept going until you fell, you will have stronger muscles, making it easier for you to do anything. By not giving up, you show you have used 35% of your potential and that you will lead a successful life.
- If you collapsed from the pain, tried another pushup right away, and kept trying until you were totally exhausted, not only will you build lots of muscle, but you will feel more energetic, confident, and that you can do anything. By pushing the limit, you show that you are using more than 50% of your potential, meaning that you will live and help others to live a triumphant life.

Striving for success is the same as doing push-ups. If you give up, you will never achieve anything in life. Only with great pain comes greater reward. Keep in mind that it is ok to fall down in life, but you have to get back up. If you stay down, you will go nowhere. If you get back up and keep going, you will achieve success.

Remember that history's most successful leaders fell spectacularly many times before they succeeded, but whenever they fell, they got right back up and kept reaching for their dreams, striving for real success. Look at Thomas Edison. He failed more than 17,000 times before he finally got the light bulb right. Also look at Abraham Lincoln. Every time he fell down, he got right back up and kept going until he became one of the greatest Presidents of the United States ever.

Don't keep yourself down. Always get back up and keep going, no matter the pain; it will be worth it in the long run.

WHY ARE SOME people able to use only 5% or 20% of their potential? What stops them from succeeding? They harbor the *four enemies of success*. Let's check out how we can eliminate them to build a successful life.

The four enemies of success are laziness, negativity, ignorance, and fear. Even though these are also enemies of other concepts in this book, they are very deadly against success. Remember: if you have the four enemies of success, anybody can beat you easily because you are weak from beating yourself. You have to fight against them and win to live a rich, powerful, and successful life.

1. LAZINESS. Be active to succeed.

2. NEGATIVITY. Focus on the positive to succeed.

3. IGNORANCE. Open your mind to success.

4. FEAR. Be courageous to succeed.

Laziness

As I mentioned earlier in The Four Wheels of Health, relaxation is important in recharging yourself, but relaxation can turn into laziness if you do it too much.

Laziness breeds the nasty habit of procrastination, making people postpone anything and everything to tomorrow, next week, next month, or even next year. Laziness infects people with a fear of hard work, blocking goal setting. Laziness then creates negativity, which causes stress; stress is not good for your health, and if you're unhealthy a lot, it's hard to be successful. In fact, I've never seen anyone who gets sick all the time have a successful life.

Laziness is your enemy, my enemy, and success's enemy. To eliminate laziness and be active, think big and start exercising today. When you exercise, you become more active, thus making yourself much more able to squash laziness.

Negativity

How dangerous is negativity? Negativity switches our focus to one that focuses on jealousy, hatred, destructiveness, pessimism, doubts, and complaints or criticisms. From these bad habits come anger, depression, and frustration that waste time, money, and energy.

Negativity makes people have a "No I can't" attitude instead of "Yes I can" attitude for success. They look for excuses and blame others instead of seeking solutions. Also, negativity creates low self-esteem and a lack of self-confidence, which causes people to disrespect and doubt others, making teamwork impossible.

Keep in mind that sometimes negativity can be good for us regarding opposing illegal, immoral, or other harmful acts and thoughts. However, negativity can destroy everything around us when it goes unchecked.

Turn your negativity into positivity by thinking, listening, talking, and acting positively, by setting and focusing on positive goals, associating with positive people, and by thinking big.

Ignorance

Although we as newborns have natural instincts (eating, drinking, self-preservation, etc.) we are born ignorant of much of the important and necessary things needed to survive and function in our world. In most cases, we can choose to learn or ignore the opportunity to educate ourselves.

When I talk about ignorance, I'm not referring to someone who lacks an academic education, but to a person that doesn't believe in continued self-education, which reflects a blocked mind. Sometimes, ignorant people assume that they're too smart to learn anything, and that also blocks many opportunities, which makes them even more ignorant.

We live in a very competitive society. Therefore, we must adapt and learn, or be cast aside. If we are ignorant, then we can't be competitive within society; and if we can't be competitive, we will have no future. Thus, learning is critical to survival. Once you have accumulated knowledge, it is yours; nobody can take it from you. Don't let ignorance keep you away from success. To eliminate ignorance and become educated, think big, open your eyes, ears, mind, and heart while you never, ever, stop educating yourself.

Fear

As I explained earlier, there are two types of fear in our lives, rational and irrational. Rational fear prevents us from doing something that may harm or kill us, which includes not putting our hands into an open flame or not walking across the street during rush hour. Rational fear also prevents us from committing illegal and immoral acts, such as using drugs and killing others. Rational fear, key to our self-preservation instinct, enables us to make correct decisions and keep ourselves alive. On the other hand, irrational fear crushes desire and hurts our potential to succeed.

In fact, there are several different kinds of irrational fear, fear that has no link to self-preservation or learned survival techniques. They are:

- Fear of the unknown.
- Fear of risk.
- Fear of failure.
- Fear of what others think.
- Fear of rejection.
- Fear of hard work.

Irrational fear can cause any of us to become self-defeating, creating within us a "No, I can't do this," attitude that turns us into quitters.

Unfortunately, irrational fears stay with most of us until we die, despite all of their consequences so they must be controlled, for they will stop you from reaching your full potential. Utilize your fears for your benefit. Don't let fear control you.

Control irrational fear by thinking big and believing in yourself to build self-confidence.

FEAR OF THE UNKNOWN

Why are most of us more comfortable walking outside during the day instead of at night? At night, it's dark outside. When it's dark, you can't see very well, and you don't know what you could trip over; where your next step might land, or if someone will come out of the shadows to attack you. Most people fear walking outside at night because it represents the unknown.

Most people are afraid of change because of their fear of the unknown, and that fear holds too many back from reaching their full potential. Believe it or not, expected and unexpected changes happen all the time: We can't survive or succeed without change.

MOST PEOPLE FEAR the unknown because they don't know how to handle it. The key is not allowing this fear to control us. We need to lead ourselves to change our lives.

Change the way you think. Don't think you need to change; think you need to improve; when you think this way, your fear will disappear, improvement becomes more positive, encouraging, and stable than the

> Confidence is the light that burns away the darkness of the unknown.

thought of change. If you still don't know what to do or how to do something, ask, study, and research to learn about what you need to improve. Most importantly, you need to think big and believe in yourself to build self-confidence to make controlling this fear even easier.

FEAR OF RISK

Risk is different from fear because we choose to take risks and they can be worthwhile or foolish, depending on the circumstances. We have all taken risks; sometimes they have paid off and sometimes they have gone awry.

A businessman will take a *worthwhile risk* by investing in a new business venture to improve and strengthen his business. Whether the businessman succeeds or fails is irrelevant. What's important is he took a chance on improving his business, instead of being afraid.

Then there is *foolish risk,* like gambling with the high rollers in Las Vegas or Atlantic City, where the player very rarely beats the house. Unlike the businessman, a gambler lacks confidence, is cocky, greedy, and addicted to the promise of making a quick buck.

The worthwhile risks are the ones we need to be concerned about. If nobody took these kinds of risks, we would still live in a primitive society.

One of the most important things that you can do to control the fear of risk is always to know the risks before you take them. If you know a risk has a reasonable chance of success, it's a worthwhile one that should be taken. Never take foolish risks, for they won't only hurt you, they will hurt others, too. Think big and believe in yourself to build the self-confidence that is needed to take worthwhile risks and avoid foolish ones.

FEAR OF FAILURE

Whether it's failing a test at school, trying to get our dream job, or even being the perfect parent, we all fail at one point or another. How we handle failure determines if we are afraid or unafraid of it. When we think of failure as a learning experience, we are unafraid of it. However, when we believe that nothing good comes from failing, then we fear it.

In fact, most of our greatest historical figures failed spectacularly before they eventually succeeded. Look at Thomas Edison. He failed more than 17,000 times before he finally got the light bulb right. Edison realized that failing was experience. Remember that failure precedes success in almost every circumstance.

The fear of failure is the biggest roadblock in setting goals. Many people, especially those who have failed already, struggle to set goals because of a fear of failure.

By refusing to give up, you give yourself a better chance to succeed because you already know what does and doesn't work. If you learn from a past failure, you can still achieve your goal. Also think big and believe in yourself to build self-confidence and help you learn from failure.

FEAR OF WHAT OTHERS THINK

Contrary to popular belief, what other people think of you is very important. As I stated earlier, 15% of our happiness comes from within, while the remaining 85% comes from others. The key, then, is to do the right thing so you don't fear what others think of you. If you think you're doing wrong to yourself and others, then stop what you're doing. If you think you're doing right by others, continue. You won't worry about what other people say or believe because eventually they will see that your actions are correct.

ALTHOUGH WHAT OTHERS think about you is important, what you think of yourself is even more important. So think big, respect others, and build good relationships with other people, but don't ever let them control your life for the sake of your own success.

> What others think of you is important, but what you think of yourself is more important.

FEAR OF REJECTION

The worst answer you could possibly receive is "no" when asking for something. However, if you fear rejection, you'll never ask for anything.

You will always wonder if you will or won't get what you want. Fear of rejection causes us to lose opportunities and puts a serious crimp into success. Simply, if you don't ask for something, you will never get it.

Also, never pre-judge other people's answers when asking for something. That isn't fair to you, or others. You have nothing to lose by asking for something.

Remember that you only live once. Think big, build your self-confidence and never let any opportunity slip through your fingers. Ask for what you need and see what happens. You might be pleasantly surprised.

However, you should never ask for anything that would be considered generally unrealistic, immoral, or harmful.

FEAR OF HARD WORK

When you fear hard work, you are afraid of putting in the time and effort necessary to make all of your goals and dreams come true. Nothing ever gets done without hard work. People who fear hard work are usually lazy or cowardly, and will never achieve success. If you fear hard work, your dreams will never come true.

Change your mindset through exercise because it will strengthen your mind so that you are unafraid of hard work. Also, learn to love yourself unconditionally. When you love yourself, you give yourself the positive energy needed to alleviate your fears of hard work and increase your self-esteem. Self-confidence will help you become the next successful leader in the world.

By working hard and working smart, you choose to be a success. As the old bodybuilding saying goes, "No pain, no gain." Think big, work smart, and hard to reach your dreams. All successful people are never afraid to work hard. In fact, they love it.

Now that you know what you need to fight against in achieving success, I will show you how to actually achieve success with the D.D.P.E. Way to Success.

The D.D.P.E. Way to Success!
You will enjoy reaching your dreams.

<u>D</u>esire. Success starts with desire.

<u>D</u>ecide. Making the right decisions is vital to success.

<u>P</u>repare. Preparation brings you closer to success.

<u>E</u>xecute. Execution of your plans actualizes success.

The D.D.P.E. method works for your personal, professional, financial, and life goals. It will help make your dreams come true.

DESIRE

Desire is "I want," pushing us to take the actions needed to make that desire into a reality. Without desire, there is no success.

However, no one can give you desire. You can be motivated and encouraged by others, but they have no power to give you desire; only you can choose to have it.

Where does desire come from? For the purpose of success, desire comes from vision, which is a positive mental picture of the future.

How does vision give you desire? Imagine that a second ago you didn't have the desire to eat, but after you saw your favorite food, suddenly you have the desire to eat. When you see a positive mental picture or vision of the future, you will have the desire to have it or achieve it.

In order to have vision, ask yourself: "Would you like to be rich and have a successful life?"

You have no reason to be poor and every reason to be rich. If you think this way, it will help you achieve your personal, professional, and family goals of success. Visualize that you can live in a beautiful dream house, that you can buy your dream car, that you can help your parents for the rest of their lives, and, if you have children, you can help them with their education. Visualize that you can go anywhere you want in the world on vacation and buy a beautiful vacation house, that you have your own jet, even visualize all the people you can help if you were successful enough. When you intentionally visualize these things, you will have vision, and from that create the desire to succeed.

Another way to have desire is to ask yourself what do you love to do? What makes you happy? What would you like to have or own in your life? Where and what would you like to be in 5, 10, or 20 years? Find these answers and use them as a gauge to determine what you want to do in your life. Doing so will help you find out what you love to do, and what you really want out of life. By doing all of these things, you will create vision. From vision comes desire.

However, desire itself is not enough to succeed. You have to have a strong burning desire to maximize your potential and succeed in life.

Why don't some people have desire? Some people don't have desire because they don't have vision and they don't have it because ignorance, laziness, negativity and/or fear have blinded them. With ignorance, these people won't know what they should be envisioning. When people are lazy, they lack the drive to make their visions real. Negativity stops their vision from appearing. Fear makes them afraid to act on their vision, which is why these people never had or lost their desire.

Always use the power of positive thinking for it will give you the strong burning desire to succeed that plants the seed of success in your life.

DECIDE

Desire is "I want." Decide is "I will do." Once you decide to do something, you are putting your desires into action; it is absolutely vital to being successful. Without making decisions, nothing can be started, therefore nothing happens in life. The greatest ideas in the world can't go anywhere without making decisions.

For example, pretend you're a high school senior who wants to go to college, but you can't decide which one to attend. What do you think will happen if you don't make a decision? Nothing. You'll be home with your parents in the fall, while the others are in college, furthering their education.

Now let's say you work in New York City and two important meetings come up in two different cities on the same day. In Los Angeles, there's a client you need to see for a very important business meeting; plus, you have to attend a special stockholder meeting in Chicago. The problem: you have to be at both meetings today. What would happen if you didn't make a decision? Nothing. Your indecisiveness will leave both business matters at a standstill.

Making decisions is where all success stories start. Look around you. Without decisions being made, you wouldn't be in the house you're living in. You wouldn't be able to drive the car in your driveway. You couldn't keep food fresh in your refrigerator. You wouldn't even be walking in the shoes that are on your feet. All of these things were somebody's brainchild at one point in time, but because they made decisions to make them, all of these things were created. Without decisions being made, nothing happens in life, period.

When you have decided to do something, you have figured out what your goals will be and what is needed to accomplish those goals. Keep in mind that there are two types of goals, positive and negative. A positive goal is one that can be achieved clearly only if there is a clear purpose and specific details on how to achieve that goal in mind. Positive goals are realistically attainable and personally beneficial, with the goal setter able to reap its rewards. A positive goal creates positive energy, guiding you in the right direction. A negative goal is unclear in purpose and in detail, unrealistic, and has no value. Negative goals create the negative energy that makes you fearful, discouraged, and frustrated. They lead you in the wrong direction while infecting you with bad habits. For the most part, negative goals are just wishes. You must set positive goals to be successful.

To set positive goals, you must believe in them. How do you believe in them? First, your goals must be clear in purpose. Then, they must be specifically detailed. Next, these goals should be realistically attainable. Finally, your goals should be beneficial and allow you to reap their rewards. The end results of taking these four steps is that setting positive goals becomes easy, giving you the confidence, energy, and hope needed to achieve your goals.

> Goals generate the direction, energy, and hope that motivate us to succeed

BELIEVING IN your positive goals is just as important as setting them. If you don't believe in your goals or think that you can't reach your goals, you won't reach them. You will be angry and frustrated instead of hopeful and energetic. Always make the effort to find a positive goal that's within your capabilities. By setting practical and reasonable positive goals, you will have a bright future.

Here's an example on how to set positive goals correctly.

Robbie needs a new car. How can he set positive goals?

1. He will clearly state the purpose of his goal.

    "Why do I need to buy a car? I need transportation to go to work."

    By establishing the purpose of his goal, Robbie will believe in it and generate positive energy toward achieving it.

2. He must provide specific details about his goal.

    "What kind of car will I buy? I will buy a brand-new Jeep 2004 model. How will I afford it? Its price is $17,000. I have to make a down payment of $1,700 and afford $400 monthly payments for the next 4 years."

This information makes the goal detailed, specific, and clear: what kind of car, new or used car, price of the car. If Robbie knows what is needed to prepare, he will be able to achieve his goal.

3. Robbie's goal must be realistically attainable.

"I will buy the new Jeep next month. How? I have $1,000 in my savings account, and I can save $700 within one month. I can handle car payments that run $400 to $500 a month.

This is a very realistic goal because he believes he can attain it.

4. He must outline the benefits of his goal, along with the personal rewards he will receive for fulfilling it.

"When I have a new car, I won't be late to work because I can depend on myself for transportation. I can help my family. I can pick up my girlfriend for dates. I will save time because I can make my schedule. Now I can hit the gym to get in shape and go back to finish my Masters in Business."

By knowing the personal rewards he will receive for achieving a goal, Robbie is more apt to set more positive goals in the future.

As the previous example illustrated, intangible and/or tangible personal rewards motivate us to set and reach goals. Such rewards help individuals, businesses, and even governments function adequately and efficiently because personal rewards strengthen us emotionally and spiritually, creating an unconscious support system that energizes and motivates us to strive for personal rewards. Would people try earning an advanced education if an elementary or middle school education allowed others to get the same kind of jobs with the same pay? No. Would pro sports teams strive for championships if they were worthless? No. Can you imagine businesses operating without personal reward?

No. Nobody works well without personal reward.

Nobody can stop you from setting positive goals if you believe in your goals and can see the personal rewards that can come from them.

LET'S LOOK AT the difference between setting positive and negative goals.

John is overweight and has a goal to lose 30 pounds in 15 weeks. He calculates that he needs to lose at least 2 pounds a week for 15 weeks to achieve that goal. In order to lose weight, he decides to stick to a structured diet and get plenty of exercise.

John's goal is positive because it is clear in purpose (lose 30 pounds in 15 weeks), specific and realistic, (lose at least 2 pounds a week for 15 weeks to achieve that goal; stick to a structured diet and get plenty of exercise), which makes his goal beneficial.

Jamie is also overweight and has a goal of losing 70 pounds in the next month. She talks to many friends about her goal, but continues to eat more junk food every day and has no real plans for losing the weight.

Jamie's goal is negative because it is unclear in purpose, not specific, and totally unrealistic. It is almost impossible to lose 70 pounds in a month unless she gets hospitalized with a serious illness or injury, and that kind of sudden weight loss is unhealthy. She will gain nothing from these goals meaning there is no benefit, except frustration and depression, among other things.

Tips for Setting Positive Goals

There are times that when you talk to people about your goals, they react badly, saying such things as, "That's impossible! You can't do it. Don't waste your time. You could lose everything." Even, "What kind of idiot are you?" When you hear these negative words, don't get discouraged. You won't achieve your goals if you get discouraged; do the following instead: don't tell anyone your goals unless you know for sure whomever you tell will support you and/or cheer you on.

Who would do such a thing to you? Could it be your friends? Even your family? Absolutely. Even family members can be discouraging. Think for a moment and I'm sure you've heard at least one family member try to discourage you from doing something at one point.

To prevent yourself from being discouraged by your family, don't tell them your goals, unless you know that they will support you 100%. You show respect for your family, prevent them from worrying and being unhappy by doing so.

At the same time, don't be discouraged or angered when others criticize your abilities. Why? Because it's better when someone is interested or concerned about you than it is for him or her not to care at all. Criticism can't damage your abilities because you are strong. Focus on your positive goals to achieve them, regardless of what other people say.

Finally, if anyone around you sets positive goals, please encourage, motivate, and praise him or her. When you praise him or her, it will also encourage and motivate you to set positive goals and help you achieve them.

Everyone has dreams and goals. We make our dreams come true by setting positive goals; goals are the steps to reaching for our dreams. Dreams are our destination and the road to them is paved with goals.

Let's work together now and write down our goals. I listed mine first and allowed space for you to fill in your goals, as well. You can make your dreams come true by setting positive goals.

PERSONAL GOALS

What is my personal goal?
To be the greatest public speaker in the world.

What is your personal goal?

_____

_____

_____

What is the purpose of my goal?
To change the world through my new way of thinking, which is a practical modern philosophy for self-improvement.

What is the purpose of your goal?

_____

_____

_____

What are my potential personal rewards?
Receiving the highest personal honors from the public that will directly help me build a martial arts university and promote martial arts to the world.

What are your potential personal rewards?

_____

_____

_____

How will I achieve my personal goal?
By planning and organizing well, always learning, practicing, executing my plans, and never giving up until my goals are achieved.

How will you achieve your personal goal?

_____

_____

_____

When would I like to achieve my goal?
In three years.

When would you like to achieve your goal?

_____

_____

_____

Family Goals

What are my family goals?
To fully provide for my daughter and son's education, preferably through Master's degrees; to build a dream house in the country to enjoy nature; and to travel around the world with my wife to learn more about the world, enjoy it, and utilize what I've learned daily.

What is your family goal?

_____

_____

_____

What is the purpose of my goals?
To provide a better future for my children, to learn about the world together with my wife, and to enjoy and promote true family happiness.

What is the purpose of your goal?

_____

_____

_____

What are my potential personal rewards?
A fatherly sense of pride, marital happiness and a worldwide education.

What are your potential personal rewards?

_____

_____

_____

How will I achieve my family goals?
Proper planning and saving money to support education and travel.

How will you achieve your family goals?

_____

_____

_____

When would I like to achieve my family goals?
Provide for my children's educational pursuits by the year 2007, and begin world travel by the year 2016.

When would you like to achieve your family goals?

_____

_____

_____

PROFESSIONAL GOALS

What is my professional goal?
To build a martial arts university.

What is your professional goal?

_____

_____

_____

What is the purpose of my goal?
To change the world, making it a better place to live.
The martial arts are the foundation of health and are
the best self-improvement program for all walks of
life.

What is the purpose of your goal?

_____

_____

_____

What are my potential personal rewards?
My dream becoming a reality. The martial arts university will become bigger than my life.

What are your potential personal rewards?

_____

_____

_____

How will I achieve my professional goals?
Through specific planning, fundraising, and building.

How will you achieve your professional goals?

_____

_____

_____

When would I like to achieve my professional goals?
In five years.

When would you like to achieve your professional goals?

_____

_____

_____

Write down your goals on paper and hang them in as many places as possible (office, kitchen, den, bathroom, etc.).

In order to achieve your ultimate long-term goals, you have to have weekly, monthly, seasonal, and yearly goals, and rewrite them whenever it is necessary.

Write down short-term goals. I have listed mine first, and have allowed space for you to fill in your goals, as well.

My weekly goal: Print convention booklet.

Your weekly goal:_____

My monthly goal: Publish magazine for February.

Your monthly goal: _____

My yearly goal: Publish yearly curriculum.

Your yearly goal: _____

By writing down goals, they become tangible and practical, whereas unwritten goals are merely wishes. Write down your goals to make things happen.

PREPARE

Preparation is a key to success. In order to achieve your goals, you must write down a clear and specific plan. A clear and specific plan is like a blueprint for a house or a map for finding a location. If you don't write out your plans, they will become easy to forget and disorganized; you will hesitate and doubt that you will achieve your goals.

In order to proceed with your plans, they must be well organized. Such preparation saves time, energy, money, reduces stress and convinces your unconscious mind that you can carry out your plans. You will enjoy going after your goals even more when you are prepared.

To prepare to achieve your goals:

1. **SET DEADLINES FOR YOUR GOALS.** Deadlines create a sense of urgency and help make things happen. If you don't set deadlines, you will slow down and may never finish your project or achieve your goal.

2. **WRITE DOWN SPECIFICALLY DETAILED PLANS REGARDING YOUR GOALS.** If you have a big goal, plan to achieve it in little steps instead of trying to accomplish it all at once. By breaking down your goal into phases, it becomes easier to achieve. Planning all of the specifics in detail will help you organize what you need along with setting a specific time schedule for execution.

3. **SET A SPECIFIC TIME SCHEDULE FOR EXECUTION.** To set a specific time schedule, organize it based on priority. Prioritizing your time will clear your mind for what is needed to prepare for execution. Without such a schedule, you will waste your time and energy.

4. **COORDINATE WHAT YOU NEED FOR EXECUTION.** Take inventory of your intangible and tangible skills, along with other useful details or talents that you may have to achieve your goal. If you don't have anything to offer or you need more than what you have, find useful tools from others and organize for execution.

5. **FIND ANY POTENTIAL OBSTACLES TO ACHIEVING YOUR GOALS AND DEVISE A PLAN TO OVERCOME THEM.** Every goal has an obstacle. Without obstacles, goals are not truly goals. Analyze these obstacles in order to prepare whatever is necessary to overcome them and achieve your goal.

6. **ORGANIZE FOR EXECUTION.** In order to execute your plan, you must organize your personal schedule to work effectively. If it's a big project, you can't do it alone. You have to organize and delegate responsibilities for execution.

7. **IF APPLICABLE, PRACTICE FOR EXECUTION.** Some of the goals you set may take all six steps to execute, but some may need one more: Practice for execution. For example, you need the six steps to plan for a trip or build a house but you can't practice either. However speeches, games, races, and even wars need planning and practice.

Example 1: Winning an NBA Championship (7 steps)

1. Set a deadline for your team goal of winning a NBA championship.
   - ❖ For example, we will have the championship title by June 20, 2004. (Today is June 6, 2003.)

2. Write down detailed plans regarding your goal.
   - ❖ Build up each team member physically and mentally with special training and nutritious food.

❖ Strengthen team building with leadership training.
❖ Get a nutritionist.
❖ Find a motivational speaker for leadership training.
❖ Strengthen shooting and defensive skills.

3. Set a specific time schedule for execution.
   ❖ Special physical and mental training starts August 10–August 30 6 hours a day, 6 days a week at the practice facility.
   ❖ Leadership training for team building starts August 10–August 30 2 hours a day, 6 days a week.
   ❖ Effective daily nutrition program begins August 10, 2003 and ends on June 20, 2004.
   ❖ Prepare to become a champion during the off-season.

4. Coordinate what you need for execution.
   ❖ Reserve a practice facility.
   ❖ Confirm all team members' schedules.
   ❖ Prepare all training equipment for training.
   ❖ Prepare nutritional food day-to-day and week-to-week.
   ❖ Hire a nutritionist.
   ❖ Invite a motivational speaker.
   ❖ Inform team members of new schedule.

5. Find any potential obstacles to achieve your goal and devise a plan to overcome them.
   ❖ Have a back-up plan in case a team member gets injured or gets sick.
   ❖ Keep motivating team members to prevent them from losing interest or breaking up the teamwork dynamic.
   ❖ Prepare emergency food in case players miss a nutritious meal.

6. Organize for execution.

❖ Organize everyone's schedule on the team to effectively delegate responsibilities.

7. Practice.

❖ Practice, practice, and practice for real action.

Example 2: Building a Dream House (6 steps)

Planning is critical in building a house. Without planning, you wouldn't know where to build, what licenses to show, what permits to attain, what materials you need, what sub-contractors or inspectors you need to hire, and how to handle any other problems that may come up during the course of construction. You can never achieve your goals without a plan.

Write a detailed list of everything you need to construct your home, and then check your list to make sure that you haven't forgotten anything. Rewrite your list if necessary so you will be prepared to achieve your goal. After you've finished, proceed through the following six steps to ensure that your goal of building a dream house is realized.

1. Set a deadline for your goal.

❖ For example, finish building a dream house by February 1, 2007 in Orlando (Today is February 1, 2004).

2. Write down detailed plans regarding your goal.

❖ French style house, 10,500 sq. feet, split plan, two stories, five-car garage, seven bedrooms, media room, practice room, recreation room, home office, and a swimming pool.

❖ Figure out how much land you need for the house and its accompanying structures (screened-in pool, pool house, sauna, gazebo, etc.), as well as for recreational use.

❖ Figure out how much capital you need to construct the house.

❖ Prepare all necessary paperwork for construction loan.

❖ Determine where you're going to build and contact appropriate real estate agency.

❖ Hire an architect and contractor for the job.

❖ Set construction deadline within the constraints of your loan, if applicable.

3. Set a specific time schedule for execution.
  ❖ Purchase the land by March 1.
  ❖ Have the blueprints by March 30.
  ❖ Hire a contractor by April 10.
  ❖ Secure the bank loan by May 1.
  ❖ Construction begins on May 15.

4. Coordinate what you need for execution.
  ❖ Determine where you're going to build and contact appropriate real estate agency.
  ❖ Purchase land.
  ❖ Hire an architect to prepare the blueprints.
  ❖ Hire a contractor.
  ❖ Figure out construction costs and prepare all necessary paperwork for construction loan (when you have seed money, which is 10% down payment).
  ❖ Find a bank to get the loan from.
  ❖ Set a construction deadline within the constraints of your loan, if applicable.

5. Find any potential obstacles to achieve your goal and devise plans to overcome them.
  ❖ Have a back up plan in case the bank says no to the loan.
  ❖ Have back up plans in case of rain during the construction.
  ❖ Have a back up plan in case the contractor cannot continue.

❖ Prepare emergency funds in case extra money is needed for construction costs.

6. Organize for processing.
   ❖ Organize personal schedule and delegation of your time.

EXECUTE

Once you put your plans and ideas into action and remain consistent until you've reached your goals, execution will actualize success. How do you execute your plans? Put your plans into action and focus 100% on your goals until you have accomplished them. Remember: the greatest ideas or plans in the world would never have been actualized unless they were executed.

There are three types of people regarding execution: watchers, quitters, and fighters.

❖ **WATCHERS.** These people always watch things happen and always ask, "What's happening?" Because they are too afraid or too lazy to start anything, or they can't start anything because they are ignorant. Even if they have an excellent plan, they're not in the game.

❖ **QUITTERS.** These people start well but whenever they meet any obstacle or hardship, they look for excuses to give up and blame others for their failure, embracing the negative instead of the positive.

❖ **FIGHTERS.** These people put their plans into action and make things happen, no matter what. They can fall down thousands of times and get back up right away thousands of times and still keep going; fighters never let failure intimidate them. They will pay any cost and never, ever give up until they win.

In order to be a fighter and achieve your goals after putting your plans into action, you have to eliminate the tendencies of failure and execute the following Seven Successful Habits.

With these Seven Successful Habits, you can now take what you have learned earlier throughout this book and apply it to your life so it becomes successful.

1. **THINK BIG AND ACT WISELY.** Success begins with thinking and action actualizes success.
2. **FIRE UP YOUR PERSONAL POWER.** Personal power is key to actualizing goals.
3. **PASSIONATELY FOCUS ON YOUR GOALS.** Passion will generate energy and focus will create a clear path for success.
4. **SAY "YES" TO ASSETS AND "NO" TO LIABILITIES.** Gain assets and eliminate liabilities to achieve lasting success.
5. **PRIORITIZE.** Prioritize your life to make each day productive.
6. **MAXIMIZE.** Fight until you win and go that extra mile to maximize your potential.
7. **HELP OTHERS TO SUCCEED:** To help others succeed makes your life triumphant.

HABIT ONE: THINK BIG AND ACT WISELY

In order to succeed, you have to be competitive. To be competitive, you have to think big and act wisely. When you think big, you gain a deeper understanding of yourself and others. Thinking big helps you discover what you want to do, making it easier to achieve your goals. It will give you vision, allowing you to see limitless possibilities, giving you hope for the future.

Acting wisely keeps you on the right path as you reach your goals, preventing you from committing the wrong kinds of actions that would throw you off the path of success. When you stay on the path of success, it also becomes easier to build and maintain a positive attitude. With a positive attitude, you become more likeable, and when you are more likeable, other people will support what you are doing, helping you even more stay on the path of success.

Always think big and act wisely to make the four enemies of success (laziness, negativity, ignorance, and fear) so incredibly small to you that you can act easily to defeat them, to have more energy towards achieving your goals, and to be competitive in the real world.

To think big and act wisely:

❖ Step out of your comfort zone.

❖ Open your eyes, ears, mind, and heart wide as you continue educating yourself.

❖ Associate with big thinkers.

❖ Set high goals. When you reach them, set your goals even higher.

HABIT TWO: FIRE UP YOUR PERSONAL POWER

The real world is very competitive. If you are competitive, you will survive and succeed, but if you aren't competitive, you will fail. The key to staying competitive lies in personal leadership, which is personal power. Physical, mental, and moral fitness are important to actualizing goals. After all, without personal power, you can't carry around all of your big thoughts and actualize your goals.

To fire up your personal power:

❖ Stick to The Four Wheels of Health (eat and drink wisely, exercise daily, recharge energy, and think positively).

❖ Think positively as you educate yourself.

❖ Build moral strength.

HABIT THREE: PASSIONATELY FOCUS ON YOUR GOALS

Whatever you focus on, you will become. If you focus on the positive, you will be positive, but if you focus on the negative, you will be negative. Therefore in order to stay positive about what you are focused on, you must visualize and talk about your goals.

By visualizing and talking about your goals, you are focusing on them 100%, which will keep your goals alive within you all the time.

This practice will give you physical and mental strength regarding your goal, along with infusing you with energy, enthusiasm, and passion. However, always use discretion in revealing your goals because there are people out there who are jealous of you, and those that are jealous of you are likely to criticize or discourage you from achieving your goals. Only discuss your goals with positive people who are goal-oriented, who will cheer you on and encourage you to achieve your goals.

However, focus isn't complete without passion. Passion is love, belief and pride in what you do. Your passion generates energy, enthusiasm, and focus, all making you the best at whatever you set out to accomplish. Passion also brings fun, excitement, and meaning into your life, helping you to have better results in whatever you do, motivating you and others. Success will be easy when you passionately focus on your goals.

To passionately focus on your goals:

- ❖ Write down your goals and put them where you can always see them.
- ❖ Constantly visualize, think, and talk about your goals.
- ❖ Eat, sleep, and breathe your goals.
- ❖ Make a habit of writing daily to do lists to maintain and strengthen your focus.
- ❖ Believe in and love your goals.

HABIT FOUR: SAY "YES" TO ASSETS AND "NO" TO LIABILITIES

In my consulting experience, I've seen three mistakes constantly being made by business owners.

1. They spend more than they make, regardless if their profit is higher than their expenses, putting themselves constantly in debt.
2. They buy a house with a huge mortgage and a luxury car with a high monthly payment to show off, even though they know they can barely afford them or can't afford them at all.
3. They start playing golf during business hours, showing that their priorities are totally unaligned.

An expensive house can't bring in any new business; a luxury car isn't going to pay the bills, and playing golf won't advertise the business.

The worst thing to happen to a business is the lack of cash flow. It's the same as the body's blood circulation. Without cash flow, a business goes bankrupt and without blood circulation, the body dies. These things happen because liabilities were created.

Remember, saying "yes" to assets and "no" to liabilities isn't just a business principle, but a life principle as well. Even if you work hard, you can't maintain your focus and succeed if you create liabilities. Only by gaining assets and eliminating liabilities will you achieve lasting success, so always develop assets, not liabilities.

To say "yes" to assets and "no" to liabilities:
- ❖ Set up a budget for the fiscal year and stick with it.
- ❖ Think big and spend wisely.
- ❖ Continue educating yourself to have the right information always, and build your self-confidence to have the knowledge and the courage in judging when to say "yes" to assets and "o" to liabilities.

HABIT FIVE: PRIORITIZE

Everyone has 24 hours a day at his or her disposal. Therefore, it is vital that you prioritize your time every day so it can be utilized effectively. When you know how to prioritize your time, it will help you increase your focus, make achieving your daily goals easier, give you a positive time management habit, and most of all instead of time controlling you, you will control time. If you can utilize your time effectively, success will be easy.

To prioritize:

❖ Develop the successful habit of writing a daily To Do List for the next day before going to sleep.

❖ Learn when to say "yes" and "no" in terms of time management. That way, you will always say "yes" to priorities and "no" to things that would waste valuable time.

❖ More tips on prioritization can be found in Chapter 3.

HABIT SIX: MAXIMIZE

Like it or not, you have to expect obstacles on your road to success. Without obstacles, you never really had a goal because goals always have obstacles. When obstacles arise, you have a choice to fight or to give up. Don't worry about failing; failure is okay. What's bad is giving up. Whenever unexpected problems or obstacles rear their ugly heads, don't be afraid to look them unflinchingly in the eye. You have to face these obstacles with grit and intestinal fortitude, and you must refuse to give up; you have to fight to win.

You have no reason to minimize your life because you only live once. Live with passion and maximize your life so you will be the world's next successful leader. You can change your life and change the world.

To maximize your life:

❖ Focus, push yourself to the limit, go that extra mile, and then go beyond that limit to maximize your potential, and never, ever give up until you win.

❖ Flexibility will give you the freedom to succeed. Without it, it's too hard to overcome obstacles. If you need to rewrite your plans because you've discovered a new idea or met obstacles in the process, don't fear taking a detour. Just take the time needed to rewrite your plans or find a better way to achieve your goal; be flexible, not stiff.

❖ You must also learn from the best, not the worst, as you do your best to maximize your life.

❖ If you get knocked down, get back up and keep going.

HABIT SEVEN: HELP OTHERS TO SUCCEED

The ultimate form of success is helping others to succeed. When you help others to succeed, you will surround yourself with a winning team. By having a winning team around you, your life will be much easier, happier and worthwhile. However, sharing involves more than just giving money to others; it also involves sharing your experience, knowledge, heart, and time.

Remember, nobody takes anything with them except their own name when they leave this beautiful world. As long as you are alive, share with others whatever you have to help other people succeed. You will live forever with honor and success.

To help others live triumphantly and succeed is to help you do the same and make your dreams come true. Truly successful people always help others to succeed.

To help others to succeed:

- ❖ Be generous instead of selfish.
- ❖ Think big and look at the big picture.
- ❖ Remind yourself that to help others succeed is to help yourself become triumphant.

SUMMARY

Every Dream Has a Price Tag

Persistence paid off in achieving the American dream. Success is a personal choice.

What Defines Success?

Peace of mind, good health, good relationships, financial freedom, and helping others to succeed.

Think Big

If you use 5% of your potential, you are a failure, 20% of your potential, you live an ordinary life, 35%, you become successful, and if you use more than 50%, you live a triumphant life. If you think big, you will be big, and success will be yours.

Four Enemies of Success

Laziness, negativity, ignorance, and fear.

D.D.P.E Your Way to Success

<u>D</u>esire
<u>D</u>ecide
<u>P</u>repare
<u>E</u>xecute

Seven Successful Habits

1. Think big and act wisely.
2. Fire up your personal power.
3. Passionately focus on your goals.
4. Say "yes" to assets and "no" to liabilities.
5. Prioritize.
6. Maximize.
7. Help others to succeed.

REVIEW OF "SUCCESS IS YOUR CHOICE"

What defines success?

_____

_____

What happens when you use 5%, 20%, 35%, or 50% of your potential?

_____

_____

How do you eliminate laziness and become active?

_____

_____

How can you turn negative into positive?

_____

_____

Why should you eliminate ignorance and educate yourself?

_____

_____

How do you control the following fears?

_____

_____

❖ Fear of the unknown

_____

❖ Fear of risk

_____

❖ Fear of failure

_____

❖ Fear of what others think

_____

❖ Fear of rejection

_____

❖ Fear of hard work

_____

What does D.D.P.E. stand for?

_____

_____

Where does desire come from?

_____

_____

Why is it important to make decisions in a successful life?

_____

_____

How do you prepare in order to achieve your goals?

_____

What is the difference between watchers, quitters, and fighters?

_____

_____

How can you always think big and act wisely?

_____

_____

How can you fire up your personal power?

_____

_____

How can you focus on your goals passionately?

_____

_____

How can you say "Yes" to assets and "No" to liabilities?

_____

_____

How can you prioritize your goals effectively?

_____

_____

How can you maximize yourself?

_____

_____

How can you help others to succeed?

_____

_____

Special

THANKS TO

You

First of all, I want to express my sincere appreciation to you for reading this book. I hope the process of reading it was as helpful to you as the process of writing it was for me. The things I learned in my research literally changed my life. I now see the world and all my relationships differently. I also see obstacles differently. Now that I understand that winning is a choice, I see that I am the only one who decides whether I am a winner or a loser. You, too, can make this simple choice that will change your life. No matter what you've done so far, whether you are winner or just a potential winner, you now have tools to build a better life.

I know that when you read the book a second time around, you will understand it a lot better. Once you change the way you think, everything will become much clearer. If you continue to read, by the third time you go through the book, it will be your daily best friend.

I'd like to ask you three big favors.

1. Please read the book at least three times through. I know that the more you read, the more you will enjoy it

2. You must start to use this new way of thinking one day at a time, in order to maximize your potential and reach your dreams.
3. Please share what you have learned with others. Success means sharing with others

I never want to stop learning, researching, and improving myself. Please visit my website www.ykkimproductions.com to see my latest developments or my seminar schedule. If I am coming to your area, I would like to meet you face to face.

In addition, now that you've heard my story, I'd like to hear your story, and any experience and thoughts from *Winning Is a Choice* that improved or changed your life. Please send your ideas, comments, or story to ykkim@ykkimproductions.com.

Thank you, my friend, and always remember to maximize your body, maximize your mind, maximize your heart, and maximize your life.

Sincerely,
Y.K.KIM

End Notes

Chapter 1

Page 12: Ghandi, Mohandis K, *Gandhi: An Autobiography-The Story Of My Experiments With Truth.* (Boston: Beacon Press, 1993).

Page 13: "Osama bin Laden." *Microsoft Encarta Online Encyclopedia 2004* (Microsoft Corporation, 2004). encarta.msn.com

Page 15: Fisher, Ian, "Arafat criticizes bin Laden in article." Orlando Sentinel, (December 16, 2002), p.A3.

Page 19: Tracy, Brian, "Building a Positive Self Concept." *The Psychology of Achievement.* Tape 1. (Chicago: Nightingale-Conant Corp, 1984).

Page 19–21: Menedez, Ramon, *Stand and Deliver.* (Hollywood: Warner Bros, 1998).

Pages 29–30: Maxwell, John C., "Theodore Roosevelt." *The 21 Irrefutable Laws of Leadership-Follow Them and People Will Follow You.* (Nashville: Thomas Nelson, Inc, 1998), pp 29–31.

Pages 33–34: "The American Presidency: Abraham Lincoln." *Grolier Encyclopedias.* (Grolier Incorporated, 2000). gi.grolier.com/presidents/ea/bios/16plinc.html

Chapter 2

Page 60: Tracy, Brian, "Goals and Goal Achieving." *Psychology of Achievement.* Tape 4.

Pages 61–62: Guralnick, Peter, *Careless Love: The Unmasking Of Elvis Presley.* (New York: Little, Brown & Company, 1999). pp 599–600, 628, 647.

Chapter 3

Pages 78–84: Choi, Suk N., *Sun-Shin Lee.* (Seoul: Kyo-hak-sa, 1992.)

Page 85: Diagram courtesy of Dr. Thomas Fisher, Professor, University of Central Florida. "The layers of self-perception."

Page 113: Wapner, Scott, "Weight Loss Firms Are Fatter Than Ever." MSNBC (March 4, 2003.) www.msnbc.com/news/880520.asp?cp1=1

Page 113: Lytle, Tamara, "We're just too darn fat." *Orlando Sentinel.* (March 10, 2004), p. A1.

Page 113: "How Many People Suffer From Addiction." (Drug Abuse Sciences, 2002.) www.drugabusesciences.com/answer.asp? Entry=31

Page 113: Center for Medicare and Medicaid Services. (2003) cms.hhs.gov/medicaid/mover.asp

Page 113: Minino, A. M., and Smith, B. L., "Deaths: Preliminary Data for 2000." *National Vital Statistics Reports: Vol. 49, No. 12 (10/09/01).* (Center for Disease Control, 2001.)

Page 113: Sherman, Mark, "$1.6 trillion spent in 2002 on health care." *Orlando Sentinel.* (January 9, 2004), p. C1–C2.

Page 125: Minirth, Frank, Meier, Paul, Hawkins, Don, *Worry-Free Living.* (Nashville: Thomas Nelson, 1989), pp 26–28.

Page 128: Lytle, Tamara, "We're just too darn fat." *Orlando Sentinel.* (March 10, 2004), p. A1.

Page 140: www.law.umkc.edu/faculty/projects/ftrals/hinkley/HBIO.HTM

Page 143: www.who2.com/tonyaharding.html

Chapter 4

Pages 186–187: nba.com.

Page 243: Interview aired on May 13, 1986. *Late Night with David Letterman* (alt.news.letterman and Lee Ann Platner, NBC Archives, November 12th, 2003.)

Chapter 5

Page 268: "The American Presidency: Jimmy Carter." *Grolier Encyclopedia.* (Grolier Incorporated, 2000.) gi.grolier.com/presidents/ea/bios/39pcart.html

Pages 269–270: Manning, Jason, *The Eighties Club.* (Jason Manning, 2003.) eightiesclub.tripod.com/id226.htm

Page 270: Bracken White. (Yale, 1996.) viking.som.yale.edu/will/web_pages/will/cases/rockctr.html

Page 271: *Hoover's Company Profile Database* (Austin, The Reference Press, Inc., 1995.) www.minidisc.org/sony_overview.html

Page 272: Breaux, John, "1998: The Year Of The $70 Billion Budget Surplus." (October 14, 1998.) www.senate.gov/ ~breaux/columns/surp1014.html

Page 273: *The Clinton Years.* (CNN Interactive, 2001.) www.cnn.com/SPE-CIALS/2001/clinton/presidency/presidency.html

Page 273: Emediaplan.com. (The Systems Private Limited, 2002.) www.emedi-aplan.com/admunch/Biographies/LeeIacocca.asp

Page 273: Lau, Debra, "Forbes Faces: Michael Eisner." (*Forbes Magazine.*) (New York: 2001.) www.forbes.com/2001/01/16/0116faceseisner.html

Page 273: "Time's Person Of The Year: Rudolph Giluani." *Time Magazine.* (New York: Time Interactive, 2001.) www.time.com/time/poy2001/poyprofile.html

Pages 273–277: Welch, Jack, Byrne, John A., *Jack: Straight From The Gut.* (New York: Warner Brothers Books, 2001.)

Pages 277–278: "Behind the Enron Scandal." *Time Magazine.* (New York: Time Interactive, 2002.) www.time.com/time/2002/enron/

Pages 278–279:" All Presidential biographical information courtesy of The White House. whitehouse.gov

Pages 281: "King Louis XVI" *Microsoft Encarta.* (Microsoft Corporation, 2003.) beta.encarta.msn.com/encnet/refpages/RefArticle.aspx?refid=761573336

Page 289–290: A-C class inspired by: Welch, Jack, Byrne, John A., *Jack: Straight From The Gut.* (New York: Warner Brothers Books, 2001), pp 158–159.

Page 297: "The Reagan Years: Reaganomics." *CNN.* (CNN Interactive, 2001.) www.cnn.com/SPECIALS/2001/reagan.years/whitehousereaganomics.html

Page 299: *Merriam Webster.* (Merriam Webster, 2002.) education.yahoo.com/search/be?lb=t&p=url%3Am/manson__charles

Page 299: Bloom, Harold, The Preacher: Billy Graham. (New York: Time Interactive, 2003.) www.time.com/time/time100/heroes/profile/graham01.html

Chapter 6

Pages 314–317: Gannon, Frank, "King of the Grill." (Washington D.C.: AARP Magazine October/November, 2003.) www.aarpmagazine.org/entertainment/Articles/a2003-07-24-kingofthegrill.html

Pages 314–317: "George Foreman." *MSN Encarta.* (Microsoft Coporation, 2003.) encarta.msn.com/encyclopedia_761564458/George_Foreman .html

Pages 320–321: Interview aired on November 10, 1999. *Meet the Press* (NBC, November 10, 1991, Volume 91.)

Pages 322–323: "The O.J. Simpson Trial." *CNN.* (CNN Interactive, 1995.) www.cnn.com/US/OJ/

Pages 323–324: "The 1960 Presidential Debates." *CNN.* (CNN Interactive, 1996.) cgi.cnn.com/ALLPOLITICS/1996/debates/history/1960/

Pages 335–337: Tannen, Deborah, "TIME 100 Artists & Entertainers-Oprah Winfrey." (New York: Time Interactive, 1999.) "Academy of Achievement-Oprah Winfrey" www.time.com/time/time100 /artists/profile/Winfery. html (Washington D.C., Academy of Achievement, 2003.) www.achievement.org/autodoc/page/win0bio-1

Pages 335–337: Sellers, Patricia, "The Business of Being Oprah." *Fortune Magazine,* April. (NewYork: Time Inc, 2002), pp 50–64.

Index

About the Author

he world's most dynamic speaker, a respected author, successful entrepreneur, and Grandmaster of the Martial Arts—there is no one like Y. K. Kim. He wants to change the world with a new way of thinking: A new, modern philosophy of personal and professional improvement through his book, *Winning Is a Choice.*

Y. K. Kim is a living testament that the American Dream is alive and kicking. He arrived in America with only his Black Belt and a heart full of hope. Through his blood, sweat, tears, and indomitable spirit, he started homeless and without a green card, and was able to overcome cultural shock, financial hardship, and language barriers to achieve a rare level of success which includes:

❖ Chairman and founder of a multi-million dollar organization

❖ Author of *Success in Martial Arts Business, Health is the Foundation of Success, Tae Kwon Do World,* and *Martial Arts World*

❖ International consultant and keynote speaker on business, leadership, and motivation

417

- Producer, writer, and star of the action film, *Miami Connection*
- Publisher of *Martial Arts World Magazine*
- Celebrated public servant, winning the prestigious Thomas Jefferson Award for outstanding public service
- Community leader, honored by the proclamation of Y.K.Kim Day in the City of Orlando
- Chairman and founder of *Martial Arts World* and the World Martial Arts Research Foundation

Grandmaster Y. K. Kim's next goal is to build a four-year Martial Arts university to provide future leaders. Y. K. Kim currently resides in Orlando, Florida, with his lovely wife and two children.

To invite Grandmaster Y. K. Kim to speak at your event, please contact him at:

Y. K. Kim Productions, Inc.
visit www.ykkimproductions.com or
E-mail ykkim@ykkimproductions.com
Phone (407) 897-6000 Fax (407) 894-5446
1630 East Colonial Drive, Orlando, Florida 32803 USA